T0082359

DEMONIC
FOES

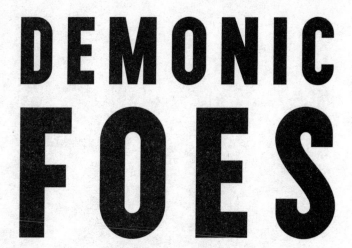

DEMONIC FOES

MY TWENTY-FIVE YEARS AS A
PSYCHIATRIST INVESTIGATING POSSESSIONS,
DIABOLIC ATTACKS, AND THE PARANORMAL

RICHARD GALLAGHER, MD

HarperOne
An Imprint of HarperCollinsPublishers

HarperCollins books may be purchased for educational, business, or sales promotional use. For information, please email the Special Markets Department at SPsales@harpercollins.com.

FIRST HARPERCOLLINS PAPERBACK PUBLISHED IN 2022

Designed by SBI Books Arts, LLC

Library of Congress Cataloging-in-Publication Data is available upon request.

ISBN 978-0-06-287648-5

22 23 24 25 26 LSC 10 9 8 7 6 5 4 3 2 1

I want to express my considerable gratitude to the individuals described in this book who have allowed me to share their compelling stories, albeit anonymously.

I thank my son Peter and many colleagues and friends, too numerous to mention, for their love and support during the whole time this work occupied so much of my attention.

CONTENTS

FOREWORD

As his past academic chairman for many years, I can attest that Dr. Richard Gallagher is a multitalented psychiatrist and a highly respected clinician who is also a valued teacher. He embarked on a serious scholarly study long ago concerning the fascinating, if controversial, subject of suspected demonic possession.

Contrary to a widespread belief, such phenomena not only continue to be reported in today's world, but they still defy easy explanation as simplistically conceived medical or psychiatric disorders. Dr. Gallagher brings his trained intellect and unimpeachable integrity to bear on the investigation of such "states of possession" and has undoubtedly directly encountered more of these hard-to-explain and intriguing cases than any other physician.

Hence, his book may well be unique in history: the serious treatment of a long-disputed topic by a superbly credentialed academic physician—a full professor of psychiatry—who can accurately offer personally informed accounts in painstaking detail of modern-day examples.

Joseph T. English, MD
Sidney E. Frank Distinguished Professor
of Psychiatry and Behavioral Sciences,
New York Medical College; Past President,
American Psychiatric Association

INTRODUCTION

The devil's greatest trick is to convince us he doesn't exist (la plus belle des ruses du Diable est de vous persuader qu'il n'existe pas!).

—BAUDELAIRE, "LE JOUEUR GÉNÉREUX"

What is said in the dark, speak in the light; and what you hear whispered, shout from the housetops.

—MATT. 10:27 (MY TRANSLATION)

In my experience, the idea of demonic possession is so controversial and so often misunderstood that I want at the outset to establish some scholarly plausibility to the notion along with my bona fides. Typical reactions to the topic reflect our nation's polarization. Despite widespread belief in evil spirits in the United States and around the world, some people find the subject farfetched, even moronic. Yet others spot the devil everywhere. And so here I detail my personal story and highlight the credibility of possessions while simultaneously offering some sober reflections on various exaggerations and abuses.

Initial medical and religious reaction in many quarters to the draft—from both well-informed academics and doctors as well as from experienced exorcists—has been gratifyingly positive. Readers may be surprised to learn that many physician colleagues of mine—around the world—agree with my findings, though they may be reluctant to speak out so openly—with some notable exceptions. For instance, a Harvard faculty psychiatrist has called this book "especially compelling . . . unquestionably by a world expert whose academic rigor is impeccable and whose personal integrity is above reproach." A prominent professor of neurology found the manuscript "most striking . . . by a witness who is completely trustworthy and one of the smartest persons I have ever met." A leading American exorcist describes it as "extremely helpful coming as the book does from America's 'go-to' medical expert on the subject of diabolic attacks. . . . Whenever I need help, I go to him. He's so respected in the field."

Demonic Foes relates unmistakable cases of demonic possession and other diabolic attacks that I directly encountered over the past twenty-five years. I did not originally volunteer to consult upon these cases; rather, I responded to requests from religious leaders for my professional opinion. And I overcame my hesitation about writing this book only after securing the permission of the afflicted men and women I agreed to help.

In 2016 I published an essay solicited by *The Washington Post*. The editor asked me to give readers my professional perspective, as a psychiatrist, of demonic possessions. The piece attracted more than a million online hits. Thousands of comments called for fuller evidence, which at the time I was disinclined to divulge. A CNN online profile of me—with an accompanying television interview—elicited a similar response. At the same time, professional colleagues and scores of exorcists were also regularly urging me as a professor and physician to report my findings and methods. Finally, scholars of "nonpathological theories" of possessions have long called for the publication of well-documented, true reports.

And so, albeit with a bit of lingering ambivalence, I decided to write *Demonic Foes*.

I have often been told, Who better than a professor of psychiatry can sort out the true cases from the many unfortunate and far more common instances of people who only *imagine* they are under demonic attack? It is not unusual for people with mental illnesses and other medical conditions to misperceive their states of mind as induced by evil spirits. As we will see, this is especially true of patients who suffer from psychoses and severe personality and dissociative disorders, as well as people who are easily prone to suggestion. I realized I was in a unique position to shed light on these knotty issues.

I have run into skeptics and naysayers, of course. I have raised a few eyebrows, particularly from the online commentariat. Cloaked in anonymity, these armchair experts are not shy about expressing their often poorly informed views. A more acerbic supporter commented that I had "disturbed the anthill" by going so public.

Similarly, most health professionals, however bright and well-meaning, have no familiarity with this subject. Because they are more aware than lay audiences how memories can easily be distorted, they tend to assume that all such stories must be either delusions or inaccurate recollections. There have been plenty of dubious "recovered memories" of diabolic attacks and satanic abuse. We cover in depth the whole controversy, but the chief accounts in this book are not of those sorts. I either witnessed firsthand the reports I present in the following pages, or the findings were independently verified by multiple highly credible observers.

Some more spiritually inclined individuals also have their reservations. Many religious academics are committed to naïve or wishful "demythologizing" in claiming that accounts of demonic activity are but myths or outdated cultural ideas and nothing else. They dismiss multiple references to evil spirits from classic texts and evidentiary documents over the centuries as anachronistic or merely symbolic.

Such conclusions would have astonished the seminal figures of most faith traditions, who had no doubt of the reality of demonic attacks. Fearing ridicule or aware of excesses, many clerics today are tentative in discussing the topic at all; others, who may be a bit too smart for themselves, discount the impressive evidence base.

Finally, the doctrinaire debunkers inevitably demand more and more "proof," to the point of making their demands impossible. They often appear a bit ludicrous in their facile dismissal of obviously credible testimonies.

Well, here is the detailed evidence aired openly. In reference to the murky world of demons, sunshine is the great disinfectant.

• • •

Different subjects call for different sorts of proof—in the case of possessions, people often want videotapes or audiotapes. Videotapes, however, are a violation of a person's privacy, and it is misguided to suppose that an evil spirit would deign to parade before a camera. After hiding or disguising themselves for millennia, why would spirits suddenly agree to an amateur filmmaker's direction? Authentic audiotapes, of which there have been many, never seem to persuade the committed skeptic. And again, such demands are naïve in expecting compliant behavior from evil spirits.

If you search in this book for laboratory evidence or controlled trials or neuroimages of states of possession, you will be disappointed. Spiritual beings don't show up on X-rays. We all use different methods of investigation in many areas of our lives. As a trained physician, I value science, and modern scientific protocols are indispensable. I accept the findings of mainstream modern science; medical practice depends upon them. But "methodological naturalism," as philosophers of science technically characterize such investigatory principles, cannot answer every question of human interest. By definition, this understandable conception of scientific methods excludes from consideration a spirit world, or any theistic beliefs, for that matter.

But historical evidence is also valuable and an important way of "knowing," too. Skeptics are taken aback when I mention that, although cases of possessions are not commonly encountered, the cumulative evidence for them throughout history has been massive. Belief in spirits and their possible influence on humans in most historical eras has been nearly ubiquitous. Anthropologists have recorded references to possessions in most known cultures over the millennia. Many in the field regard those unfamiliar with the nature of these reports to be ignorant, or as one researcher put it, the equivalent of today's "flat-earthers." Most anthropologists take these spiritual experiences quite seriously, however odd, though they may remain personally agnostic.

Nonetheless, throughout history, exaggerated reports of satanic crimes and mayhem have been common, too. I am well aware of periodic hysterias, including the witch hunts of the sixteenth and seventeenth centuries, as at Salem, whose targets were often cited as being possessed. As a psychiatrist, I lived through the more recent fiascoes during the 1980s and 1990s of "repressed memories" and the "satanic panic." As an attending physician at that time on a psychiatric unit for patients suffering from various personality disorders, I had to combat such nonsense daily. We don't want a repeat of such shameful episodes.

But if you discount out of hand all of the historical evidence, or if you presume you can subject spirit entities to experimental trials before believing any of these accounts, you will never grasp the subject.

President John Adams called facts "stubborn things." The goal of this book is to present the persistent but unequivocal factual evidence of demonic possessions and assaults in a contemporary context; open-minded readers can then interpret that evidence for themselves.

Many Western secularists cannot conceive of the existence of demons. But belief in a spirit world—and attacks by evil entities—is more mainstream than widely assumed. Large majorities around the world believe in a spirit world and in states of demonic possession. In this country, an early third millennial poll found that 70 percent of citizens believe in evil spirits, and just over 50 percent of Americans believe in the possibility of demonic attacks on humans. Just who is out of the mainstream here?

Differing theories abound, of course. In addition to the traditional view of diabolical attacks, possessions have most often been ascribed to various states of disease, especially in the contemporary world. To try to explain at least some of the unusual features of possessions, other commentators propose latent human "psychic" abilities, pushing theories that have never been verified on credible scientific grounds. A widespread credence in pseudoscientific notions about "paranormal" events is growing, and even religious experts have sometimes fallen for "parapsychological" theories.

Less skeptical observers down the ages have recognized the evident reality of spirit attacks but have attributed possessions and other such assaults to spirits other than demons. Certain cultural traditions blame malicious dead souls, ancestors, poltergeists, vengeful deities, sprites, or goblins. Despite the various theories about spirits, there are striking commonalities to the varied types of possessions reported across widely divergent cultures throughout history. Whatever the explanation, the common element remains that a spiritual *attack* of some kind occurred; if such an attack can't be ascribed to an *evil* spirit, words lose their meaning.

At the same time, I recognize the need to warn the overly credulous against harmful exaggerations and superstitions, or just common misconceptions. This field is prone to hucksterism, hyperbole, and human stupidity. Exploitative individuals may act on their mistaken perceptions that individuals are suffering from demonic attacks when to a professional eye the afflicted are obviously psychiatrically or medically impaired. Even worse are the sad episodes of physical abuse by ill-advised efforts to "liberate" victims. These abuses are not new. Historical and current efforts to expel demons by aggressive or dangerous means, such as through beatings and torture, remain as inefficacious as they are ignorant and at times sadistic. Problems caused by spiritual entities require spiritual help, which eschews all violence.

Another frequently ignored note of caution is the need to recognize the *rarity* of possessions. Most doctors will never see such a case; even the vast majority of clergy are unlikely ever to encounter a genuine possession. Many believers are surprised when I state that of the 25,000 or so formal patients I have assessed in depth over the course of my career during my normal professional workday, *none* were possessed. The cases I've concluded were possessed were always either sent to me by clergy or found me only after hearing of my expertise first and seeking me out on their own. No ordinary patient has just strolled into my office and then been surprised by a dumbfounding diagnosis of "possession"!

The soundest approaches to discernment require considerable expertise, not mere intuition or guesswork. Many people are also surprised to learn that the criteria for discerning spirit possession are quite strict and based on the recognition of a genuine "syndrome" whose features are as exacting as any other medical diagnosis. That our culture has now grabbed on to wild theories about the paranormal as well as exaggerated intimations of demonic attacks only exacerbates the confusion of those people seeking help.

• • •

Demonic Foes is my attempt to enter into a meeting place between pop culture—which sensationalizes the paranormal and the supernatural— sound spiritual judgment, and serious psychiatric and scientific study. It is of necessity an interdisciplinary approach.

The best way to illustrate this, in my opinion, is to tell my own personal journey of transformation from skeptic to believer to expert.

To ground the discussion in reality, I explore along the way some of my more complex and compelling cases, outlining my own investigative methods while explaining how each case relates to and informs modern culture, history, religion, and psychiatric theories.

Of the many cases I have seen, I highlight the following:

A young woman, a self-described Satanist, who levitated for half an hour during her exorcism in front of eight witnesses—a "once in a century" case, in the words of her two experienced exorcists.

A housewife whose hearing was blocked whenever anyone mentioned anything related to religion and who uttered vile blasphemies during recurring trancelike, possessed states.

A professional woman who suffered from unexplained bruises, spoke several languages completely unknown to her, and during her states of possession periodically ran amok, potentially wreaking havoc on herself and her reputation.

A petite woman who in her possessed state threw a two-hundred-pound Lutheran deacon across the room.

In such cases, I've worked hard to develop a system of investigation based on my psychiatric training and experience. To begin, I never officially "diagnose" someone as being "possessed." I do this for several reasons. First, it is not a clinical diagnosis that can be shoehorned into a conventional and scientifically responsible psychiatric diagnostic category. Because possession is a spiritual problem—not a psychiatric one—no laboratory or cognitive or mental status tests exist to register that information using medically established categories. Instead, I ask one basic question: Do the patient's symptoms have a natural or scientific explanation?

I may begin to answer this question, as need be, through a physical exam and standard rounds of medical tests, such as blood work to search for chemical abnormalities. I especially make sure the patient isn't suffering from an odd seizure disorder or other undiscovered brain damage. To rule these out, I may schedule a brain scan or an EEG, if indicated. If appropriate testing is negative, I rely upon a full narrative assessment and symptom survey that I always conduct. I also generally interview friends and families to confirm all details reported by the patient.

To the untrained eye, many possessions may be thought to fall into the psychiatric categories of various psychoses and severe personality and dissociative disorders, or they may seem to happen to individuals who are prone to suggestibility. However, for well-trained psychiatrists and other health professionals, possession differs from such disorders in significant ways. I outline in detail these symptoms and signs throughout this book, along with both the medical and spiritual criteria involved.

In those rare instances when I cannot determine a natural or scientific explanation for a person's condition, I refer the individual back to the priest, rabbi, pastor, imam, or other spiritual adviser who sent that person to me. The men and women of faith make the final *official* determination and arrange for spiritual help, if the patient is in need of such.

I take my responsibilities as a physician seriously, so I remind those who are mentally ill and who only *think* that they are being attacked by evil spirits to seek psychiatric help. The field of exorcism is littered with examples of careless deliverance groups and lay amateurs who may use questionable and sometimes outright hazardous forms of "liberation" on people who are struggling with depression or another mental illness.

A major attempt to moderate mistaken diagnoses and excesses came through the founding in the early 1990s of the International Association of Exorcists. I knew most of the founders personally and acted for a time as the association's scientific adviser. In the United States, Catholic Bishops have appointed about one hundred or so exorcists to combat serious demonic conditions. They routinely expect psychiatric evaluations. Other denominations have mounted similar, if perhaps less prominent, efforts. None of these sensible developments, however, should blind us to the continuing scattered abuses among poorly led "teams" of the overeager, especially among fundamentalists of all faiths in both the developed and undeveloped worlds.

• • •

My having earned the trust of numerous possessed individuals, as well as my privileged position as a psychiatrist, allowed them to open up to me not only about the strange features of their presentations, but also about their backgrounds and many intimate aspects of their personal lives. All these factors are crucial in judging whether a person is undergoing a true demonic attack. Patients in their profound and varied suffering will often tell a physician, and especially a psychiatrist, matters that they wouldn't reveal to anyone else. These details commonly include shameful behaviors, such as briefly turning to the occult or even satanic practices, that may make them reluctant to divulge their past indiscretions to clergy, let alone spouses and close friends. In some cultures possessed individuals are shunned and isolated; a few around the world are even physically punished or killed. As a consequence, these individuals often keep their stories hidden. In the United States, they usually fear institutionalization.

I work hard to distinguish carefully as a scientifically trained physician what "science" and good historical testimony can and cannot demonstrate about episodes of possession. And I take these individuals' trust in me very seriously.

All the understandable demand for proof should not blind us to the inescapable reality that tortured individuals are at the center of these assessments. They are not looking to illustrate a theory or prove their credibility. They are in enormous pain and want relief. I've often looked into the eyes of those who are suffering and been moved by the terror that I see. Few of them fully understand what is going on or why they are in a constant state of torment. But they believe their whole body, mind, and soul are under attack. Should one just ignore their distress?

Yet surprisingly, most often their own behavior and attitude are also essential to their liberation. As the Catholic Church teaches (along with similar beliefs in other denominations and many religions), the Rite of Major Exorcism is not a magic formula that will cast out demons automatically and completely liberate suffering victims without effort from the afflicted individuals themselves. Exorcists are not wizards, and often a long, grueling, and terrible struggle ensues for victims to be free of what ails them, just as it would be in a normal psychiatric case with a typical severe mental illness.

Exorcisms are not magic bullets. In the end, that is why I'm placing my professional qualifications on the line to write *Demonic Foes*. I want to enlighten the public as to the import and reality of these admittedly rare phenomena and what must be done for someone to receive help. I want to see tormented people set free from all things that would oppress or destroy their lives. I've dedicated my life to fighting the ravages of mental illness, and I've put the same sort of passion into working with people who may suffer from demonic possessions or lesser attacks, however controversial such conclusions may seem to some of my peers.

While I know I can't persuade the hard skeptic or critic, my hope is that *Demonic Foes* will reach out to the vast middle ground of people who are open to the ideas that we live in a world that is both seen and unseen and that these two realms can influence each other in unimaginable ways. A segment of that invisible world seems to be mysteriously but remarkably hostile to human beings and seeks their physical and spiritual destruction. On rare occasions, like some kind of cosmic terrorist, that segment shows its true colors. The public in recent decades has learned to its horror that vile humans may practice unspeakable acts of terrorism; perhaps the suggestion that spiritual entities of a similar brutality may also engage in acts of spiritually motivated savagery has thus become more believable.

I thank the many people who allowed me to share their compelling stories. I especially express my gratitude to the avowed Satanist presented in this book, who not only permitted but encouraged me and my colleagues to report her striking narrative. I well recognize the flamboyant, almost phantasmagorical nature of her strange story; however, it is not unprecedented in any of its individual details, and I provide parallels to even the most bizarre features of her situation from other historical cases.

Neither she nor any of these victims were patients of mine; I would not write about them if they were. Almost all of the cases found to be of an "extraordinary nature" (the traditional term) have instead been sent to me by educated and knowledgeable clergy of many faiths or other credentialed mental health professionals who have requested my opinion. In recent years, a few assaulted victims have found me on their own after learning of my experience online or from interviews I've given or articles I've written.

There is always a balancing act between discretion and the benefits of disclosure in the coverage of sensitive matters. Following standard ethical practice in medical reporting, in the pages of this book I have honored these victims' own wishes, in the phrase of one, to "get the word out." Still, I have concealed or changed irrelevant identifiers— names, locales, ethnicities, physical descriptions—that have no real bearing on the factual basis of these case descriptions. I am committed to privacy in communication. The media have frequently asked me to invite such individuals to be interviewed and to speak out in public, but I will never ask anyone to do so, though more than a few have been willing on their own to reveal themselves.

On the other hand, the need to enlighten readers about relevant particulars is essential, which is why I have not changed any specific details of the case accounts. Only a meticulously accurate recounting of all examples is worth reading. In the following pages I do not take any literary license or exaggerate facts; nor do I downplay the astonishing nature of some of the material, however impossible it may seem to readers.

I do not name any exorcists who have wished to remain private or who have not given me explicit permission to reveal their identities, although a number of my contacts in that role have by now reported abbreviated tales of their own. Workers in this unusual vineyard are not hard to find. With increased numbers and a perceived need for public education in the face of widespread confusion and hyperbole, many exorcists or their lay assistants are now willing to describe the nature of their work more openly. Too often, however, their sober testimonies are short and ignored by a wider audience.

A fitting reluctance to speak out by some witnesses of possessions may reflect an appropriate discretion and prudence. But too rigid an adherence to secrecy can be counterproductive, once proper safeguards are ensured. Overly strict concealment of accurate, if disturbing, facts has kept this subject in a cultural fog. Some knowledgeable observers remain afraid to disclose anything of substance, which allows the ignorant or critical to dominate the discussion.

A special thanks goes to a special physician, my former academic chairman and a past president of the American Psychiatric Association. Dr. Joe English told me once that he had encountered a rare but unequivocal case of possession early in his own career. He knew my professional goal to educate the public about the many fallacious notions that have long surrounded this complex subject and to ensure that psychiatric patients receive proper care, not misguided rituals. In their limited knowledge, both dogmatic materialists and overzealous but poorly trained religious people may cause real harm by hindering or delaying victims from obtaining the particular help they need, be it spiritual or, much more often, medical or psychiatric in nature.

I've always believed that a doctor should not refuse to get involved in such cases. As I said, I have merely answered calls for help. For any person of science or faith, it should be impossible to turn one's back on tortured souls. *Demonic Foes*, with the authorization of a few of those souls, and my thanks, represents their accounts as much as mine and is dedicated to them all. I celebrate their willingness to share their stories when so many advise caution or diminish and ridicule the reality and significance of these victims' profound suffering.

• • •

Finally, I bear witness in this book to the underlying spiritual realities that give meaning to these victims' travails. Exorcisms are not the most significant aspect of the practice of healthy religions. At their best, sound spiritual traditions place their emphasis on love of, service to, and compassion for other human beings—and also on divine love. "God does not need our love," a fine thinker made the point recently, "but he desires it just as surely as he wishes that we love one another."

Confusion about spiritual matters in the world is perpetual. Too many modern people see a divide between "faith" and "reason," and that misperception colors much discussion of the subject matter of this book. This dichotomy, however, is not the traditional view. We have inquiring brains for a reason. Social scientists emphasize that how one is raised and other social factors strongly influence the development of one's religious or spiritual ideas and attitudes, but these factors are never determinative. As adults, it is immature to never question them, or, conversely, to never try to learn more about their reasonableness and factual basis.

And surely, one cannot—should not—be expected to profess an "unreasonable" or unquestioned faith without being open to evaluating the evidence that history offers us. *Demonic Foes* presents examples from a larger body of such evidence concerning a subject area that is often misunderstood or ignored.

Like most things in life of real value, one must remain persistent and authentic in pursuit of the truth, unshackled by one's upbringing or cultural preconceptions or what conformist opinion dictates one should believe. At a time when many people have lost all sense of the sacred and of the supernatural, and when institutional authority is viewed with suspicion, that need is more of a personal challenge than ever. I believe that the value of identifying and attending to the reality of this sobering topic is worth the effort and that its implications warrant reflection.

PART ONE

SKEPTIC TO OBSERVER

There are more things in heaven and earth, Horatio,
Than are dreamt of in your philosophy.

—SHAKESPEARE, *HAMLET*

CHAPTER ONE

INITIAL JOURNEY

The Interested Student

Growing up as a baby boomer in the suburbs of New York City, I was instilled with a deep Yankee skepticism. I didn't give much thought to the idea of a devil, let alone the strange idea of demonic possession. Reports of diabolic assaults and the paranormal, we all believed, were topics for the tabloids, like aliens and Bigfoot; and Halloween was a time to make fun of all that nonsense about witches and goblins and black magic and the evil eye. I remember a neighbor's mother giggling over her son who was dressed in a black-and-red costume as a "cute little demon."

My generation was educated during a historical period of settled faith in rationalism. As part of a middle-class United States, I and others of my generation took for granted our time and our country's specialness—our faith in our democracy, its material progress, the great achievements of modern science, and its overthrow of superstitious ways of thinking. I learned in school an American pride and patriotism and, I was later to reflect, an easy dismissal of "Old World" habits and folk beliefs.

Later, when I pursued history and religious studies seriously as a classics major at Princeton University, I began to take more of an interest in such strange and unorthodox ideas. I was struck by how pervasive notions about evil spirits and ongoing supernatural events had preoccupied the ancients and the medieval world, and how even educated people reported a lively belief in spirits and trance states of communication with gods and dead souls. Though I was beginning to entertain a nascent fascination with such ideas, I was more interested at the time in developing my growing interest in the human mind. I immersed myself in my studies in languages, literature, and philosophy and had an early exposure to psychoanalytic ideas, which I hoped to pursue in earnest.

After graduating from college, I lived for a year in France, where I taught in a high school and played on a local semi-pro basketball team. Our team did well and, as a big fish in a smaller pond than in the US, I averaged about thirty points a game. I loved the rabid French hometown fans, who were always worth an extra fifteen points against all visiting rivals!

When I wasn't on the court, I behaved like every other unattached single male on an adventure in a foreign country: I drank excellent wine, ate delicious French food, and imbibed too much of the Cointreau made in nearby Angers. The worlds of the so-called paranormal and diabolism that had intrigued me back home were the furthest things from my thoughts.

That is, until my brother John met a local witch.

John had been living and playing on another team in a region known for its active interest in athletics. One day he told me he had been talking to an elderly woman who claimed to be, in her words, a "good witch." During their conversation my brother mentioned that he had suffered from warts on his hands since he was a teenager. She told him she could cure him.

Despite my skepticism and ribbing, my brother couldn't shake the idea.

The woman recommended what she called a kind of folk healing. She told John to perform a midnight ritual on a bridge on the outskirts of town. He was to recite a short incantation and then throw three beans over his shoulder into the river; she stressed that he "had to believe."

When John woke up the next day after having followed her instructions, the warts were still on his hands. That afternoon, he went back to the woman, who told him the ritual hadn't worked because he hadn't "*really* believed." He promised to try again, this time in earnest.

The next morning, my brother came to see me, his voice filled with excitement. His warts had disappeared. Like a typical younger brother, I told him he must be getting a bit soft in the head. I dismissed it as a case of mind over matter, documenting in an admittedly superior manner cases of relief from minor maladies that had occurred through the power of suggestion.

"Well, I don't care," John said. "Something all of a sudden worked after all these years of useless creams and freezings."

Although I remained skeptical, the incident deepened my interest in various theories about traditional healing practices, and I became fascinated with psychosomatic medicine, the vagaries of our complex immune system, and the enormous power of our brains upon the state of our physiology. Because I was planning on going to medical school when I returned home, I filed away the incident in my mind. By that point, I had already read the historical theories advanced by Sigmund Freud and his peers documenting the prevalence of what they then called the bodily effects of "hysterical" states of minds.

Freud and other early analysts stressed that unacknowledged emotions and impulses could directly lead to overt medical conditions, sometimes as dramatic as paralyses. Later, these states were called "conversion disorders"—mental conditions in which patients experience specific neurological symptoms without an organic cause or coherent physical explanation. As a medical resident at Yale, I later came to see excellent examples of these phenomena firsthand. For instance, I examined a hospitalized young woman suffering from a mysterious leg paralysis that

had no plausible physical or anatomical explanation. During one examination, she admitted that her deepest wish was to "kick real hard my
son-of-a-bitch father."

Freud was influenced by Jean-Martin Charcot, an animated and famous Parisian physician during the late nineteenth century. An avowed
secularist, Charcot was hostile to religion, and Freud applied his own
theory of hysteria to religious phenomena, including demonic possession. Freud argued that the "demonic possession" of a seventeenth-
century artist was an example of mental pathology wrongly mistaken
for a diabolic attack.

As it turned out, I played a basketball game near the small town
of Loudun, which I learned was the site of an infamous seventeenth-
century case of supposed multiple possessions at a convent there. In
the 1630s, several Ursuline sisters claimed that demons were assaulting
them. During their alleged possessions, the nuns screamed and gyrated
in bizarre ways and, supposedly, spoke several foreign languages unknown to them. The case was a sensation and still remains controversial in France. At the time, some exorcisms were conducted in public
and drew crowds of curious onlookers. Aldous Huxley detailed these
events in his 1952 book *The Devils of Loudun*. A campy film adaptation,
called *The Devils*, starred Vanessa Redgrave and premiered in 1971.
The movie's graphic violence and nudity caused a storm of protest at
the time, though I doubt many viewers took the subject matter seriously. I certainly didn't. Huxley persuaded me that, with all its confusion and sensationalism, the Loudun case was a likely example of mass
hysteria. He concluded that the episode was politically tinged and the
product of severe emotional disturbance of a few cloistered and sexually repressed Catholic sisters.

What made the case even more intriguing to me, however, was the
involvement of two infamous priests, Urban Grandier, a wealthy and
well-connected pastor of the town, and Jean-Joseph Surin, a Jesuit.
Grandier, who was famous for his effrontery and wandering eye, was
accused by his political rivals of seducing the nuns and casting spells

on them. They even produced as evidence a Latin document that was purported to be Grandier's pact with Satan. Under horrendous torture, Grandier maintained his innocence. His inquisitors burned him at the stake.

To atone for the nun's—and Grandier's—reported sacrileges, Surin invited a demon to attack him and, later, wrote a fascinating, detailed account of his alleged years-long ordeal with the spirit. Whether Surin was actually possessed or simply mad remains a point of historical debate.

The noted French neurologist Jean Lhermitte much later concluded that the supposed possessions represented psychological pathology. His 1956 book *Vrais et faux possédés* (*True and False Possessions*) undoubtedly influenced Huxley's view.

However, one religious scholar pointed out that to draw the same simple conclusion as Lhermitte, one would need to discount a good deal of the contemporary records. Many reports claimed to have credible evidence of the nuns spontaneously speaking foreign languages. One would also need to dismiss as inaccurate multiple descriptions in the extant sources of the nuns' wild and anatomically inexplicable gyrations and impossible contortions. Years later, a local French professor asked me, "Have you ever known a bunch of nuns going berserk, who just happen at the same time to be highly gymnastic?" This scholarly man concluded that, though the nuns were likely not all possessed, there probably had been some demonic phenomena evident in the village. He speculated that perhaps the nuns suffered from lesser attacks of what is known as "oppressions," or diabolic "vexation."

• • •

I put much of this interest on hold during my busy years of medical school and, after an internship in internal medicine, my psychiatric residency training at Yale. During my medical training, I became well-versed in the many inexplicable twists and byways of the human psyche. Indeed, true scientific exploration opens up new doors, new questions, and new possibilities. This is especially so when it comes to the mysteries of consciousness and of the human mind and spirit. I concluded that there were other ways of knowing things that didn't depend on whether that knowledge could be quantified through a laboratory experiment or a rigid scientific test. I came to feel that the evidence for the strange psychic phenomena history repeatedly throws at us—especially the hard-to-explain but well-documented spiritual experiences in all cultures—also deserved rigorous "scientific" exploration.

Aside from a few confidantes, I rarely shared this interest with any colleagues—and I still don't, mostly, unless I am asked about it. Looking back, I suppose I thought most of them simply indifferent to this subject; others I imagined might even be critical of my fascination and look a bit askance upon a fellow psychiatrist early in his career who took this realm seriously. At the same time, I can now acknowledge that I have not really experienced, then or since, any overt hostility to my studies in this area.

Around the time that I graduated as a resident and post-doc fellow from the Yale psychiatry program, a somewhat inaccessible literature about a modern possession was emerging within the mainstream. Various investigators, inspired by the commercial success of William Peter Blatty's 1971 novel, *The Exorcist,* and the movie that followed, were digging up previously unreleased facts about the events that had inspired the fictionalized account.

I was fascinated to learn the real-life details of this sensationalized story, and, though I was already convinced that Blatty had borrowed features from various historical accounts of exorcisms, including the Loudun case, I was particularly struck that the movie had primarily fictionalized an account of a putative actual and present-day possession.

Blatty's fictional story was said to have been modeled on the real-life possession of a young boy in Maryland, starting in 1949. Original sources pseudonymously called the boy Roland Doe, but in the age of investigative curiosity, the boy was later rechristened Robbie Mannheim. Raised Lutheran, Robbie was ministered to by his pastor, the Reverend Luther Miles Schulze. He had stints in hospitals, but doctors couldn't explain the case features, and psychiatric treatment had no effect. Robbie remained possessed for a long time.

As portrayed in the film, troubles began with poltergeist-like phenomena—inexplicable noises and "scratchings," a vibrating bed, objects flying around, a tipped-over chair. Multiple accounts claimed that up to forty-eight people witnessed these strange happenings, including Reverend Schulze, who attested to such occurrences when Robbie stayed with him in his home for an extended observation. Robbie's condition eventually progressed to symptoms more typically associated with possession: involuntary trance states; vitriolic expressions of hatred toward religion, delivered in a diabolic-sounding voice; and other paranormal abilities, including speaking in Latin, a language that young Robbie did not know. At one point, according to witnesses, Robbie's room became frigid, a not-unprecedented occurrence during exorcisms, I later learned.

A variety of clergy performed multiple rituals of exorcisms, first according to Lutheran, then Episcopalian, and finally Catholic procedures. Several Jesuits in a St. Louis hospital eventually conducted the successful series of exorcisms years later. The priests related that a loud noise accompanied the actual moment of Robbie's deliverance. The Jesuits compared the sound to a "thunderclap." After his successful exorcism, Robbie went on to marry, have children, and lead a successful life.

Before his death in 2017, Blatty acknowledged that his fictional story was most prominently based on the Mannheim possession but was also a composite. For instance, Blatty modeled the character of the priest-psychiatrist in his book and screenplay in part upon Father Surin, who had similarly offered himself to the demon as ransom for the original victim.

At the same time, Blatty intended the two priests in his novel—

Father Damien Karras and Father Lankester Merrin—to represent two contrasting points of view. With his heavily lined face and white hair, Father Merrin symbolized the old-school Catholic Church and its belief in literal evil spirits. He doesn't waver from that belief even as he conducts the exorcism that will end his life. Father Karras, on the other hand, begins the story with the conviction that the young girl Regan MacNeil demonstrates signs of an unknown psychiatric disorder despite the evidence pointing to possession. Only after running every physical and psychological test possible does Father Karras change his mind, finally acknowledging that something inexplicable, something demonic, is going on.

The personal transformation of Father Karras proved especially fascinating to me. I probably only later realized how seminal it turned out to be to my much later academic pursuits and direction: a trained psychiatrist who *investigates* the matter from an analytic and scientific point of view and then—and only then—comes to believe firmly in the reality of demonic possession.

Like Father Karras, I have since walked in two worlds—the world of scientific psychiatric investigation and the world of exorcism. And I've spent much of my time over the years deepening my understanding of both, which to some seem incompatible, though in my opinion they are not so at all.

After my four years of residency, I took an academic position as an attending psychiatrist at Cornell–New York Hospital–Westchester's long-term division. I was part of a team treating very troubled individuals on a specialized inpatient unit for patients diagnosed with severe borderline personality disorder. These patients are highly unstable and troubled and frequently have been abused. Working with such challenging patients was a stimulating experience right out of my residency.

The treatment "milieu," or program environment, had been established and guided by the clinical principles articulated by our hospital director, Dr. Otto Kernberg, one of the foremost psychoanalysts in the world. At Cornell, I also got involved in research, helping develop more rigorous interview methods and assessment scales for evaluating degrees of traumatic experiences in the backgrounds of our inpatients. Our results, as one of several research groups publishing early findings confirming high levels of abuse in their case histories, were eventually published in a monograph in *The Journal of Personality Disorders*, of which I was lead author. I found both the clinical atmosphere and the academic work in Westchester engrossing but also time-consuming. Once again, I had to put out of my mind any interest in possessions and other such topics in what I came to think of as "religious phenomenology," which I still considered a side avocation.

Before I left New Haven, I gave some serious, if fleeting, thought after my training to pursuing formal graduate work at Yale in the academic study of the history of religion. After working at Cornell for a time, though, I began to think that I had turned my back on that option, perhaps forever. I decided to enroll at the Columbia University Center for Psychoanalytic Training and Research and entered the required training analysis with Dr. Kernberg. I was soon asked to teach the course at Cornell Medical College on the life and work of Freud. Slowly but surely I was becoming known as someone skilled in psychopharmacology, and I was starting to think about applying for research grants. A conventional career as an academic psychiatrist was taking shape.

But one morning in the early 1990s an unexpected visitor—an elderly Catholic priest—knocked on my office door and asked whether I could help evaluate a woman. The priest told me he was one of the few official exorcists in the United States.

CHAPTER TWO

A PRIEST COMES CALLING

Observing External Oppressions

The priest was dressed in clerical garb, draped from head to toe in black, except for the identifying patch of his white Roman collar. A bit stooped in posture and out of shape, he was winded from his short walk across the campus. He had the air of a rumpled scholar, probably because his pants were in desperate need of a pressing.

Father Jacques, as I'll call him, worked as a chaplain in a state psychiatric hospital and served as a part-time assistant in a parish a good distance away.

"Forgive me, doctor," he said. "I need help with an odd situation. I want you to evaluate a woman's condition." He added, "I'm no expert in your field," though he seemed to know a fair amount about patients with mental disorders.

Then he told me that a woman, who had traveled two thousand miles to meet with him, was demonstrating signs of what he called a demonic oppression, a state that he defined for me as a diabolic attack short of a full possession. While this spirit continued to attack the woman, it hadn't taken control of her body—the definition of a demonic possession, Father Jacques told me. Out of caution, though, he admitted that he wanted the opinion of a psychiatrist after a hematologist he had consulted had ordered some blood tests and concluded that no medical illness could explain her odd symptoms.

In my career, I had encountered many psychotic patients who *imagined* they were getting attacked by demons. I told Father Jacques as much and admitted that, though open-minded, I retained a deep skepticism of demonic possessions.

"This is why you are the perfect man for the job," he said, laughing.

To this day I'm not entirely sure why Father Jacques chose me. Perhaps one of the religious scholars with whom I'd conversed had mentioned my name to him. I was also known by local priests to be Catholic myself.

Despite my ambivalence, I confessed a curiosity that I might learn something from the kind of case that had begun to fascinate me as a physician, at least on a theoretical level. I was struck that this articulate man wanted to introduce me to a real-life, modern problem case that might prove demonic in nature. But I was also wondering whether I wanted to get involved with him professionally, not knowing how credible or superstitious he might be.

• • •

A few days later, Father Jacques brought to my office a pleasant Mexican woman. I'll call her Maria. A devout woman, she was dedicated to her children and charitable work. Maria reported no psychiatric symptoms or any past psychiatric treatment. Happily married, she enjoyed her life. She felt fine—except for a striking complaint. She told me that she was being beaten by invisible spirits. "It usually occurs when I'm in bed," she admitted, a bit embarrassed. "I can't see them."

Her husband, Alejandro, corroborated her story, telling me how he would stand by helplessly while Maria absorbed these recurring blows.

"Out of nowhere these bruises appear all over her body," he said.

Since the couple were Catholic, Maria and Alejandro believed the devil was targeting her, possibly for her religious zeal and "good works." Or perhaps, Maria added, a "*brujo*, a nasty man," or sorcerer, had put a curse on her, although neither she nor Alejandro could explain why he would single her out.

My job was to evaluate whether there might be any diagnosable mental or physical illness behind Maria's bruises, some of which were still visible on her arms. Could she and Alejandro both be delusional? A shared psychotic condition called *folie à deux* exists, but neither appeared paranoid or impaired in any way. Could Alejandro be beating Maria and making up a story to hide his abuse? But he seemed a gentle man, clearly enamored of his wife. And why would they have traveled so far and involved Father Jacques and me in their ruse?

I could find no standard pathology to explain this bizarre symptom. Although I did not believe the couple's hypothesis of a possible hex, I was struck by the sweet nature of this woman and the couple's sincerity and good sense. I wanted to be careful with the case, though. I ordered a battery of tests, including a physical exam, repeat blood work (especially tests for clotting abnormalities), an EEG, and a CT scan. All were negative. The only physical ailment were the bruises on her body. Her mental status exam—a series of questions about her cognitive abilities and her emotional state—was also normal.

While her bruises showed a superficial resemblance to a few disorders such as psychogenic purpura, her history was very different from any conventional organic pathology. Psychogenic purpura, which is also known as the Gardner-Diamond syndrome, consists of temporary skin swelling followed by multiple ecchymoses, or bruising. Psychological stress and trauma are thought to contribute to this rare condition. But Maria reported no such early manifestations of skin swelling. She was also mentally healthy and reported no significant stress, other than the physical beatings, which she described as outright blows to her body. In our conversations, Maria's story remained consistent and coherent.

I eventually told Father Jacques that I could find no diagnosable psychiatric or medical condition.

"I suspected as much," he said.

Some time later, Father Jacques told me that, through a series of his and her parish priest's deliverance prayers and through Maria's own redoubled spiritual efforts, the attacks gradually decreased and, over time, went away completely.

• • •

Over the years, I have met with many people who similarly claimed to have been beaten by spirits. Some even said they were choked and scratched, a claim supported by photographs. They would usually offer a personal explanation of their own—sometimes plausible, other times not at all. After consulting other physicians or their clergy, most had come to believe evil spirits had targeted them. None of this, in my professional opinion, was evidence of psychosis or someone being overly prone to suggestibility.

"There is always *some* cause," Father Jacques would always tell me. "These things don't just happen out of the blue to victims. And these people are not mentally ill."

Soon after Maria's case, Father Jacques invited me to meet a young African woman who was possessed. This was the first case I saw of demonic possession. We met in the basement of an ornate rectory where I observed him and another priest perform a "major exorcism," as the authorized prayers of the formal Roman Ritual are known. After the rite, I was convinced that this woman had indeed become liberated from her long-standing possessed condition.

I believe Father Jacques wanted to show me different cases of possession and oppressions in their many manifestations during my ad hoc training in this odd new field. I had already encountered some gruesome stuff in my work with abused patients at Cornell and sociopaths at the Yale Psychiatric Institute. Still, I wondered how I would react sitting in a room by myself with a fully possessed person, as I expected would eventually happen.

As I gained experience with oppressions, I became aware that I was at first primarily being asked to comment upon what are labeled *external* oppressions, which demonstrate bodily symptoms. Such cases most often confuse spiritual advisers, who have considerable trouble distinguishing such *physical* signs from an organic illness, especially if few other features are present, as is often the case. Most priests or ministers or other clergy seeking out Father Jacques were not themselves able to know for sure whether such symptoms didn't just comprise an odd illness unfamiliar to their untrained eye.

The causes of such attacks proved another important indicator of their validity. In diagnosing external oppressions, I kept in mind that I needed to consider the *totality* of the various components of a demonic attack that prove most persuasive, or "pathognomonic," as we say in medicine. Make no mistake, these attacks should not be haphazardly diagnosed; they required no less a discernment as those made in medical practices. Only when the various features of a possession or oppression are both typical and singular enough to characterize a traditional diabolic assault does one gain the true conviction that an accurate discernment is being conducted. This diagnostic confidence is more easily obtained when the particulars partake of the "paranormal."

Unlike most (not all) possessions, people who are oppressed retain consciousness at all times and do not lose full control of their actions. They do not generally have the same level of aversion to the sacred, as seen universally in the possessed, because in a possession an actual demon is directing, not just harassing, the victim. The evil spirit hates the sacred things or beliefs; the victim doesn't. But that discernment rises to the level of "moral certainty" called for by the church, especially when the victim presents, as well, with a clear historical rationale for the attack.

Possessions and oppressions can, in my view, be consistently distinguished from both mental and physical disorders by an expert. But one needs a lot of experience. It is especially important that spiritual advisers, who often know little about psychiatric or medical disorders, work closely with mental health or medical professionals when dealing with oppressive situations. It helps to have a thorough knowledge of both medical/psychiatric illnesses and typically oppressive features as well as an appreciation of the likely causes.

• • •

A good example of how tricky these investigations into the causes of oppressions can be occurred in another case I saw, not long after my consultation with Maria. This man, whom I call Stan, was referred to me by a clergyman, to whom Father Jacques had given my name.

Stan was a tall, middle-aged man from the Pacific Northwest. Highly intelligent, he worked in a technical field. I found him reasonably composed and stoic, but his wife told me she was terrified by what was going on.

Like Maria, Stan also felt he was being beaten by, in his words, "some spiritual force." He complained that he was periodically scratched and occasionally choked, again in his words, by "some kind of weird, unseen assailants." The scratches, which he showed me, were mostly to his neck and face. He also brought me photos of past cuts that crisscrossed his legs and torso. Some psychiatric patients cut themselves for a variety of reasons, often masochistic ones, but Stan and his wife firmly denied he was engaging in self-mutilation. Before meeting with me, he had already been evaluated by a number of physicians. Though they were all puzzled by his story, none believed he was emotionally troubled, psychotic, or lying. All medical testing done in this case, too, had been negative. To verify Stan's story, I talked to both his primary doctor across the country and his specialists. No one had any idea what was going on with this seemingly otherwise healthy man.

Upon further questioning, Stan admitted to exploring various spiritual traditions throughout his life. For years, he had questioned the Christian beliefs of his upbringing, and in his adult life, he had briefly explored Eastern religions. For a time, he also "seriously investigated" Islam under the tutelage of a Muslim co-worker. He impressed me as being a genuine seeker of spiritual truth. But by the time he came to consult me, he had long returned to his Christian roots. Stan denied any period during his life when he had pursued any overt "occult" practices, which is often a telltale cause in a diabolic case.

I was puzzled. Thanks to Father Jacques, I knew genuine oppressive attacks don't just arise out of the blue. Though I pressed Stan, he firmly denied omitting any serious, potentially relevant, and more suspicious factors in his personal history.

After I met with Stan, Father Jacques telephoned me. "I *do* think it's an oppression," he told me, "but he isn't giving us a plausible cause yet. Would you be willing to meet him a few more times to get a better feel for this guy?"

I liked Father Jacques's caution.

Since Stan had come so far at no little travel expense, I agreed to extend his visits with me. As always with these sessions, I made it clear to Stan that I was a consultant to the priest and not in any way his physician. Because I was a psychiatrist and because Stan was looking for a spiritual discernment, I emphasized that Father Jacques would make the eventual official *spiritual* diagnosis.

I came to find Stan a brilliant man, well-read and knowledgeable about religious history. He had even learned some Hebrew to grasp better the nuances of the Old Testament, or Tanakh. For several sessions, however, I remained convinced that he was hiding something.

Then at our fifth meeting, he finally blurted it out. "I know you've been pressing me about an explanation for why all these peculiar symptoms are occurring. Please forgive me, I didn't mean to take advantage of your generosity, but I have a confession to make."

He hesitated. Throughout our meetings, Stan had always exhibited an intense, but congenial manner. His apprehension here caught my attention. I knew whatever he was about to tell me had been weighing on him, perhaps for years.

I could only think to say, "Go on."

Then he told me that as a young man he had briefly turned to Satanism—"of a sort," he added defensively. Stan admitted that he had spent a few weeks worshipping Satan and even "promised his soul" to that figure if he received favors and experiences in return. It had been a foolish impulse and undoubtedly a transient misjudgment, but the entities he had called upon seemed to have taken him at his word and were still exacting their price.

"I really thought it was nothing," Stan said. "My 'flirtation,' as I called it, was extremely brief, only for a few weeks or so at most."

His wife nodded.

"I had also been smoking a lot of pot at the time, which I haven't done in recent years at all, but maybe the weed affected my judgment. You know by now, Dr. Gallagher, that I'm a sincere searcher for the truth, but also, I guess, I'd describe myself as someone who's always been hungry for 'spiritual experience.' That's the best way I have of putting it."

That made sense to me. As a kind of "New Age" seeker, Stan was in constant search of a concrete experience that would satisfy his spiritual yearning. Many Westerners turn to Eastern religions for what they perceive to be a more "direct" connection to a spiritual realm. Some of them, unfortunately, flirt with occultism and even diabolic pursuits.

By then, I was learning in depth how various elements from a victim's personal history were involved in the genesis of these weird, oppressive phenomena.

In Maria's troubles, for example, it seemed clear that she was being punished—not because she had engaged with the occult but because, as such a devout and charitable person, she became a target for demonic foes. As I had learned by this time, oppressive phenomena of beatings and other sorts of physical attacks had been reported throughout history in surprisingly sound documents. And such historical records often document that the kind of oppressive assaults Maria endured frequently affect fairly saintly individuals in response to their continued devotion to God and their steadfast rejection of Satan and his realm.

By contrast, Stan had turned to outright diabolism, which instigated his external oppression. He'd been "caught" in an imprudent bargaining with forces beyond his reckoning, and however he tried to justify his brief lapse in judgment, he was paying a punishing price.

I wasn't sure whether the *brujo* Maria had mentioned had something to do with her condition. Seeing her case in a whole different light from Stan's, some spiritual experts refuse to use the word "oppression" at all in characterizing her suffering. Rather, they prefer a term like a diabolic "attack on the holy." But I doubt demons quibble about wording as they ply their mischief.

Yankee rationalist that I remained, as well as a trained physician unlikely to jump to occult hypotheses without a lot of evidence, Maria's theory about a sorcerer putting a curse on her seemed all too crude, too superstitious to me at the time. But later cases, where curses and hexes and the like proved all too common parts of the story, gave me pause. I was seeing firsthand that occult factors in a person's suffering, or healing, were by no means the silly or benign phenomena most people supposed. I was reminded of my brother John's contact in France with the "good witch" who had healed his warts and started to take his experience more seriously.

As Stan's story illustrates, a person who starts to follow Satan but later tries to turn away may be especially vulnerable to evil spirits—or an individual who seriously dabbles in the occult and "opens a door," as it is put, but then attempts to reform his or her life and return to serious religious practices. Like organized crime figures, once a person pledges to the group and knows the players, the organization hardly wants to let that person leave without exacting its revenge. Such people "know too much."

· · ·

Later, I met another person who had turned naïvely but seriously to occult pursuits. A psychologist I knew had examined a woman around fifty years of age who seemed to be suffering serious oppressive symptoms. According to Father Jacques, the troubled woman had extensive past experiences with the occult. Originally from India, she had immigrated to the United States, where she became a citizen and successful businesswoman. But then she began to experience all sorts of strange and painful paranormal experiences.

Hinduism is the major religion in most of India, and many Hindus believe in both malign and beneficent deities. This woman had been a student of what's known as "Kundalini awakenings," which are generally described as experiences that range from feeling a "cool breeze" or heat to spasms at the base of the spine, visions, alternate states of consciousness, and, adherents claim, possible "enlightenment."

To understand and best assist some of the cases Father Jacques was introducing me to, I needed a fuller knowledge of each person's underlying beliefs. Before my visit with this Indian woman, I read as much as I could about the phenomenon of Kundalini awakenings. To my surprise, there was a large amount of research literature on the topic, however controversial. The Sanskrit word *kundalini* means "coiled snake," and the term refers to what is called divine energy (in Sanskrit, *shakti*), which is believed to be located at the base of the human spine. The concept is also identified with a "serpent goddess," and students such as Carl Jung and Joseph Campbell were intrigued by its symbolism and its original spiritual significance.

Prominent among the four major schools of yoga, Kundalini yoga has centers throughout the world, including a number in New York City. Many of these centers emphasize their neutral physical practices—of breathing, exercise, and meditation—often without any mention of underlying Hindu beliefs. Whatever one makes of these notions, many adherents of Western religions with traditional ideas about evil spirits have argued that its undoubted "paranormal" elements, as claimed by those who have undergone these awakenings, have diabolic roots. Predictably, some secular critics have characterized these awakenings as simply nonsense or deluded, an idea hotly denied by traditional Hindus.

In any case, this woman had in recent years turned to Catholicism and had become convinced that she had opened herself to demonic forces through her Kundalini practice and was seeking relief from her very painful experiences. She wanted deliverance from what she had come to believe were attacks by malign spirits.

The core of her complaints, which also entailed a number of odd "internal" experiences, again mostly consisted of painful physical ones. Though she experienced very real pains, her physicians could never discover a medical reason for them. In addition, she also reported occasional unseen blows and several times felt strangled by "spirits," similarly to what Stan had suffered. She felt she was being punished for her past interactions with what she now believed had been malign spirits. Interestingly, she stated that the pains were increasingly torturous when she attended Mass and became unbearable when she neared the Eucharist. (In the years since, I have heard many similar complaints from oppressed men and women who experience an increase in pain while in a church and especially when close to communion hosts.)

During our work with this woman, Father Jacques introduced me to another priest who had been consulted on the case, Father Malachi Martin. Martin was a noted but controversial figure in the religious world for his radical views about old-style Catholicism and the conspiratorial inner workings of the Vatican. Both priests believed this woman was being diabolically attacked, and her psychologist had already assessed her psychological state as otherwise normal. Father Jacques wanted me to hear about her Kundalini experiences and to meet the elderly Father Martin, as he was still calling himself although he had resigned as a Jesuit years earlier.

To augment my research, I listened to Father Martin's experience with other demonically possessed individuals. He still had a heavy Irish brogue and seemed a bit of a "character"; a lively and charming man, he did not have long to live (he died in 1999). Our relationship remained cordial, though I confess to having a mixed reaction to him and his work. By then, his 1976 book on the subject of possession, *Hostage to the Devil*, had long since become a bestseller, surpassing even Blatty's in popularity in the genre.

But he had been criticized for taking considerable poetic license in his reporting of possessions. A bit of blarney? I was never sure. I have been told on good authority that Martin did not really have much personal experience in the field of exorcism; he called himself an "assistant" to cases and skirted going through "proper channels." Some reviewers thought he perhaps had based his account on a number of real cases that he had heard about and then fashioned into five "stereotyped" subjects, each proving a general ideological point about the modern world.

Some commentators also have argued that he exaggerated the toll taken on the exorcist, overemphasizing the idea of exorcism as a personal duel between demon and priest, rather than as a prayer for God's intercession. Perhaps he did this for dramatic effect.

Martin is also alleged to have maintained that more than half of psychiatric patients in asylums had been demonically attacked—an unwise judgment, if he indeed held that view. I regret never pinning him down on whether he truly took that position or had ever mentioned that statistic, which Father Jacques and I both regarded as absurd. Whatever liberties Martin may have taken with his reports, he was familiar with many records of the historical practice of exorcism and the long experience Catholics have of dramatic possessions and oppressions, and so he, too, genuinely contributed to my early understanding of this odd field.

• • •

My serious education in the nuances of these matters had clearly begun.

As one of the most knowledgeable Catholic exorcists in the United States, Father Jacques was asked to see a large number of people suspected of being diabolically attacked all around the country. Our association and his prominence in the field soon allowed me a broad exposure to an unusually large number of amazing cases, though the workload often proved a bit onerous, as I continued to fulfill my clinical and academic responsibilities.

As our collaboration, and friendship, eventually grew, I regularly accompanied Father Jacques on many trips. During our long car rides, he told me about his background as a priest, delving into his vast store of tales about possessions and other sorts of demonic assault. Catholic bishops in the United States regularly authorized Father Jacques to perform exorcisms, so they clearly respected my friend's judgment and discretion. In the years since, the US Catholic Church has appointed more exorcists, which is why this generation of exorcists doesn't encounter anywhere near the number of cases Father Jacques and eventually I routinely saw.

At the time, I hadn't understood Jacques's prominence in the field and, hence, his involvement in cases all across the country. I also hadn't realized how often Jacques would be calling me to ask for my opinion. So I soon had to make some hard choices. I wanted to help Father Jacques and the people he was sending my way. They were confused, often tortured individuals. Even if psychiatrically troubled, as some turned out to be, I didn't want to ignore their pain. If nothing else, I knew I could generally help them sort out the more precise nature of their difficulties, whether psychiatric/medical or demonic, and secure the kind of help they so desperately needed.

I also had to admit that the field intrigued me. These were certainly not the sorts of cases I had heard about in medical school. Was

I going to commit to this strange, new endeavor? As a rough rule, I decided that I'd try to do my best to help out whenever I was asked. Since I hadn't gone out of my way to seek out this field, I trusted that events would help dictate my level of participation, which allowed me to think of my involvement as in a way providential.

But I wasn't prepared for the next case Father Jacques literally brought to my door.

CHAPTER THREE

JULIA, THE SATANIC QUEEN

Her Possession and Her Remarkable Abilities

The night before I met Julia, something unnerving happened. My family loves animals, and at that time, a French bulldog and two cats prowled around our house like longtime relatives. All three always got along well. The cats often curled up next to each other on our bed at night.

But one night around 3 a.m., loud screeching sounds startled me and my wife out of our sleep. Our two normally docile cats were going at it like champion prizefighters, smacking and clawing at each other, intent on inflicting some serious harm. My wife grabbed the female cat and I held on to the male. As we separated them into two different rooms, they continued to growl and bristle. My wife and I got back into bed, mystified, but wrote off the tiff as perhaps caused by some bad cat food or one too many sniffs of catnip.

The next morning, Father Jacques rang our doorbell. He was standing at our front door with "Julia." She was dressed in black pants, with a dark purple blouse hanging loosely around her slight frame. I guessed she was in her late thirties or early forties. Her short hair was dyed jet black, and her black eyeliner extended to her temples—the style I later learned that was favored by her fellow cult members.

Dressed again, as always, in his clerics, Father Jacques had his hands in his pockets, avoiding eye contact.

"This is Julia," he said. "She has something to confess."

With a smirk Julia gazed at me.

"How'd you like those cats last night?" she asked.

I stared at her, taken aback as much by her manner as by her astonishing statement. She regarded me with that smug smile, evidently pleased with herself.

"What are you amused about?" I blurted out.

Her smile widened as she leaned against the doorframe.

"Look," I finally thought to say. "I respect Father Jacques, and he asked me to see you. But let's not have a repeat of last night, understand?"

My thoughts came fast and furious. *What the hell am I saying? Could she really have had anything to do with the cats?*

Unperturbed, Julia just stood there with the air of an honored houseguest, offering no apology.

For the rest of the day, I tried to collect my thoughts. *What in God's name have I gotten into?* This was the first time I had ever doubted or even questioned my involvement with Father Jacques. To get a few things off my chest, I called him, throwing away common courtesy and asking, "What on earth were you thinking, bringing her here?"

He apologized profusely and told me she had arrived earlier than he had expected. He had wanted to make sure I was around so we could meet with her as soon as possible. Jacques was eager to get my input, though I already knew he was convinced that she was possessed.

"Striking while the iron was hot," he put it, since he didn't seem to trust that her motivation to get help would last long. He further astonished me by admitting that a similar thing had occurred in the house of another psychologist who had interviewed Julia. The man's wife subsequently forbade him from having anything else to do with "that horrible woman" after their crazed cat tore up their living room couch.

"Now you tell me," I said. I felt annoyed, invaded.

Father Jacques went on. "She can be provocative, but she does seem to want our help, at least for now. She needs our help, the sooner the better, I think. Her cult doesn't want to let her go and will do anything to stop our continued exorcisms."

According to Father Jacques, Julia was a truly exceptional case even for a serious possession. As a rare Satanist and the "high priestess" of a satanic cult, he further explained, Julia had been granted certain "special abilities." Because her cult had threatened him directly, he said, Father Jacques was convinced her stories were credible.

I agreed to see her at my office the next day.

During the exorcisms of most full possessions, the evil spirit may on its own (or may be forced to) manifest itself and display its remarkable preternatural powers. Even outside the exorcisms, and critical to the diagnostic process, victims in their periodic possessed trances frequently display at least some of the classic signs of their state. Evil spirits may speak foreign languages; show supernormal strength; or reveal "hidden knowledge," that is, display an awareness of matters they have no natural way of knowing—akin to what psychics claim to be able to do. Of course, it is the demon who has such powers, not the victim. In a possession, the demonstration of these paranormal abilities is precisely what proves that a foreign evil spirit is present and in control. Despite occasional protestations by so-called parapsychologists and spiritualists, human beings on their own have none of these powers.

But Father Jacques explained to me that a powerful diabolist like Julia who has explicitly committed herself to Satan, who worships him, may be granted some "privileges" of this sort "on their own." That is, the contention that Satan grants his devotees the ability to demonstrate psychic powers not only outside an overt possessed state, but also in their normal conscious state. Under Satan's power, they perform these paranormal feats through no inherent ability of their own but are able to draw upon demonic sources of power in a strange way.

Cases of individuals who have such a level of "favors" are, in my experience, very rare, even more uncommon than in a more typical possession. But Julia, I was soon to discover, was hardly typical. She openly exhibited these features and delighted in her "favors."

• • •

When Jacques and Julia arrived the following day, I ushered her into my office. Instead of greeting me, she strolled over to my large windowsill, which was filled with small wicker baskets of forsythia, and without a word, started watering my plants. Again, I was struck by her effrontery, her almost complete disregard for formalities or everyday courtesies.

"I'm into the life of plants. *We* love plants and animals. Well, maybe not *all* animals, I suppose." She chortled at her little joke. "But we're unlike stupid Christians who hate nature, have you noticed?"

Through the months of our discussions, Julia always insisted that she desired to be in tune with the "natural world" and that was one reason she was a practicing Satanist. She interpreted traditional religion as unnatural and repressed. "My philosophy is this, doc," she told me. "Indulgence instead of abstinence. Vital existence instead of spiritual pipe dreams. Vengeance instead of turning the other cheek." It sounded like her cult's formulaic motto of sorts, and she even wrote it out for me once.

She liked calling me "doc," which I took as a good sign. She seemed to trust doctors more than priests. Having heard how she talked to priests, I expected her to treat me the same way. But I think she knew I would call her out on any discourtesy, and, as it turned out, she gave more respect and heed to my views as a physician than to the admonishments of priests, however obviously well-intentioned on their part. She wanted my perspective on, as she called it, this "possession business."

"I know I'm possessed," she said. "I space out and then don't recall what happens. They tell me a voice comes out of me. I don't know. I don't remember anything. It's a demon, I'm sure. It's not Satan. He doesn't bother himself with small things like that. But it comes from him. Everything is under his control. I have long followed the Master and done everything he wants for years."

I was struck by the calm and rational way Julia talked about her condition. It wasn't what I had expected. She stood in front of my office window, staring at the neighboring buildings and surrounding wooded area. I had chosen this office specifically for this view, and I regularly took in the scene, in much the same way Julia seemed to be enjoying it. If I hadn't known what she was enduring within her spirit, I easily could have mistaken her for one of my usual patients. She struck me as intelligent and in firm control of her emotions. She did not seem to me the unbalanced or limited person I had been suspecting.

I decided to dig a little deeper, hoping she would reveal to me some crucial detail about her story that would allow me to gain a better understanding of her situation and her mental state.

"Why do you think you became possessed?" I asked.

She claimed not to have a clue, which I found odd. "Well, Satan is certainly in charge, so he must have his reasons. But I don't understand why. And, no, I don't like it. It's always unwise to oppose the devil, but I decided to seek help. The cult would hate that, too, so I told them I would infiltrate the church and get any priests I met in trouble. I assume they believe me, but I'm leery and afraid they'll turn on me. But I just sense I have to get rid of this possession. I heard only priests or ministers can help me. Can psychiatrists? I don't think so. I'm not crazy, that I know." I was impressed by her frankness, including about the priests.

She finally sat down in front of my desk, easing into our conversation. I decided to let her talk, which she seemed eager to do. I figured out quickly that she liked the fact that I just listened. In that, she didn't prove immune to something I've observed in my years as a psychiatrist: if you say little, people often tell you everything. Plus, she knew that I was taking her seriously, not charging her a fee, and not automatically assuming she was mentally disturbed or pushing for a hospitalization.

She mentioned that Father Jacques had taken her to a couple of psychologists first. Jacques had told her that in their view no psychological explanation came close to explaining her strange condition. As believers, both agreed she was possessed. She went on to say that Jacques wanted the opinion of a physician, however. She took some glee in telling me that the original "shrinks" were a little scared of her.

"Then he put me on the phone with a Jesuit priest he knew. He seems to know a lot of people, big shots. This priest was also a psychiatrist. I couldn't stand the guy. He was a real smartass. He said he couldn't tell me his full opinion over the phone, but he went out of his way to tell me he thought my thinking was 'off.' Can you believe the nerve of the guy? Here he was giving me some dim-witted opinion even though he never met me and didn't know all the facts. Him and his stupid, heavy red curtains."

"How do you know he has red curtains?" I asked. "You told me you spoke to him over the phone."

Julia laughed and lit up, visibly excited. With a glimmer in her eyes, she explained that she had some "powers." One of them, she claimed, was what students of the paranormal call "remote viewing."

"I can also wreak havoc whenever I want."

I was learning fast here. My characteristic incredulity faded by the minute, with every new piece of information Julia presented me.

"But I don't want to get into that now," she said. "You'll see soon enough." She promised to tell me the truth, but she wasn't ready to tell me everything about her devotion to Satan, or anything about the cult or its leader and participants. "It might be better for you not to know anyway, if you get my drift, doc."

In my previous conversations with Father Jacques he had assured me that he was positive Julia was involved with a committed group of avowed devil worshippers. I also knew she claimed to be a kind of satanic witch—a claim that still seemed fantastic to me, despite her continued candor. Still, I was starting to believe her story, or rather I wasn't ruling out its veracity on the basis of this conversation. At least she didn't give me the impression that she was deluded or simply trying to cause a stir with sensational stories.

She told me she was not some pathetic "loony bird," as the Jesuit had implied. "He told Father Jacques I should probably be observed in a hospital." For the first time, Julia got annoyed. "I have never had any need for psychiatric help in my life."

Despite her growing anger, she said all this with such conviction that I again was surprised by the coherence of her vehement reasoning.

"You won't do that, will you? Put me in the hospital against my will? Father said you're more open-minded than most shrinks and have some experience with people like me."

I told her that I wasn't in the habit of putting people in the hospital unless they are a danger to themselves or to others. Julia visibly relaxed.

"I think I trust you. You seem an honest guy, I can tell. I trust Father Jacques, too. He's actually very sweet. He's sort of a wimp, but good-hearted. I just hope he knows what he's doing. I'm not a big fan of priests. Some seem dense to me. Others are worse, if you get my drift."

I'd heard enough and decided not to push further. I wanted to make sure that Father Jacques had told her that I wasn't serving as her physician, that I was an unpaid consultant to him, so there was no real confidentiality. I asked whether that was an acceptable arrangement to her, and she readily agreed.

I felt compelled to add that her talking to me was voluntary and that I wasn't going to do traditional therapy or push any medication. Rather, I was going to explore her beliefs and the ambivalence she brought to seeking exorcisms. I told her she could visit with me from time to time, or not, as she chose and as Father Jacques suggested, though only as long as she didn't in any way try to mess with me or my family. I had been tempted to add "again," thinking about the incident with our cats. If she decided she wanted a regular therapist or needed medication, I would try to arrange something.

She laughed again. She repeated that she had no need of either and that she wasn't a crazy person. She said she wanted additional exorcisms and realized Father Jacques strongly wanted her to talk to me about her fears about moving forward.

She was more thoughtful and brighter than I'd thought likely of someone who had joined such a shady cult. Her intelligence, I later guessed, was why she later assumed more of a leadership role in the group as so-called high priestess, as if she were pagan royalty.

She then chewed on her lip. I sensed some confusion on her part, a quiet vulnerability hiding beneath her outward boldness and tough exterior. "Can people really recover from this sort of thing?" she asked.

"Yes, they can, and you can," I said, with a confidence now based on my experience with several, admittedly less dramatic, cases of possession. "But there isn't a quick fix. You have to work at it. You have to want it."

After Julia left, Father Jacques elaborated on her situation. He believed she was possessed because she had become a Satanist and had turned to an evil lifestyle, though why it was her specifically who had become possessed, he couldn't say. "It's always a mystery why one person with such a background might become possessed, but not another with similar intentions. I believe she has consented to serve Satan in a more dramatic and explicit way. I wonder just what she was willing to promise for her special privileges with Satan and her elevated standing with the cult."

Father Jacques didn't know too much about this group, but knew Julia had at times been living with several members. She had undergone a few exorcisms with little result, but Jacques remained optimistic. Given her refusal to break definitively from her cult, however, I wondered whether "Pollyannaish" was a better description of Jacques's expectation.

I was becoming increasingly aware that, once again, he wasn't asking me for a diagnosis. Instead, he wanted a better understanding of Julia's seeming ambivalence about continuing the exorcisms. He hoped I would be able to help unravel her motives.

Father Jacques confirmed that Julia had previously met with the two psychologists. As part of my consultation I telephoned them to corroborate Father Jacques's impressions. I knew and trusted the work of the first one. After interviewing Julia a few months previously, he had concluded she wasn't psychotic. The second psychologist agreed. "She doesn't seem at all delusional and has no reason to make things up," he told me. "Although she may like intimidating people with her accounts, I don't think she exaggerates. She gives a lot of specific details. I would question her motives if she were lying at the very time she is asking for exorcisms of her own free will. It seems counterproductive to get help from the church to acknowledge still being in the cult."

Neither man believed that Julia had any overt psychiatric disease, even though they felt, as I did, there were clear features of a "personality disorder," that is, ingrained and poorly adaptive character traits—in her case of an unsavory and long-standing nature. Both concluded there was no clinical or conventional explanation for the paranormal features that seemed to follow Julia and that her overall story seemed credible.

Father Jacques entertained no doubts.

• • •

Shortly after my first office visit with Julia, Father Jacques, Julia, and I were speeding along a highway in the priest's old Chevy, searching for a suitable venue for the next exorcism—at least, that's what Father Jacques told me we were doing. I later realized that he wanted the three of us to spend some time together so I could observe Julia in a more casual setting. I sat in the front passenger seat and Julia was in the back, alone with her thoughts. I wanted to talk to her, but Father Jacques's erratic driving distracted me.

"I'll be the assisting exorcist," Father Jacques said, swerving the Chevy between lanes and riding the brakes. "The chief exorcist is an interesting character. You'll meet him soon."

From the back I heard a deep, raspy voice, "Leave her alone, you fucking monkey priest." Startled, I turned around and saw Julia glaring at us, her fists clenched. "She is *ours*. We will never let her go. You'll be sorry, you stupid monkey priest." The "monkey" part I've always felt a fair indication of how evil spirits view us humans.

The voice was coming out of Julia's mouth, but it wasn't really Julia. Her face had taken on a distant, even vacant look. She went on like this for ten minutes.

Suddenly, the voice stopped, and Julia reemerged from whatever state I had just witnessed. She had no idea what had just happened. I asked her whether she remembered telling the priest anything. She did not, and she asked us what had been said, where we were, and how far we had traveled.

After that trip, I lost any lingering doubts about her situation. But I still wanted to question her further, especially about her boast of being a satanic witch, a claim that still seemed fantastic to me.

A few days later, she and I met again, this time at Father Jacques's office. Not hesitating, I dove right into how she viewed herself and her status in the cult. She told me that she enjoyed her powers. She took great pride in them. *A funny sort of pride*, I was thinking, considering their source. Smiling, she promised their demonstration soon. I encouraged her to continue.

"You have to realize that I'm the priestess of the cult," she told me. "I'm their queen, Satan's queen. I trust him alone."

She pressed further. "Why do you think people worship Satan? People usually think we are just superstitious or crazy and delusional and make things up. Well, I'm not nuts and have never seen or needed a headshrinker. You think we become Satanists because we're stupid? It's because we get a *lot* in return. We worship Satan because he looks after us and grants us big favors."

Julia stated matter-of-factly that her psychic "abilities" were the traditional privileges of a high-status devil worshipper. "They're my due," she said. She didn't quibble about the term "witch" but felt she was actually of a higher status than most witches. She relished her role and insisted that her paranormal abilities were typical only of a "powerful witch, not a run-of-the mill one."

Her clear-eyed appreciation of her "gifts" intrigued me. In my years as a psychiatrist and psychoanalyst I had never encountered a person like Julia before. In addition to her apparent capacity to view people remotely, Julia's powers included an accurate knowledge of others without having direct contact with them. She once told me how my own mother had died by the precise cause of ovarian cancer, which she had no way of knowing without a special source of knowledge. She did the same with other people, too. Some of this awareness falls under the category of "hidden knowledge." Like speaking foreign languages, it is another of the classic signs of possession, as noted.

Later, I called Father Jacques to discuss proposed dates for Julia's next exorcism. Suddenly, another voice interrupted our telephone conversation, hissing, "We said LEAVE HER ALONE, YOU FUCKING PRIEST. She belongs to US, not you. You'll be SORRY."

The voice was the same unsettling and creepy one I had heard in Father Jacques's Chevy. As clichéd as it sounds, I felt the hair on the back of my neck stand up, and I nearly hung up the phone in a startled reaction.

I asked Father Jacques whether he had just heard the voice, too. "I've heard a demon's voice come over a phone line like this in a number of cases," he said, "always the more severe ones."

I reflected that I again felt invaded, even more so than by the incident with our cats. *They can intrude on my own phone,* I was thinking. *Just how far can these nasty creatures manipulate our surroundings, even our belongings?* I imagined that the battle lines were drawn more starkly. I was being targeted, too, at least to a point. Because I was trying to help Julia, our demonic foes now considered me part of the problem. What else was in store?

I always believe that skepticism should start out governing all these investigations, but it is difficult and foolish to hold on to disbelief in the face of such overwhelming evidence. After observing Julia on our trip, reflecting upon her knowledge of the cats, and now hearing the disturbing voice over the phone, I lost any lingering doubts about her dire situation. Something beyond a medical disorder clearly was occurring here and in a manner far beyond what I had observed in previous cases.

I could not diagnosis any mental or physical reason that could explain these events. It had long been difficult to see Julia's state as any sort of psychiatric disturbance, particularly when so many inexplicable and peculiar events were simultaneously happening. From my work on inpatient units, I had seen many cases of so-called multiple personality disorder, now more properly labeled dissociative identity disorder. This was hardly that. Although such patients "dissociate," this exchange and the other paranormal features I had experienced firsthand with Julia convinced me that this case entailed phenomena far beyond what any psychiatric patient presents. I wondered again just what I had gotten myself into.

Before the next scheduled exorcism ritual, I had another long talk with Julia when she returned to the area. I was direct, asking her: "Why are you hesitant to keep going on with the exorcisms? And yet you are the one *requesting* them."

She didn't say anything for a long time. I was trying to imagine her emotional state. Oppositional and ornery? Manipulative and scheming? Fearful? I felt all these options were on the table.

Finally, looking down, she said, "I'm scared. I'm suffering. I need to get rid of this."

"Tell me more about that," I said.

She sighed and finally recounted what she called a "long story." She hadn't had an easy life. She had been baptized a Catholic and attended Catholic schools but never took religious beliefs seriously. Her family life "wasn't so great," something I fully expected to hear. But she was reluctant to provide much detail about her parents or criticize them either.

When she was a teenager, a priest took an interest in her. "I soon found out what *that* was about," she stated. Julia told me he had sexually molested her. Strangely, she didn't think it had affected her much, although she noted that it certainly drove her away from the church. Sexually naïve at the time, she was curious about sex and, she told me, mostly enjoyed the physical contact before fully realizing what sex was all about.

She dismissed it as her "dalliance" but admitted that the molestation did more than disillusion her about the church. She felt it eventually contributed to her attraction to a local group of Satanists in the area that an acquaintance told her about one day when she complained about the priest.

I was aware of the toll such sexual abuse takes, especially from an expectedly trustworthy authority. I felt Julia minimized her trauma and other stressors of her youth and family life. I was also thinking that she was probably opening up more to me than she had to anyone else, which I took as a sign that maybe she was willing to accept help.

But I had to remind myself that I wasn't serving as her therapist, and so I didn't want her to become overwhelmed by her powerful memories. I had seen patients fall apart after sessions where they first ventilate such traumatic issues. Still, Julia continued to describe these painful memories in a matter-of-fact manner and didn't seem overwhelmed. Because of my training, I knew she was omitting many details, but I let her continue without pressing her. It was hard to be sure of a confident formulation of her dynamics. I was curious, for instance, about her early family life and what her cult was like. But because I was explicitly *not* her therapist, I decided to let her go on at her own pace and choosing. Her tale lacked key details, but I got the sense that, in turning to this bizarre cult, she may have been looking for a substitute family.

"I fell in love with its leader, a powerful guy named Daniel," she admitted. "He was the first really strong man I had met or had relations with. Very handsome and domineering, a little dark-skinned—not like that pale priest who looked like he'd spent his life in a library. Daniel had an air of danger. I know certain women go for the 'bad boy' type. I guess I was one of them."

A search for pleasure—the point of existence—was at the core of how she thought of herself. This, she stated, was the typical thinking of true Satanism. Julia explained how the cult eventually made her its queen. She called herself Queen Lilith, after the name of a legendary demon seductress. The cult also worshipped Asmodeus, "the demon of lust," she added. What she really liked to call herself, though, was the Queen of Voluptuous Delights. She had signed letters she'd sent to Father Jacques with that title, as he later showed me.

Sex was obviously a big piece of all this. Sex seemed a part of many weird cults in some way, shape, or form. The women, especially the younger and more desired ones, were often sought after for their "favors"—until, that is, they weren't. Male leaders often restricted the females to their own pleasurable purposes, excluding "lesser" male followers from the delights of such benefits.

Julia developed a taste for kinky sex. "I was pretty perverted," she told me, grinning. "Still am."

She'd been flattered that the priest, a smart and educated man, had found her enticing, but she didn't seem especially clingy or obsessed with him, as many patients with borderline features tend to become. She was hardly impressed with his sexual prowess, describing him as inexperienced and fumbling, though a "nice, gentle man." She recounted without much emotion that he eventually got kicked out of the priesthood. She thought he may have later killed himself.

By contrast, she stated, "sex with Daniel was like something I fantasized about, rough at times, but it excited me to no end." Orgies with the other members of the cult were a frequent occurrence, as well, which Julia also found arousing. She liked that the men in the group all wanted to have sex with her. Julia did get jealous to see Daniel with other women, but she felt that was the life she had chosen.

She enjoyed the orgies, which she called "parties." But sex was often a part of their more elaborate rituals, too. She hesitated to tell me much about these periodic ceremonies, which she called Black Masses, in parody of the traditional Catholic Mass. Scholars date such rituals to at least the Middle Ages and some to even earlier times. Though these rituals have varied widely over the centuries, sex and bodily fluids have often played an integral part in them. Julia told me little other than that they would dress in robes and use stolen eucharistic hosts during ceremonies.

Daniel—who ran the ceremonies dressed in full satanic garb—was the most powerful member of the group. He was devoted to Satan and prayed to him all the time, which is why, according to Julia, he, too, received so many privileges in return. His powers eclipsed Julia's. He had some kind of profession, Julia said, but from a communication of his that I was shown, he appeared a vile and not exceptionally bright guy—an obvious narcissist.

Julia originally thought he cared about her in a special way, but she was beginning to wonder whether his feelings had changed. She was getting older and told me she wasn't sure she could get pregnant anymore.

"Meaning?" I asked.

Julia hesitated before answering my question. I could sense that she was debating how much to tell me. She chose her words carefully and spoke defensively.

"I was the cult's main breeder," she said. "I could get pregnant easily, which gave me a special status in the group. We had someone who could perform abortions, a physician's assistant, I think, a repulsive guy. We used fetuses for ceremonies. Daniel encouraged it and said he and Satan would honor and reward me greatly for this 'service' and be eternally grateful for my role.

"I sure wanted to be in good with Satan. He could deliver the goods. People paint his kingdom as eternal torment, but I doubt that. It's some kind of society, I suppose, even if there are some punishments and stuff. There is that in this life, too. And there I'd have a high status, I was promised. So, I was excited to do this benefit to him in some strange way. Plus, Daniel was pleased with me, too."

Julia said Daniel told her that people had been doing this kind of "service" to Satan for centuries. The group considered themselves pagans, he argued, and he claimed that a lot of pagan cultures were essentially demon worshippers, but the Aztecs did far worse in sacrificing *living* humans—mostly women and children.

I was repulsed, but said nothing. Later, I heard similar stories from a few other individuals, though I was rarely sure of their credibility; I generally doubted their veracity, though a few such stories seemed credible to me from their details, in addition to Julia's. I once asked an assistant district attorney whether such a thing as using a dead fetus in satanic rituals was illegal. "Well, technically, yes," he told me. "But no one is going to prosecute someone for that. Plus, how are you going to obtain evidence?" He asked me whether I knew of any ongoing examples. I told him that everyone who spoke of such "offerings," as Julia called them, claimed they no longer engaged in that behavior.

As Julia recounted her role in these demonic ceremonies, she seemed untroubled by her past actions. What seemed to bother her the most was her fear that Daniel no longer loved her. "For the first time in my life I had felt really special," she said. "Daniel had singled me out. It started out when I was a cute teenager. It was really intoxicating for a while. But now I'm not so sure. I'm getting older and wonder whether Daniel still cares for me. He said 'okay' when I told him I'm just trying to cause some mischief with the priests by seeking their advice and maybe get them in hot water if I can. He'd love that, trust me, and so would Satan. But I'm not sure if he still cares what happens to me. I don't think I can breed now and wonder whether I'm, you know, 'expendable.'"

I was struck by her openness and also took notice of her ongoing fear. But I wondered whether everything she described was fully accurate. I didn't have a good feeling about what she was saying—or how she was saying it. During our meetings her attitude about seeking help would shift dramatically from genuine hopefulness and a vague search for God and forgiveness to an outright rejection and special hatred of Christianity. Privately, I questioned whether she really wanted the help except during moments of transient desperation.

Though somewhat hindered by Julia's unwillingness to reveal too much, I attempted to get a better feel for her personality in the hope of better understanding her hesitation. I felt sure by then that she had some entrenched features of personality disorder that were interfering with her ability to make a firm commitment. Patients with border-line personality disorder are often inconsistent in their intentions and attitudes. Julia didn't seem a fragile person, as many such individuals are, but she also had other character defects that, despite her apparent frankness, made me question her motives. She was a bit grandiose and could be quite critical and belittling—behavior that was suggestive of some narcissistic traits. I suspected she was desperate enough to attempt to cause trouble for Father Jacques, perhaps to ingratiate herself with Daniel. Maybe, I considered, she was trying to have it both ways—trying to rid herself of the possession while not alienating or even leaving the cult.

I knew enough by then about how victims of such demonic attacks needed to work at their own spiritual liberation and to understand that they had to strongly commit to their spiritual health. I told her exorcisms weren't magical incantations, like the chants of a witch doctor. But she didn't seem able to take in my advice, perhaps being too afraid to think things through fully.

* * *

By the time Julia agreed to continue her exorcisms, I had met the "chief" exorcist, a diocesan priest in good standing from a neighboring state. He called himself "Father A.," which I imagined as his nom de guerre.

Father A. had a wealth of practical knowledge and wasn't afraid to let victims know where he stood and what they would need to do to be liberated. He either introduced me to or told me about many of the cases he had seen, most of which had had successful outcomes. Not everyone liked him; a few priests found him too dictatorial. But I knew, like Jacques, that he always had the best interests of those he was trying to guide uppermost in his mind.

Julia had originally approached a local priest, who sent her to Father Jacques and Father A. Though discreet about his work, Father A. was probably the most experienced exorcist in US history. As far as I know, he only once broke his public silence by appearing on a radio program to discuss Julia's case, her exorcisms, and the outcome. In the process, he revealed some specific details about her situation that I have never been comfortable exposing. I told him so at the time. He apologized, but he nevertheless felt that leaving some kind of public account as the exorcist in charge was important for the historical record.

He and Father Jacques always kept me abreast of their dealings with Julia. I also spoke to several other participants of her past exorcism sessions—all honest, God-fearing souls who knew what my role was. They promised scrupulous accuracy with me about what they observed at Julia's previous rituals as well as at any future sessions.

Julia told me once that her cult and especially Daniel despised Father A. so much that he was their number one target. "He's the one the cult really hates," she told me. "He's a special priest. Oh, how they would love to get him."

I pondered whether Julia had become preoccupied with him. Perhaps here was another strong male figure she was drawn to.

One day, out of the blue, Julia told me she could "see" Father A., just as she had earlier told me she "saw" from afar the office of the Jesuit psychiatrist whom she disparaged. I gathered it was more of a clear and very powerful image in her head than something she literally saw with her eyes.

I wasn't going to let her off this time by allowing her to avoid my questioning. "Well, that seems impossible," I said. "What in the world are you talking about?"

She calmly claimed that she could "see" Father A. "in a blue windbreaker and khakis," walking along the seashore near where he lived. She had never visited his home and knew nothing about where he lived. She called this ability on her part her "projections," a term she used idiosyncratically, not in the psychiatric sense.

I immediately called Father A. on his cell phone and asked where he was and what he was wearing. "I'm usually in the rectory at this hour but decided to take a walk tonight," he told me. "I'm saying my breviary along the shore in my khaki pants and a windbreaker."

"What color is your windbreaker," I pursued.

"You must be talking to Julia. She's something else, isn't she?"

Julia could also tell me when Father A. was in physical pain. I have always wondered whether she had anything to do with causing that pain. Her and Father A.'s own views were that Satan sure did.

• • •

I met with Julia a couple more times before Father Jacques proposed the exorcism sessions were to start up again. Although I did not expect I could attend the actual rituals, I continued to probe her motives and her openness to a genuine break with her past. She continued to be strikingly frank with me but remained frustratingly noncommittal. Eventually she agreed to resume getting help, without a firm resolve to leave her life as a Satanist, so I remained pessimistic about her outcome.

In anticipation of the resumption of the exorcisms, Father A. brought me up-to-date. He was more worked up than I had ever seen him.

"She seemed to get cold feet before the last session," he said. "We talked to her for over an hour about giving the exorcism a try, but she balked. She looked more scared than I had ever seen her."

Father A. took a deep breath and said, "But the events afterward proved scarier." Julia had needed a ride back to where she was staying, and Father Jacques had promised to drive her, given the late hour.

"You know Jacques by now," Father A. continued. "He is so good-hearted that he can't say no to people. Stupidly I agreed we'd drive her. How could we do otherwise when it was too late to do anything else? Big mistake, though."

They all three got in Father A.'s Chevy, with Julia again in the back seat. They noticed rather quickly that she had returned to her possessed condition. Wearily, Father A. described her state as "the usual stuff," by which he meant boasts from the demon, statements that she had promised herself to Satan, and taunts that the demon would never leave her.

Then with a thin smile, Father A. said, "Then the real fun began."

I raised my eyebrows, curious to learn what happened next. I was still learning the many bizarre wiles and strategies of our demonic foes, but I was surprised when Father A. said, "That's when the spirits appeared!"

Father Jacques had previously instructed me how evil spirits can affect our own senses and material reality, which makes it difficult, if not impossible, to tell the difference at times between what's real and what isn't. Because both he and Father Jacques saw the same things, Father A. believed the spirits were altering material reality at that point and reflected their ability to assume, visibly, various shapes when appearing to humans.

"They appeared, *seemingly*, in front of the windshield—fleeting, wavy, dark things," he said.

As Father A. started to pull the car over, the headlights of the Chevy went dark, along with all the dashboard lights. Driving blind, Father A. veered the car into a small ditch, shaken, no doubt, but unhurt. There they were, stuck on a dark country road without any way of seeing where they were going—or where they could get help.

I asked Father A. how Julia reacted to all this. He snorted and said she seemed just fine. He described the same annoying smirk I had witnessed so many times before. It was unclear when she came out of her possessed state, and so she may have missed the real action. "She never thanked us, of course," Father A. ended.

I remember thinking that they should hardly have expected gratitude and were lucky they were still alive, given their poor decision to drive a possessed woman home at night.

• • •

Two weeks later, following Julia's next exorcism, Father A. telephoned me again. This time, he told me that he feared Julia might never agree to attend another session.

The ritual began on a cold evening in the late fall on the grounds of Father Jacques's parish in his well-heeled suburban town. The "team" included eight people: Father A., the chief exorcist; Father Jacques, who assisted Father A.; two nuns, one of them a nurse; and four laypeople recruited to help, a woman and three strong men.

Everyone gathered in a chapel in the small house where Jacques lived. Julia was half an hour late, and when she finally arrived, she was hesitant and nervous—perhaps already under some "influence." Nevertheless, she signed the requisite forms to proceed.

Father Jacques started the formal prayers, using the older Latin version of the *Rituale Romanum*, which includes the classic text for exorcism from 1614, his preferred source for the rite. As the litany began, Julia rapidly entered a full trance. "Soon the 'voice' was expressing itself, again adopting its typically arrogant tone," Father A. told me over the phone. "It protested that no one had a right to liberate this woman because she had freely promised herself to Satan, a typical sentiment of evil spirits. The creature or creatures was trying to bully them all and employed the usual complaints, blasphemies, and boasts. 'We won't ever leave. STOP. GO.'"

According to Father A., the ritual continued for at least two hours, and the demon repeated the same sentiments throughout the exorcism. Though the demon generally directed its animus to Father A., it also regularly taunted the two nuns, calling them "whores" and "sluts."

I imagined the scene in my head. The participants would have surrounded Julia, in case they needed to hold or restrain her. All of them would have taken direction from Father A., who commanded the room and was exacting in his methods, as I knew from past experiences.

With a possessed female, Father A. always ordered the women to hold the victim, in part to preempt any later charge of misconduct by the males present. On this night, the two invited nuns and the laywoman had their hands directly on Julia's shoulders and arms, ready to grab her if she struck out or bolted. This time it proved necessary. Father A. told me that from the beginning of the exorcism ritual Julia was straining with considerable strength. She tried to grab Father A.'s stole from around his neck. Fortunately, her arms and hands had been restrained. Everyone wondered how Julia could sustain this effort over two full hours, but they recognized that they were struggling against the power of the evil spirit's supernatural strength, another classic sign of a genuine possession.

"And then," Father A. continued, "it happened."

"What?" I asked.

"Julia levitated right out of her chair. For half an hour."

All the witnesses later corroborated this story. Julia visibly rose about a foot off the chair and, in the clear impression of all attendees, would have ascended higher if it hadn't been for several of those present, including all the men, laboring mightily to hold her down. Later, one witness commented to me, "She would have gone to the ceiling if we hadn't stopped it. Was it an attempt to escape or scare the participants? It's hard to say, but everyone was shaken."

Levitation is a rare but well-documented event in religious chronicles, including past and current exorcisms. I tried to imagine their astonishment and fright.

Father A. paused. He seemed fatigued and discouraged, absent in the conversation in a manner I wasn't used to.

"Father," I now pressed him, "are *you* still here?"

"Sorry, Rich. I'm feeling a bit pessimistic as I'm telling you this. The demons—because I thought multiple ones were involved—kept up their constant barrage and seemed to get stronger as I grew more tired. One told us that Julia had invited them in and had received many favors in return, so she had no right to be freed of their presence." He hesitated again. "Maybe they know her intentions better than any of us. I had already been wondering whether she ever felt interested in renouncing them at all."

Then Father A. recounted a long list of the more dramatic phenomena he had encountered during the long session. The demon, or demons, frequently writhed in pain upon any contact with holy water he sprinkled on Julia, yelling, "Stop! It burns!" On the other hand, Julia had never had any reaction to tap water during any of her earlier test assessments, though her possessing spirit, of course, would not have been told which water had been blessed.

During the rituals, including this one, Father A. told me, the demon often spoke in several foreign languages Julia didn't know. According to Jacques, who knew the language well, the demon spoke articulate Latin.

At some point during the last ritual, the room became distinctly frigid, and then the temperature spiked drastically, making the room stiflingly hot. "It was like we were standing right next to a boiler and someone turned it up to maximum strength," Father A. told me. Also, loud cries and groans and other raucous, animal-like noises interrupted Father A.'s prayers, making him feel like he was in the "middle of a dangerous jungle," he said. "Rich, I felt like I was at the gates of hell."

Other exorcists have over the years reported to me similar happenings, and I have encountered many such examples in the historical literature. But, as I reexamine the extraordinary testimony in Julia's case, confirmed in exact detail by all the participants, I'm still struck by the almost unprecedented force of her possession. Combined, these features appeared to me to clearly represent the response of a powerful enemy fighting desperately to keep controlling a woman who had specifically dedicated herself to Satan.

The intensity of Julia's exorcism surprised even Father A. and Father Jacques. The display seemed intended to frighten them away or, they surmised, to prevent Julia from abandoning the cult or continuing to reveal its nefarious behaviors to perceived interlopers. Other experienced exorcists later commented to me that Father A. and Father Jacques should have prevented such "theatrical" manifestations by commanding the demon or demons not to create such havoc. But given the immense pastoral experience of my two exorcist friends, I feel that in this case they encountered a spirit, or spirits, too powerful to control.

When the session ended, Julia rapidly emerged from her trancelike state. Like most (though not all) possessed people, she characteristically remembered nothing, though the exorcism had lasted a little over two hours.

• • •

The sad ending to this story is that Julia was never delivered from her demonic presence. This was an unfortunate case of an avowed Satanist reluctant to break from her involvement with her cult and to stop her devil worship, which would require considerably more of a change of mind and dedication on her part. After this spectacular session, Julia chose not to pursue continued exorcisms, though she was offered the opportunity to resume if she wished.

I believe that Julia was probably deathly afraid of the cult—and Daniel in particular—and was simply never fully committed to getting spiritual assistance; or perhaps she wasn't emotionally ready to leave the group. Either way, she found it difficult to commit to the help of exorcists.

I increasingly mistrusted her motives, too, because in subsequent meetings, she told me stories made up to discredit many of the priests she had known in her life, including Father Jacques and Father A.

Her ambivalence was best illustrated in one of my last conversations with her. I already knew that she enjoyed her high status in the cult but feared she was becoming less attractive to Daniel. She seemed preoccupied again that she couldn't breed anymore, calling it a "big blow" to how she was now treated. She also told me that members who had tried to leave her cult had been dealt with harshly. "You don't want to mess with Daniel," she said. "He's too close to

Satan. I did want at least to get rid of the possession, but now I'm not so sure what I should do."

I listened closely. Her fatalistic tone and use of the past tense were new, which made me believe, as Father A. did, that we were losing her.

"Jesus, God, whatever. I understand nothing of all that. Where were they when I needed them? But Father Jacques keeps telling me I have to turn to them, whatever that means, and renounce Satan. Renounce Satan! Are you kidding me? How can I do that? Who knows what'll happen to me? This isn't someone you want against you. Trust me, I know. He's punished me plenty already."

Julia then went on to talk in a manner surprisingly reflective.

"People think hellfire comes from God. That's not true. It comes from Satan. That's how he disciplines his subjects. He has to have some way of punishing people, at least from time to time. He's done the same to me."

Julia complained about experiencing a burning sensation from her own diabolic tormenters.

"What's it like?" I asked.

"Not like a material fire. Kind of a spiritual type, very hard to explain in words. You don't get burned up. But it does hurt—like Hell, I was going to say!"

She laughed a little, without mirth.

Gruesome as such comments seem, Julia is hardly the only demonically attacked individual who has complained to me about experiencing a burning sensation from their evil tormenters, in addition to a variety of other pains.

Satan, according to Julia, was still her Master, and she continued to place some crazy hope in him. She still worshipped him, she admitted, calling this demand for devotion to Satan a direct challenge made to all humans and "to what Christians call their God."

These last statements didn't entirely surprise me, but after our time together I felt disheartened. I reminded myself that my aim was solely to assist her, if I could. She didn't owe *me* anything.

"I've been punished by the cult, too, in the past," she added. "They can be sadistic. They call it 'the discipline.' They'll lock me in a box for hours, that kind of thing. I don't really want to talk about it. I've told you too much already. I'll probably get punished for doing that, too."

I countered that, although she had given up at the time, it was never too late for her to change her mind. I agreed that she couldn't have it both ways, though. To leave that life once and for all, I told her, she had to abandon the cult and cease praying to Satan, regardless of her fear. Sensing she had made a firm decision for the near term, I added that Father Jacques never gave up on anyone.

She said that she had tried to be loyal to him, too, despite telling Daniel she aimed eventually to "get" Jacques and Father A. She realized we three genuinely cared about her, which was at least something positive, I thought. But I felt that I was clutching at straws and that she seemed much more concerned about Daniel's reaction.

"I've probably ruined my relationship with him now," she said. "He always knows too much. I thought I'd at least get rid of the possession, but I no longer believe that'll happen either."

She hesitated, but then resumed talking with more confidence, as if she had at last resolved what the immediate future would bring her. She called it "taking a break."

Then she surprised me by giving me permission, almost encouragement, to tell her story someday. She didn't want me to identify her directly or reveal where she lived or other known associates. "Okay? I know you're a professor. It's the least I can do, to maybe warn some other vulnerable people," she said.

I think she wanted to give me a last gift, or perhaps soothe her conscience. I realized again, for all her bravado, she was a conflicted and tortured person—and probably had been for much of her life. I kept thinking of the word "trapped," which is how I saw her at that moment. She was probably too confused and scared to make a rational decision, I concluded.

And here, as I was getting a sense of a looming ending, I felt I'd obtained a fuller grasp of why she felt the way she did. She always felt threatened in some way—either by the cult or by the stipulation the exorcists were making to overturn her lifestyle, or by the loss of Daniel's love and attention. Maybe until that moment she had never fully grasped the true price she had to pay, the real-life demands and not the "magic" that had become so much a part of her mentality.

• • •

Several months after Julia's last exorcism, at Father Jacques's strong urging, we visited her in her southern hometown. She remained reluctant to carry on.

As I was traveling home by plane from our meeting, my wife and my secretary both received a phone call from a man posing as a "priest and friend." He told them that Father Jacques and I had been in a serious car accident and were in critical condition. Without answering any more questions, he hung up. Fearing the worst, my wife frantically tried to locate the hospital where I supposedly had been taken. It wasn't until several hours later, when I routinely checked in by phone from LaGuardia Airport in New York, that they learned I was fine.

A few weeks later I was walking along East 29th Street in New York City and noticed two women in their thirties following me for a few blocks. They were adorned with prominent black eyeliner makeup, as Julia often had been, and dressed in the eccentric manner peculiar to the group with which she was involved. When they saw that I had spotted them, they veered off around a corner onto Madison Avenue, and I never saw them again.

I spoke with Julia only one more time. A year after the last exorcism, Father Jacques asked me to call her and check her health status again. Julia confided that she'd been diagnosed with terminal cancer but said she wanted to be freed from demonic influence before her death.

To me, Julia still sounded ambivalent. She told me she would have to "think about" giving me permission to get a report from her oncologist. Then she never contacted me or Father Jacques again, although Jacques tried to reach out to her several times before his own death some years later. I was never able to verify with certainty whether or when she died. Though doubtful, I hope she is still alive, of course, and was still just looking for some brief contact with us to see if we still cared.

PART TWO

INVESTIGATOR AND DIAGNOSTICIAN

. . . beauty is mysterious as well as terrible. God and the devil are fighting there and the battlefield is the heart of man.

—FYODOR DOSTOEVSKY, *THE BROTHERS KARAMAZOV*

CHAPTER FOUR

TROUBLES OF THE SPIRIT

Diagnosing the Spectrum of Possessions

I was learning rapidly about this strange battlefield. More often than not, this relentless clash for the hearts and souls of men and women tells a tale of confusion and human ignorance, and pain for so many. And, yes, it involved a real battle by vicious foes who could also assail victims, oddly enough, *physically* in the rare but by then multiple circumstances I was witnessing. Once attacked, people do not escape their clutches easily without a struggle, as I had seen so many times.

If I was going to consult in such a wide variety of situations and properly advise people, I realized that, like any good doctor, I had to keep learning my new trade and investigate every relevant facet of the field.

After those early cases, I spent the next years delving into both the history and the present reality of demonic activity and exorcisms. I studied every book I could get my hands on about the subject—pro and con, religious or secular—some dating back centuries and written in various languages. My knowledge of Latin and ancient Greek proved especially valuable in reading classical and medieval accounts of possessions and exorcisms.

At the same time, I became connected to the wider exorcism community. I consulted for and taught a rapidly growing number of official

Catholic exorcists and some of the most noted practitioners of "deliverance ministries" in the United States and around the world, generally Protestants, but also Catholic "charismatics." In addition to my work with Father Jacques and Father A., I was starting to receive calls from many non-Catholic and non-Christian victims, too.

In the process, I came to learn the strict criteria that allowed me to understand the varieties of demonic attacks and those psychiatric conditions that have always confused so many people. I needed to keep my hat on as a physician and firm believer in science. But I also needed to remain open-minded and compassionate about the immensely suffering victims of this stark and obscure world I had stumbled upon, or that had stumbled upon me.

• • •

I came to see by that early stage that the major task of physicians in working with exorcists is to differentiate what may be termed troubles of the spirit from troubles of the mind. The former are also called "extraordinary attacks" of evil spirits, which include possessions and oppressions. These conditions exist on a continuum, representing a spectrum of penetration by demons. In turn, each of these conditions needs to be distinguished from what believers call "ordinary" influences of evil spirits upon humans, or simply temptations. Human beings are also perfectly capable of sinful or evil behavior on their own, of course, though there are plenty of people who prefer to blame their misbehavior on demons.

Before I encountered Julia, I had already seen about eight or nine cases of what I regarded as full possessions. I define those as cases where the evil spirit *completely* takes control of someone, such that the victim has periods when he or she has no remembrance of such episodes. I have since seen scores more such possessions and a much higher number of cases of oppression, which are far more common than possessions. Because of my involvement with the International Association of Exorcists, I have heard reports of hundreds more of each type, but that hardly implies they are anything but rare conditions, as I still know them to be.

• • •

About four years after my dealings with Julia, I met another seriously possessed victim—a man from Chicago I'll call Juan. His case ended much more happily, an outcome that generally occurs when victims are more diligent in working at their liberation.

Juan was fifty-one years old, a big and well-muscled man with a string of tattoos up each arm. At our first meeting, despite his unwillingness to admit it, I could sense his anguish and vulnerability. His wife, Stella, seemed equally desperate. As a teenager, Juan had become involved with a neighborhood gang, turning to a life of crime and violence. "It was an 'okay' life but dangerous, and I wanted more, a lot more," he said. A fellow gang member told him that if he turned to Satan and "the dark side," he would be much more successful and operate under Satan's protection. "I became a devil-worshipper, I guess, and used to pray to Satan for everything I wanted."

For a couple of years, Juan got everything he desired—girls, fancy cars, money. "I was having a ball," he told me. "I was king of the heap." He started recruiting other gang members into the occult, which he believed added to his good fortune.

Specifically, Juan committed to Santa Muerte (Holy Death), an iconic Mexican folk saint that many occult members of Hispanic descent have appropriated for their diabolic causes. Some members of the infamous MS-13 gang are avowed devotees of Santa Muerte, and according to police reports and newspaper stories, they petition the saint for favors in a kind of perverse reversal of praying to saints for intercession.

Also known as Mara Salvatrucha, MS-13 started as a Los Angeles street gang of Salvadoran immigrants who had fled their homes following the civil wars of the 1980s. Eventually, MS-13 spread to a few other US metropolitan centers, including in Northern Virginia and Long

Island, where they quickly developed a reputation for drug dealing, child prostitution, robbery, and other acts of violence, from beatings and stabbings to murder. A number of ex-gang members have openly testified to their worship of what they regard as demons. "Sometimes when we wanted to find out if people were snitching on us, we would summon the devil," a former member who called himself Speedy told the *New York Post* in June 2017. "We used a Ouija board to call him."

Speedy and other former members of MS-13 have also described their experiences under a kind of "variant" possession, an unmistakably *voluntary and temporary* state of possession. For brief periods of time, they went through the typical trance state, markedly increased their strength, and gained the ability to uncover detailed and previously hidden information about complete strangers—all of which are characteristics of the possessed condition. "Once, the devil took over my body," Speedy told the *Post*. "I didn't know what was happening and it took 10 members of the gang to hold me down. In a trance, some gang members would give up names of people to target. It was a loyalty test, and we called it 'taking a soul.' If the devil gave you a name, you had to go out and mess that person up. You had to take their soul."

In Juan's case, however, his possession was not temporary nor voluntary. When the police finally moved in on his drug operation, he was convicted and sentenced to a lengthy time in prison. But in jail he started to experience states of possession, slipping into persistent and prolonged trances during which the telltale voice of a demon spoke in foreign languages unknown by Juan.

A prison chaplain confirmed Juan's story and performed exorcisms while he was incarcerated. During these in-prison rituals, the demon reportedly exhibited remarkable feats of strength, fighting off a number of burly men holding Juan down. "The exorcisms helped, I think," Juan told me. "But the evil spirit has come back, or probably never fully left."

By the time I met him, Juan and Stella were already trying to become regular churchgoers. But they reported that the demon was resuming its worst attacks against him, hindering them from attending services. "Juan'll go into a trance and then say all kinds of horrible, God-hating things," Stella told me. Like Julia, he was often prohibited from entering a church, held back by some kind of force he found difficult to describe. "That's not Juan then," Stella told me. "And when he's out of those states, he remembers nothing of them. He still speaks Latin in trances, because I recognize some of the words from when I was a kid at Sunday Mass."

Stella swore that one night, during one of his trances, Juan elevated above the bed. "He was up in the air, I swear to God!"

Juan proved a tough case, but unlike Julia, he was committed to getting help. He underwent a series of exorcisms, some of which I attended. His demon professed never to leave, a common characteristic in possessions. The cursing, the belligerence, the obstinacy, the boasts—all were in evidence. But it soon became obvious that the grip of the evil spirit upon Juan was weakening. The difference in his outcome compared with Julia's was that Juan was committed to getting rid of the demon by working on his own spiritual state; Julia had not been.

From time to time, he and Stella would get discouraged, and Juan would fall back into some bad habits, such as drug use. To his credit, though, he always picked himself up again and recommitted to his spiritual growth. By the time he seemed fully delivered, he was praying daily and attending Mass regularly. This struggling and humble man calls me from time to time to update me on his well-being.

• • •

Like Juan and Speedy, occultists have for millennia summoned spirits to grant favors or communicate through them. Edgar Cayce, who is sometimes called the father of the New Age movement, regularly did just this to great acclaim during the first half of the twentieth century, a practice that others in this field continue. Celebrity clients such as George Gershwin and Woodrow Wilson came to Cayce for help, as did thousands of others.

For various motives (often pecuniary) people who call themselves psychics or spiritualists or necromancers claim they can invite spirits to take them over and speak through them. They also claim to receive from what they think is a benign spirit world (or what they often claim is a deceased human) closely guarded secrets about other people or healing powers. They may, of course, be frauds, but a surprising number deliver accurate information, or the same hidden knowledge so typical of a possessed state. Even some police departments sometimes rely on psychics, at times claiming to have received remarkably helpful hints, though more often finding their information imprecise or inaccurate.

In any case, differing groups open themselves up to demonic sources of knowledge and have always done so; however, they generally vehemently deny that their source is diabolic. One prominent spiritualist I know, who claims he can put himself into a trance and routinely receive such valuable info, is unusual in acknowledging that many spiritualists are actually communicating with demons without knowing they are doing so, though according to him these spiritualists remain rare.

Unlike such mediums, Juan realized that his interaction with a spirit was neither temporary nor voluntary, and it was hardly benign. Thankfully, he came to understand the dangerous state he had put himself in through his seeking assistance from the devil, and he eventually mended his ways.

• • •

By the time I had talked extensively with both Julia and Juan and seen their differing outcomes after exorcism, I had certainly encountered enough genuine cases of possession and oppression even at that stage to be confident of my ability to tell the difference between people suffering from possessions or oppressions and people who were medically or psychiatrically impaired. I had had the advantage of my early tutelage from Fathers A. and Jacques, but I was also simultaneously making myself conversant with the careful literature on this subject.

In his 2005 book *Glimpses of the Devil: A Psychiatrist's Personal Accounts of Possession, Exorcism, and Redemption*, author and psychiatrist M. Scott Peck concluded that two cases he had seen were diabolically attacked. I have always been struck that, though an intrepid and open-minded explorer in this field, Peck was starting from scratch in relying exclusively on his own observations. Trusting his own intuition and his limited clinical exposure to genuine cases, he once described a diabolic attack as a rare *mental* condition. I could not disagree more. Though they do entail a cognitive aspect, diabolic attacks are *spiritual* disorders. Dr. Peck appeared to have no awareness that theologians and other thinkers had long drawn up a set of specific benchmarks to definitively classify the differing kinds of diabolic assaults. What's more, exorcists are fully expected to be learned in these matters, though they also are strongly encouraged to use the naturalistic expertise of physicians and are never supposed to just "guess," as I believe Peck was wont to do. Instead, exorcists must arrive at their conclusions with "moral certainty."

Once Father A. asked Dr. Peck whether he'd care to witness an exorcism. Peck readily agreed but insisted upon a hefty fee. Father A. withdrew the invitation. "I was doing the good doctor a favor," he later told me, "because he had much to learn." Dr. Peck also did exorcisms himself—an unwise decision as a physician.

I made sure I didn't make the same mistakes as Dr. Peck. I already knew well that exorcists and other spiritual authorities had for centuries written about the various types of demonic states, their differentiation, and their *spiritual* treatment. They knew that no medical or psychological assistance would be of any help.

The two major conditions—possessions and oppressions—exist on a continuum, from relatively minor to severe and incapacitating. In each, a recognizable pattern emerges, and like any disorder, accurate diagnosis requires a grouping of signs and symptoms that constitute a specific condition, what we call in medicine a true *syndrome*. Contrary to what many superficial students of this subject often assume, spiritual disorders are no different; their diagnoses are (or should be) rigorously conducted, too.

• • •

Diagnosing possessions (at the risk of some repetition here) is a complicated process. As with many complex subjects, not everyone agrees on its strict definition, with either a broader or a narrower view of the term "possession" variously employed by different thinkers over the centuries.

The essence of a possession is the actual *control* of the body (never the "soul" or will) of a person by one or more evil spirits. At its *full* manifestation, victims no longer are acting on their own accord; the demon has taken charge of their functioning and, periodically at least, their consciousness. The evil spirit tends to manifest openly only intermittently; that is, the spirit seems to come and go as it pleases in most serious possessions, though it apparently never really "leaves." In this "complete" type of possession, subjects do not remember at times when the full "takeover" by the evil spirit occurs; it is outside their awareness, and they have no later recollection of the demon's activity. (As we will show, however, here—as always, it seems—there are also exceptions.)

There are also said to be "temporary" and "voluntary" possessions, too, as just noted about Speedy and, I'd argue, Cayce, when subjects also often have no memory of what occurs during their altered states.

As opposed to more serious mental illnesses—where the rule is generally a fairly continuous level of disturbance for prolonged periods, albeit with exacerbations—in severe possessions the demon seems to "do its thing" and then generally lies low for a while; it even apparently more definitively "leaves" in some of the voluntary cases. In rarer cases, the victim's usual consciousness may be "submerged" by the demon's action for a much more extended period, though that behavior is the exception, not the rule.

In a serious possession (and at least especially during the involuntary type, the sort we are mostly discussing in this book), the spirit openly acts belligerently, especially attacking anything of a holy or religious nature. The entity refuses to leave the victim's body, while attempting during a typical exorcism to have the affected individual assault, or at least try to escape from, those restraining it. The extreme aversion to the sacred—frequently the initial symptom to appear—is an invariable feature of such a possession. The demonic voice, if and when it announces itself, tends to use vile and blasphemous language with a decided arrogance.

Accompanying signs vary greatly but are generally found together in the worst cases. As previously noted, for centuries, the official manual for exorcists emphasized as strongly suggestive the following *three* signs: the ability to speak an unknown language, the awareness of hidden knowledge, and various abnormal physical signs, especially immense strength, but also humanly impossible bodily "movements," extreme contortions, and even the rare levitation. All these classic features are not always present, but they recur often enough in serious possessions to serve as helpful diagnostic indicators. Quite often they may only fully appear during an exorcism, in themselves confirming that some entity beyond the human host is unequivocally operating.

The presence of a foreign creature, a spirit, in the victim is precisely what those classic signs unequivocally indicate, since it is a common-sense conclusion that humans have none of those abilities. The bizarre nature of these features formerly was termed "supernatural" or "preternatural" (beyond nature). In the past century, we have tended to label them "paranormal," a modern, quasi-scientific word, as I've argued, intended to be descriptive in a neutral way but with strongly pseudoscientific associations.

It is important to look for other potentially characteristic features, too, also frequently present during possessions. For example, the evil spirit often has the capacity to be able to distinguish blessed objects from ordinary ones, such as holy water, from which the spirit may recoil. (Hollywood seems to love portraying this reaction in particular.) But evil spirits are always crafty and duplicitous, and I have seen how sometimes demons can restrain an outburst in reaction to holy objects or ceremonies, presumably with some fair effort, to mislead witnesses— one of their principal aims. Once, when an evil spirit in a possessed man reacted with extreme repugnance to a blessed religious medal, the man grabbed the medal and threw it across the room. Then he calmed down and lied, "Oh, that stupid thing didn't bother me a bit!"

Less commonly present but associated with some traditional demonic possessions may be a remarkable ability of the possessed person to affect the surrounding physical environment, especially during exorcisms. These doings include the ability to emit intense, raucous noises of various sorts or to make a room hot or frigid or to exude remarkably powerful, sometimes sulfurous smells. All witnesses to Julia's sessions testified to the periodic appearance of all these phenomena.

Still other signs may not appear at first blush paranormal at all, but generally appear, too. Being common, they especially serve to confuse more casual onlookers to conclude that nothing out of the ordinary is going on. For instance, witnesses might have believed Julia's aversion to churches simply reflected her hostility to religion. But in the context of other signs, her physical discomfort in holy spaces was yet another indication of an entity's presence and its inability to tolerate the sacred.

Once one has witnessed a number of these possessions, it is impossible to credit their appearance to anything but distinct creatures entirely separate in their identity from the human host, real entities with spiritual faculties beyond the human. They even are forced to name themselves at times. These spirits display obviously distinct and unattractive personalities of their own and intentionally use their preternatural talents in perverse ways. They hate their human hosts and take satisfaction in tormenting them.

Satan may, in rare instances, grant his devotees the ability to demonstrate psychic powers not only outside an overt possessed state, but also in what seems their everyday conscious state, as with Julia.

Even so, they perform these paranormal feats through no inherent power of their own. Instead, they are able to draw upon their demonic sources more freely than most possessed individuals. As we saw too, Father Jacques had explained to me that a powerful diabolist like Julia, who explicitly committed herself to Satan, may be granted some "privileges" of this sort.

It should go without saying that mentally ill patients do not exhibit these paranormal traits, though people unfamiliar with psychiatric disorders sometimes imagine so. Such patients obviously cannot levitate, as both Julia and Juan did (or any of the other fifteen or so cases I've either encountered personally or had well verified, not to mention the cases documented in many historical records, like that of "Robbie Mannheim"). Nor do mentally ill patients possess accurate hidden knowledge. Those fed often remarkable info from spirits are hardly "cold readers," as is sometimes suggested. Neither can mentally ill patients or other humans spontaneously start to speak foreign languages expertly without having previously studied them. And yet possessed individuals frequently do so. Finally, though some manic and extremely agitated patients may display a high level of vitriol, energy, and force, they never exhibit anything close in degree to the massive level of preternatural strength or the impossible contortions seen in many possessed individuals. This difference in degree and in kind is well-illustrated by the much lesser level of strength, however abnormal, seen in the manic or psychotic patient's periodic bursts of increased energy and might.

The comparisons simply don't hold up to careful scrutiny. Psychotic individuals may have fantasies and false impressions of occultlike communication or "thought reading" of others, but such delusional states in psychiatric patients are nothing compared with the humanly impossible frequency and uncanny accuracy of such displays of knowledge in those who are possessed. Truly possessed individuals do not engage in "thought reading" at all; they are merely fed information by spirits themselves.

Some other superficial resemblances to psychiatric states may be present in possessed individuals—a high level of agitation, for instance. This is another way that demons attempt to hide and confuse witnesses. But aside from surface commonalities like severe hostility, these resemblances are highly imperfect, especially in intensity—one among many reasons the true expert can differentiate these cases from what I call "counterfeit" (medical or psychiatric) ones without too much trouble once one knows all the facts.

Critics have offered explanations more implausible than the realities. Rare cases of so-called cryptoamnesia, for instance, when individuals have been able to speak or at least to mimic the sounds of a language to which they were exposed in their youth, have been documented. However, these cases display nothing like the fluency that possessed victims routinely display. One victim I met spoke perfect Bulgarian, though she had never once been exposed to the language at any point in her life. An American priest of Bulgarian descent, the target of the spirit's spoken-word vitriol, confirmed the language. Several possessed victims I have encountered spontaneously spoke either Latin or Greek without previous knowledge. More typically, many demons easily follow the Latin prayers of Catholic exorcists and then may comment in either Latin or English. Being highly intelligent and having observed humans for millennia, this capacity seems characteristic of evil spirits, though it may serve to confound onlookers, again, to surmise some deceased human is appearing.

An even stronger sign of a possessing spirit has been the obviously paranormal one of levitation—which may be the most dramatic feature of *The Exorcist*. Still, also often surprisingly to most people, levitation and extreme physical contortions do not necessarily constitute a possession. Many historical observers have claimed that various holy figures and gurus as well as a number of modern spiritualists have also levitated. Some argue that these latter cases show diabolic influence, though not necessarily a possessed condition.

The notorious nineteenth-century medium David Dunglas Home

allegedly levitated multiple times in front of scores of witnesses, as amply reported in the European press. In the seventeenth century the Franciscan friar Joseph of Cupertino, who was saintly and obviously not possessed, also levitated. About Joseph the writer Colin Wilson, who was no friend of Christianity, in his classic 1971 study *The Occult*, wrote, "The weight of the evidence is such that we know that Joseph of Cupertino was able to fly when he was in ecstasy as well as we know that Napoleon died on St. Helena." When more literal-minded people claim that levitation is impossible because of the laws of gravity, the natural reply is that spiritual beings are hardly subject to materialist principles. Can one not imagine that heavenly—and "fallen" angels, too—might well be capable of flight?

Various theories try to explain away any and all of these features. But the critical point, I always emphasize, is the general principle that no *single* factor—not even levitation—in any suspected case should be taken to prove a possession definitively. Instead, it is the *total* package that constitutes definitive proof of a possession, one displaying the rigorous criteria demanded by Catholic authorities and other sensible religious practitioners. For such an episode to warrant authorization for an exorcism with the certainty required, *clear* signs of preternatural activity in the context of other typical manifestations must be present and well-documented. A careful gathering of all the hard evidence following the strict guidelines for assessing cases are the keys to proper evaluations.

To repeat for emphasis: in the final analysis, as with all scientific conclusions about complex subjects, it is the *sum of the hard evidence*, either for or against such a conclusion, that should be the deciding factor.

Finally, *context* matters, too. Possessions don't come out of the blue: the person's historical situation or background that led to the demonization is critical to consider, too. This truth applies to both possessions and oppressions and is elicited by a good historical interview. The primary motive of the typical individual who may become possessed has been to turn to evil because they want something in return. Both Julia and Juan turned to the demonic world for special favors, and it proved hard to turn back. Another possessed young man once told me he had explicitly "promised" his soul to Satan when he was about seventeen years old because he was unhappy with his life. He wanted revenge on others and to be popular with girls. He suffered from one of the most severe possessions I have ever encountered.

Invite the devil in, and he will try to take over the house.

Still, even most individuals who participate in variations of satanic or lesser occult practices, or who have simply performed evil deeds but don't fully commit to Satan, may suffer only from less intense forms of demonic harassment, such as oppression or, more usually, no overt demonized condition at all. As always, there's that mystery—as well as the rare exceptions that disprove any hard-and-fast rule. One doesn't always need to turn to evil or the occult to become possessed, as the strange case of "Manny" shows.

Manny grew up in Ohio after his family immigrated to the United States from their native Philippines. He excelled at school and was always one of the most popular and well-liked students. He told me he had almost married a girlfriend he'd dated for a few years; however, at the last minute he changed his mind and called off their engagement, because he wanted to enter a religious order.

According to Manny, the woman's Filipino parents were enraged at his last-minute change of heart and "put a strong curse" on him. Along with some of her close friends, her mother allegedly turned to folk traditions to invite an attack upon Manny by evil spirits. This "sorcery" must have been the cause, Manny told me. His condition turned out to be an actual possession, though a decidedly milder one than many of the others I had seen. During his subsequent exorcisms, a few of which I attended, a demon spoke, as typically sarcastically and belligerently.

Manny's possession lasted about a year, while he was substitute teaching in a Catholic high school, having deferred his application to the religious order. Several diocesan priests conducted a series of rituals, which helped him greatly. During the exorcisms he revealed hidden knowledge; for instance, Manny had never met me but the demon sarcastically commented on associates of mine and told me that an upcoming lecture on demonic conditions I had been asked to conduct would "do no good." The severity and hours-long duration of his physical struggles during the exorcisms were without question diabolically induced.

Like Juan, Manny worked at getting better spiritually. During the series of exorcism rituals, the episodes when the evil spirit manifested itself gradually grew briefer and eventually dwindled to nothing.

While most people in the United States find curses or hexes implausible and superstitious, a growing number, including Manny and his family, still believe in such potential sorcery and are convinced that such things can lead to diabolic harassment or, in rare circumstances, possession. This general skepticism is not a bad thing; some societies become crippled by a proliferation of such mistrustful and exaggerated views. Maria, I remembered, had thought a local *brujo* a factor, too, in her oppression. Whether these traditional "dark arts" can cause a full possession, as defined above, remains up for debate. Some religious commentators claim other factors must be operating as well—there must generally be a *vulnerability* of sorts. But tens of thousands of people around the world claim they have been victims of such sorcery or black magic. Anthropologists strongly attest to widespread acceptance of these notions around the world to this day.

In recent decades, there has also been a growing belief that "ancestral" factors—*past* hexes and curses or, somehow, bad "influences" from nefarious members of one's own lineage—can affect descendants, too. Many people, in my view, take this theory a bit far. I spoke to a woman once who insisted that a distant ancestor had put a curse on her possessed son. What she did not know, as he himself confided in me, was that her child, now a young man, had spent years immersed in an intense pursuit of occult practices. For obvious reasons, he had never told his parents about these long-standing activities.

In my experience, more obvious causes for specific demonic attacks almost always reveal themselves in time; one usually doesn't have to play Sherlock Holmes to unearth them. Though others vehemently dispute this notion, some people continue to believe that even misdeeds of the distant past may be relevant in select situations. It is implausible in my view that such a remote cause would turn out to constitute the most crucial factor when more immediate issues prove obviously germane. Moreover, evil spirits are known for sowing as much confusion as they can.

Critics of this genuine popular development among many deliverance ministries nowadays feel such searches often prove unfruitful. Some commentators believe the trend represents mostly just another demonic strategy stimulating superstitious fears by playing upon the suggestibility of the gullible with smokescreens of little relevance. Those claiming scriptural support for such a viewpoint are countered by other scholars who find their biblical references torn out of context and such arguments unfounded. This debate goes on. In addition to befuddling victims and their families, another motive of evil spirits may often simply be to intimidate people and waste their time as they focus on more remote factors.

In any event, it's important to keep a balanced opinion about these contentious debates. Cultures can (and have) become preoccupied with such ideas, retarding their progress toward a healthier view of human causation. In any case, *overt* diabolic attacks are so uncommon and generally involve such unusual and strikingly rare background features that the average person should not worry that a demon attack might "just happen" to them, or that some ancestral curse will ensnare them or their children. Yet such fears persist, especially among those unfamiliar with a less sophisticated view of these issues.

Classically, during the vast majority of states of possession, especially full possessions, a demon will manifest during a victim's trance state as an independent agent and hostile force but outside the host's awareness and later memory. However, in certain more unusual cases, the victim *is* aware of the demon's appearance and its assumption of control (fully or for the most part), yet has no ability to act on his or her own. Victims have described this latter state of mind as being akin to watching a movie of their own activities.

This was the case during all of Manny's manifestations and all of his exorcism sessions, including the one I witnessed. He told me afterward that he knew exactly what was going on throughout the entire ritual. To his horror, he experienced his possessions as a passive, constrained observer, unable to exert any agency over the possessing spirit.

Manny proved this special kind of case. He was somewhat vulnerable to the curse placed on him, it appeared, or so he believed, but on the other hand, presumably because of his sincere religious vocation and practice, he seemed more spiritually prepared to withstand the demonic attacks. The demon could gain a tenuous toehold, true, but it was never able to take full possession of Manny's consciousness. After a relatively few rituals, the demon was forced to leave.

All of which illustrates the spectrum and varieties—but also the limits—of these strange states of possession caused by our demonic foes. Manny's case demonstrates the frequent inability of evil spirits to truly penetrate those who are spiritually "armed," to use a traditional term. And it shows the demons' failure to defeat the countervailing spiritual opposition, provided by exorcists and others who lend their support to those who are wise enough to turn to them for help.

In short, the latter forces are the inherently stronger ones in the long run. In the process, those who sincerely resist the devil prove the ultimate victors, even in these cosmic microbattles that presage the ultimate struggle between good and evil more broadly, a battle in which we all appear to be engaged, whether consciously or not.

CHAPTER FIVE

DIAGNOSING THE VARIETY OF OPPRESSIONS

Just as there are various kinds of possessions, there is also a wide variety of oppressions. The large diversity of oppressions is yet another way that evil spirits sow confusion and discord. The terminology related to what Father Jacques always called oppressions has varied historically and stimulated endless debate. One venerable differentiation (though an oversimplification) of such attacks is defining them as being "internal" or "external."

Maria and Stan, discussed in chapter 2, are prime examples of external oppression—that is, they seemed to be pummeled physically by "outside forces." The case of a woman I call Sara is a classic exemplar of an "internal" one. In these cases, the senses and mental processes are more directly attacked, stimulating endless puzzlement and controversy among skeptics.

Sara, a good Christian woman devoted to her family, came to see me one afternoon in great turmoil and told me her lengthy story. She was of sound mind and sound body. She had no psychiatric history; she was not depressed and seemed mentally healthy to me. The story she told me was consistent and coherent. I could detect no sign of any typical emotional or medical illness.

However, acknowledging how crazy it sounded, she told me that "angels" were giving her "messages." I asked Sara to describe what these "communications" (her word) sounded like. I wanted to know whether she was *hearing* voices, a sign of psychosis, or whether these communications seemed more in line with "thoughts" or "unheard" but coherent statements.

Sara responded that there were no "sounds" and she "in no way" heard voices, but that they were not "thoughts" of hers either. No, she insisted, these communications were not something she was "hearing" or merely thinking at all, of that she was certain.

"They don't really 'speak' to me," she told me. "I hear *nothing* with my ears. I just get this very strong sense of a 'message.' It's very clear and articulate; I'm *sure* about that. It's a long and perfectly straightforward message from somewhere, strange as that is to say."

"And what is that message?" I asked.

She seemed embarrassed. "Well, it *is* very intelligibly expressed in many ways but doesn't really make a lot of sense to me. They say they have an important mission for me. I am to report some special ideas from God himself to the world about something as yet undisclosed. They are asking whether I'm prepared to take on that important task."

I have certainly experienced many troubled or attention-seeking patients who had some "special sense" about themselves. Their alleged communications with "outsiders" sometimes resemble Sara's a bit, but they tend to be shorter, more bizarre, and disjointed. Rather than resisting these messages, such patients may relish them. Almost invariably they occur in individuals with a psychotic history, such as those who suffer from schizophrenia or bipolar disorder.

But Sara was *not* like most psychotic patients. She functioned extremely well, had close relationships, and was in no way self-preoccupied or grandiose, as many such patients may prove to be. Sara had already tried medication, albeit reluctantly, but she and her doctor both concluded that it had absolutely no effect. Her humility, loving and unself-ish character, and down-to-earth manner further disabused me of any suspicion about her mental health.

"Look, I'm no special person," she told me. "I'm no saint or any-thing. I don't believe for a second that anyone well-disposed to me would choose me as a prophet or something. And so, I'm confused, as I said."

Reserving judgment, I was thinking what I could say that might prove hopeful for this woman. I wanted to let her know that I had an open mind about these matters, but I couldn't yet give her a definitive opinion.

"I admit it is puzzling," I told her. And then I urged her to contact clergy in her church to help her determine whether the "communica-tions" had a spiritual rather than psychiatric cause.

Sara smiled and said, "But they sent me to you!"

I wanted to see how this would evolve. Though I already had strong suspicions of the true nature of her experiences, I maintained my customary high level of caution about such complaints. I encour-aged her to continue her personal religious practices and to stay in touch.

"If your troubles are spiritual in nature," I told her, "these are not the sort of things medication would normally resolve. Call me in a month or so, Sara, and we'll talk about how this all develops."

She called me exactly three and a half weeks later. She was excited that the messages had shifted in the interim.

"It changed a few days after we talked. Now they say they are dead souls. They don't give me a lot of information, but I am to receive further instructions."

"What do you make of this development?" I asked, though I wasn't surprised by it.

"I think it's bogus. Why would they change their identity? Do they think I'm stupid? I don't even believe dead souls can communicate with us like this. The Bible condemns such stuff in the strongest terms. These are not experiences I sought out, and I would never go to a medium and communicate with the deceased, as I know the Bible warns against. So, there's got to be some other explanation."

I was impressed again with her sober thoughtfulness. I agreed in my own mind but also didn't want to lead her on. I again encouraged her to stay in touch, and on the basis of other cases, I expected to hear from her soon.

I was not disappointed. About a week later she called me again. She sounded more confident. "Well, Dr. Gallagher, now I know what's going on. They've finally told me who they are. They admit they are demons. So, they were lying. That makes sense to me because they have lied and bothered me for a long time now."

Despite this breakthrough, Sara was not out of the woods yet. Other obvious paranormal experiences continued, which convinced me all the more that her case was indisputably diabolic in nature.

Many well-trained psychiatrists, unfamiliar with this arcane terrain, would without any hesitation automatically diagnose gross psychosis here. But these were not customary "hallucinations," and Sara was not mentally disturbed in any other way. These were not the fragmentary "voices" psychotic patients usually experience but were coherent and comprehensible messages. Because Sara was not "hearing" anything with her ears—as schizophrenics generally do, if they hear voices—I couldn't even classify these as "voices" at all. When asked again, she reported that she was "mentally experiencing" them (again, her term) but was clearly convinced they were not the result of her imagination. However one interprets that claim, they were significantly different in her description from typical auditory hallucinations.

One hypothesis, sometimes labeled the "psychotic continuum theory," has taken the position that all such auditory experiences arise from "brain events," or neurological issues of some kind, but can be essentially "nonpathological." That view seems farfetched here since the two experiences are so qualitatively different and are found in very different sorts of "hosts" (that is, those with paranormal features versus those found in typical and obviously psychotic patients). Both are also to be distinguished from individuals who simply have "lively imaginations." Neither can be explained as being the mere fruits of overactive thinking, as anyone would conclude with confidence after talking in depth to either of these groups of very different sorts of people.

The *context* of Sara's condition was a critical element as well, just as in the discernment of possessions. Sara had already been subjected to a medication trial, which had no effect. This lack of efficacy also at least suggested the unlikelihood of any characteristic mental pathology. Furthermore, Sara's *historical* context was one of a woman demonic spirits might well want to harass and confuse, or perhaps just embarrass. Like Maria, she may have been targeted because of her sheer goodness and devotion to God and others. She certainly felt "attacked," or at least strongly "bothered" in her view, and was undergoing weird but nonpsychiatric symptoms, apparently paranormal in nature. Her odd state was not happening, it seemed, because she had turned to evil or unsavory occult practices; she denied any of those factors in her background.

Based on my previous experience with spiritually active persons like Maria, Manny, and others, I was optimistic about Sara's long-term outcome, a confidence that in time was fully vindicated. She received no psychiatric treatment or medication, and yet today she is free of the "communication" that she knew from the start she didn't have to heed and that didn't mean she was a psychiatric patient.

The most significant aspect of Sara's experiences may well be in showing that evil spirits habitually lie about their true nature. One of the major aims of demons is to confuse human beings, and throughout history they have repeatedly feigned being dead souls or angels, or, perhaps, the deities of pagan religions. Evil spirits take delight in stimulating superstitious and frightful beliefs in people about their real nature, which is why they try to obfuscate their diabolic identities.

Such obfuscation is also an attempt to create havoc with our belief systems. Demons disguise their aims sometimes by faking what may otherwise be supposed to be what are known as "private revelations" (thought, that is, to be a genuine, if rare, experience in saintly souls, for example), with their "messages" often serving as fodder for the tabloids and sensational social media.

With Sara, the demons eventually declared their true identity to her, only under the pressure of her receiving spiritual assistance, it appeared. In many exorcisms spirits reveal their identities only under extreme duress. In a famous case in Iowa in the mid-twentieth century the possessing evil spirit maintained it was the soul of Judas Iscariot. Only after the priest had conducted sufficient exorcisms to loosen the spirit's hold on the affected woman did the possessing spirit tell the priest-exorcist with great reluctance that it was all a pretense and that it was indeed a demon.

One could multiply this example many times throughout religious history—when an exorcism demonstrates the false pretense under which an evil spirit attacks its victim, only to be forced to declare in the end its real demonic identity. A prominent exorcist commented to me early on in my work once, "The game is half over when the evil spirit can pretend no longer and, after great resistance, is compelled to reveals its true name, in effect indicating its real mission has been to confound and attack."

Other victims have told me that other intentionally misleading "messages" include ideas like the impending end of the world or bizarre ideas about Satan's "real" intents, or sometimes suggest sadistic and frightening notions of the afterlife. More than one person has told me that spirits claimed Satan was now ready for a truce with God and that the lucky recipient of this happy message was to inform church authorities.

These messages come from otherwise coherent and sane people, though such people may be unsophisticated in their beliefs. It certainly explains one way that some "false prophets" or visionaries throughout history may have come up with their odd and misguided notions. Our demonic foes are ever bent on confusing those who are vulnerable to their tricks.

Unlike many other people, Sara had the good judgment from the start to sense the true nature of the spirit behind the communications she was receiving. If nothing else, such attacks upon good and holy people disprove untrue assertions that no sincerely spiritual person can be seriously assaulted by evil spirits.

As Father Jacques recognized, spiritual advisers, who often know little about psychiatric disorders, should work closely with mental health professionals, especially when dealing with cases of internal oppression, like Sara. This need parallels the value of working with physicians when encountering external oppressions, which more commonly tend to mimic *physical* illnesses, such as happened to Maria.

Admittedly, terminology here becomes convoluted. Americans involved in this field still tend to employ the word "oppression" widely, as Father A. and Father Jacques always did. But not everyone uses the same terminology, and the word "vexation" is commonly used as an alternative. For instance, the International Association of Exorcists uses "vexation" to refer to external oppressions, though in the past, this term was at times confined *only* to demonic attacks on spiritually holy individuals. Other spiritual writers have simply called the latter "attacks on the holy." Some experts also make finer distinctions between what they label "full" versus "partial" possessions; in most circles in the United States, partial states might simply be called "severe" oppressions. So, sometimes differing uses of these terms can be understandably confusing to the public.

I am sometimes reluctant to provide people with too-rigid guidelines concerning the parameters of these states, in any case, not only because of the wide variety of examples that could be given, but also because so many of these terms and phenomena are endlessly deliberated and confusing, at times even to genuine experts. I have often witnessed heated disputes accompanying discussions of oppressive states, involving as they do much subtler states than the more dramatic and more obvious possessions. Oppressive conditions of all sorts can easily appear simply as psychological aberrations or odd medical anomalies to the inexperienced.

In broad strokes the diagnosis of an oppression is not all that different from the diagnosis of a possession. To discern an oppression requires a preternatural or at least highly anomalous symptom as well as a likely cause. And here, too, the most frequent reason for an oppression is the same as for a possession: the victim has turned to sinful or occult practices, albeit in highly varied ways and generally less intensely than in possessed people.

The distinction drawn between an external and internal oppression is also somewhat more complex than supposed for other reasons. First, many victims have elements of both and the condition may also go on to a full possession. Second, when one talks about an evil spirit attacking someone from the "outside" or dwelling "within" a person (as in a possession), this language is loosely used. Since spirits are not material beings, all we really can say is how they are "acting" upon someone, although people certainly feel "invaded" in all these attacks. Again, this reflects the power of demons to affect—at least in circumscribed ways—the *material* world.

Still, I have recognized the wisdom of these traditional categories. In Sara's case of an internal oppression, there was such a powerful influence on the imagination or the senses that one was hard-pressed to attribute the experience to anything but an *inner* spiritual assault.

I have seen many examples of oppressions over the years. Some of the cases were truly bizarre, though most were more limited in their manifestations and almost prosaic in the crude manner in which victims were afflicted—internally or more often externally. Quite a few individuals, including Julia, as we have seen, have told me they seem to be interfered with whenever they try to pray or go to church.

Oppressed individuals may also experience an unexplained pain upon entering a church or waiting in line to receive communion.

Those afflicted often run to a doctor when these problems first arise (as they should!). Physicians may order some tests, which prove negative. They may tell patients that there seems to be no serious impairment. Or, doctors may suggest that the pain is "all in their head" and that perhaps they should consult a mental health professional. Of course, that may well be sensible advice, and some psychological explanation—like a conversion reaction or psychogenic pain—may be operating. But not always.

Probably just as frequently individuals who are externally oppressed may report scratches, bruises, or other marks on their skin. Many such individuals have shown me their lesions or provided pictures of them. Here, too, it is sensible to rule out any physical causes, as I did from the beginning of my contact with Maria. When no common medical explanation for these sorts of cases can be found, one may entertain the more remote possibility that a paranormal or preternatural factor is involved.

In cases of a true oppression, I almost always hear what sounds like a probable *spiritual* precipitant, just as in a possession. As we have seen, a typical backstory might include the admission on the part of afflicted individuals that they had turned to occult practices at some point in their lives. Or they may have gone through a time when they were estranged from sound spiritual practices and turned to behavior they later recognized as shameful, sinful, or outright evil. Paradoxically, the overt condition sometimes began when they turned back toward their religious observances or otherwise turned away from their past behavior, a turn in their lives that seems to enrage evil spirits.

Eventually, victims may intensify their spiritual efforts and seek out spiritual support for prayers and specialized assistance. Then, sometimes rapidly, but more commonly after a longer period of effort, these individuals finally get relief. Many in the mental health field with whom I have discussed such outcomes are astonished to discover that all the odd symptoms they may have seen in a case disappeared after spiritual assistance.

Then there are more flamboyant examples of oppressions. For instance, one man, who came all the way from London to consult me, claimed that Satan was having a "constructive" dialogue with him. The gist of this idea was that Satan had decided to reconcile with God after all these eons and was just waiting for church authorities to recognize this breaking news. Just like Sara, this man was not "hearing" this message with his ears but experiencing it strongly and clearly in a mental (he used the term "telepathic") way. Besides this claim, he was completely coherent, functioning well in his life, and had no history of mental illness or delusions.

This man tried to persuade me to publicize this message to the world. I disabused him of the notion that this would be a good idea, let alone a sound interpretation of his experiences. He eventually sought help from an exorcist in addressing what was an evident internal oppression. He lost his "communication channel" with Satan and came to recognize how he had been duped. His life took a much happier and fulfilled course without the strange internal drama he had been unwittingly roped into before realizing its true nature.

Another woman, a housewife from Delaware, claimed to have multiple visions and direct messages from "the Trinity." She showed me pictures of the apparitions she had photographed on the walls of her church. I certainly didn't believe they were genuine saintly or divine appearances, and I knew by then to recognize them as likely diabolic tricks. She showed me typed records of the messages that she said she had taken down verbatim from God himself. I commented on how amazingly ungrammatical God was if these allegedly verbatim communications were accurate!

Most people, hearing about such individuals, of course, assume that all these people are just crazy, or perhaps merely highly imaginative. It has been of interest to me as a doctor, however, that they all tend to talk of their experiences in much the same manner and, like Sara, in no way like a psychiatric patient. It is also striking that after seeking the proper spiritual help, almost all such individuals no longer suffer these highly idiosyncratic experiences and get past this period in their lives without any residual problems.

I suppose one could try to write such people off as eccentrics, but all came to feel eventually that they had been tricked by demonic foes.

CHAPTER SIX

TROUBLES OF THE MIND

False Cases and Other Medical Tasks

There are the individuals attacked by evil spirits who need careful discernments and spiritual help; then, of course, there are the much, much larger number of people who just *imagine* or are deluded that they are squaring off against demonic foes. Sadly, people with certain problems too often find it preferable to believe their complex problems have simple solutions and that a magic "deliverance" will "cure" them.

Around the turn of the twenty-first century, Father Jacques asked me to consult on another case that was confounding him. Though he had not yet visited with this young woman, as he usually did before referring someone to me, he was intrigued and puzzled by the details of her story. He asked me to accompany him on his initial visit with her and her almost cultlike religious group, whose members traveled on special "prayer missions" around the country.

Father Jacques assured me that the group was widely considered to be well-intentioned and pious, made up of harmless individuals genuinely dedicated to serving and praying for congregations and religious organizations. According to Father Jacques, its members all joined voluntarily, and its leader was an evangelical minister with a decent reputation. Father Jacques didn't know all that much more about them, but he appeared unconcerned that it was an unhealthy or dangerous arrangement.

And so I agreed to go with him, although I had some lingering suspicions.

One hot summer morning, Father Jacques and I pulled into the parking lot of an old, urban church. In the distance, in the middle of the ground's yard, I could hear a small group of people singing hymns. There were about twelve singers in all, mostly young women.

As we approached the group, an older man rushed over. Powerfully built, he extended to me a too-firm grip. Without introducing himself, he asked to talk privately for a minute.

His manner reminded me of a drill sergeant whose commands usually go unchallenged. Lowering his voice, he said, "I have this girl in our troop, the youngest. She's a nice girl, but I'm worried about her. She says she's getting attacked by evil spirits. I'm not a Catholic, but she and some of the young'uns are, and a lot of fellow ministers I know advised that I consult a priest of her own faith.

"I used to be in the military, and we run our group a bit like a platoon, so she'll do as I ask. I want Father Jacques to say some prayers over her and see what happens."

The reverend, whom I'll call Wayne, told me that "Satan himself wants to destroy us." Wayne was convinced that demons were assaulting Lily, the group's newest member, and he had no doubt that evil spirits were indirectly trying to stop the group in their mission.

"Everyone gets a physical before they can join the group, so I know her health is fine. It's a spiritual problem, I'm sure," Wayne added.

I had yet to say a word, but I was already put off by the reverend's dogmatism and surety about what the young woman may or may not have needed.

"It's Satan's way of attacking the group," Wayne said. "That's my opinion. None of my girls or guys need a shrink. I don't believe in Freudian mumbo-jumbo, but Father insisted we invite you to give a doctor's opinion. So, I'm game for any thoughts you have."

I wasn't too sure of that last sentiment.

The young woman in question had been watching us talk. She was twenty-two and had joined the group only a few months earlier. She was tall and thin but looked physically healthy.

I'd been expecting to talk to her alone in the rectory office first, but Father Jacques had other plans. He had sensed what Wayne was expecting. "Well, Dr. Gallagher," Father Jacques said in front of everyone, "let's go into the church. I want to say some prayers there."

By this point, I was familiar with Father Jacques's methods, which he saw as an attempt to provoke a reaction from an evil spirit, if one was in fact present.

We all entered the large Byzantine-style structure, noted for its striking restored and beautiful stained-glass windows featuring prominent saints. Father escorted Lily and Wayne to the first pews in the front near the sanctuary. The rest of her peers he directed to sit a few rows back. He opened with some traditional prayers, such as the Our Father. Then he calmly explained that he was going to make some special petitions to God, but it would be a private ceremony. I knew he wanted to demystify the morning's activity for all the young people before dismissing the group from the private ritual.

"So only your boss, Lily, that tall fellow over there, who is a doctor, and myself will stay," he told the group, and asked them to walk over to the rectory until we had finished.

At these words, most of the troupe started to leave. A couple of them, I thought, seemed disappointed not to be able to witness the show. I imagined there wasn't too much excitement in these young people's everyday lives, so some may have been eagerly anticipating what awaited Lily.

As they filtered out, Father Jacques turned to Lily. With a soothing voice, he said, "Young lady, I've heard a little about you, but I want to know more about what you've been going through. It's not easy to join a whole new bunch of friends and travel around to strange places every week, is it?"

Lily nodded and said little at first. She looked anxious. I got the sense she was a lonely young woman, even surrounded by members of her little community. For the moment, she was doing her best just to take it all in. Eventually, she started talking in a clear and coherent manner, which assuaged my concern about her possibly suffering from depression.

With some prompting, she began to tell us what had been happening to her. She'd been excited to join the group and saw it as an honor to have been allowed to become a member. She liked the idea of being with other young adults, other spiritual people near her age, because in her earlier public schooling, she told us, religion had been ignored or mocked. A few weeks earlier, however, she noticed some "strange feelings" and got a strong sense that an evil spirit might be influencing her. She would get a vague thought that a demon wanted to punish her for her choice to enter the prayer group. A few times, she lost control of herself and started responding involuntarily to the "suggestions" of an "inner voice," not a hallucination, she believed, but "strong thoughts." She then acted strangely—by rolling on the floor and "things like that." Because she never lost consciousness, she was fully aware of what was happening, though she claimed she couldn't control it. Upon our questioning, however, she admitted that such behavior *might* be "a little bit under my control."

Still, she was mystified about what was happening, offering only that a demon was likely directing her. Father Jacques pointedly asked Lily whether she had experienced any painful attacks or other paranormal experiences. She told him she had not.

"Well, Lily, we'll figure it out, trust me," Jacques told her. "By the way, have you read anything about things like possessions or exorcisms?"

I had had the temptation to ask Lily the same question, but at that point I held back because I knew I was going to interview her one-on-one later that morning. But I was already skeptical that any genuine demonic condition was involved here.

Lily brightened at Jacques's question. "Oh *yes*, Father." She said she'd always been an avid reader about religious matters and in particular had devoured a few books about how evil spirits can attack people, even saintly people. She once attended an assembly by a televangelist who allegedly cast out demons in front of hundreds of people, and she had been mesmerized. She'd loved the book *The Exorcist*, even more than the movie, which she still considered her favorite film. She wondered whether something demonic could be happening to her because she'd had these same urges to act in such bizarre ways.

Jacques asked, "How so?"

"Well, as I said, I feel I just get these weird sensations. I may get an impulse to throw myself on the floor or something. Religious items kind of irritate or repulse me too. Stuff like that. Intense *feelings* inside me mostly, I guess, but I get compelled to do things in a way that doesn't seem to be me."

Lily added that she knew Father Jacques was an exorcist and she'd read some of the articles he'd written. She was thrilled to finally meet him, she said. *Too thrilled*, I was thinking.

Jacques then explained to Lily that he would start to say just a few, short prayers. These did not entail a formal exorcism, he made clear. He called them "provocation" prayers, which didn't follow a strict script.

"Just to see what happens," he told her, "if that's okay with you."

I knew Father Jacques occasionally used such kinds of prayers, addressing demons who were potentially present without presuming that they were. He was not "casting out" evil spirits in any formal way. In his description to me, he was "praying that our Lord allow evidence of their presence, *if* such is the case." Some exorcists, mostly in foreign countries, start by intoning the words from the *Rituale Romanum* itself as they closely monitor the reaction of the potential victim. Over the years, some experts have told me that they regard this technique of a "provocation exorcism" unwise, because it is likely to stimulate a victim's suggestibility, strengthening the notion in the person's mind that they are being attacked by demons.

In any event, with Lily's permission, Father Jacques started his provocation prayers, which generated a more rapid response than certainly either of us expected. Almost immediately, she collapsed to the floor, careful, in my view, not to hurt herself.

I was thinking, *She's not wasting any time, is she?*

She hissed and growled. She wriggled, then raised herself up and walked over to the sanctuary as if in a daze. She then fell down again, even crudely "slithering" like a snake while glaring at the tabernacle.

And then, just like that, she came out of it.

I didn't believe her actions were anything more than histrionics. It was too obvious a "performance," to me at least. Lily never went into a real trance and seemed purposeful in her activity the whole time. There was nothing paranormal or not easily imitated by someone mimicking an imagined affliction. I felt sorry for her and had the impression of someone "trying too hard."

Father Jacques probably had the same view, because he wrapped up the brief session quickly.

I held my opinion before speaking to Jacques afterward, until I had the chance to interview Lily alone. In a private office in the rectory, I avoided commenting upon what had just happened. My task, as always, was to develop a deeper sense of Lily's emotional history, her family dynamics, and her background.

Lily was cooperative and, again, seemed to relish the attention. She told me that her father was an alcoholic and had left her mother and younger sisters many years earlier. Lily had what some clinicians call a "father hunger" and, not surprisingly, had readily put herself under Wayne's authority. As the dutiful daughter of a single mother in a large family with many siblings, she seemed never to have rebelled. In my opinion, she harbored a lot of unconscious anger as a model "parentified" child, forced to assume a role with her younger siblings of an assisting caretaker to her depressed mother. Her school years were unhappy, because she had an intense personality with a self-righteous manner and was immature for her age. She never felt attractive to boys. She admitted that she didn't have many friends.

In Wayne, Lily found the strong father figure she never had, and she was quite eager to find a more accepting peer group. The hope, I felt, was that her fellow members might not only admire her religiosity, but also accept her "specialness." By undergoing what she seemed sincerely to believe an assault by an evil spirit, she could use this supposed attack as a validation of her self-worth as a singularly targeted spiritual warrior. I wasn't surprised when she told me her favorite saint was Joan of Arc.

From the start, Lily displayed a classic example of a needy and suggestible character structure. I asked a few more questions about her mood, past hospitalizations, any former drug use, and the like. She denied any of those problems. I concluded that she probably had a strongly histrionic personality disorder with narcissistic features, as well. She was not psychotic, and though there were hints of a maladaptive coping style, I did not think she truly dissociated to any degree.

After our meeting, I conveyed my impression of her to Jacques. As usual, it increased my trust in his judgment that he had a similar, lay opinion of her behavior. He readily agreed to my more technical professional assessment as I explained some of the psychological terms I was employing.

When we met the next day with Lily, all three of us—myself, Father Jacques, and, to his credit, Wayne—told her she wasn't suffering from a diabolic attack. She seemed to grasp the gist of what we were telling her, finally admitting to Wayne her long and distressed relationship with former peers and her family, including her disappointment with an absent father. Lily seemed most worried about getting kicked out of the group, that she would no longer be allowed to continue her mission work. Despite its itinerate vocation, the group offered her a safe place from the emotionally complex world she had been struggling to navigate.

At her young age, Lily already had a track record of applying repeatedly to enter a religious order, *any* community that would take her. As it turned out, every other group had turned her down until she was accepted into Wayne's community. She must have been relieved to hear that her new prayer team had finally given her that opportunity, although her reprieve was only temporary.

Later, I was sad to learn, Lily was still seeking such a haven. She continued to try to join other religious congregations, which refused to admit her after their own psychological assessments. I had suggested to Wayne that he get her into psychotherapy and have her recognize that a religious vocation is not an escape from life's painful challenges.

Without being truly out of touch with reality, that is, to the point of gross psychoticism or a "thought disorder," individuals of highly suggestible natures can come to believe all sorts of things about themselves from their overactive imaginations alone. This occurs especially in the context of a mistaken or naïve set of beliefs, extremely poor self-insight, and a facilitating environment or subculture. Lily fell victim to all three. Her behavior, strange as it was, was not something all that unexpected, given how intensely her peer group readily thought evil forces might be antagonistic to their spiritual mission. This sense, probably a bit paranoid in nature, was also shared by the only authority figure on the scene, someone who should have corrected her. But I believed Reverend Wayne was only too ready to jump to the same conclusions as Lily, probably for many of the same reasons. That inclination on his part made it all the more likely that she could succumb to assuming such a role within the putative spiritual drama being played out in her little group. In addition, her ill-digested and uncorrected exposure to similar ideas in books and movies prompted a powerful psychological identification as a spiritual victim.

Lily's case in some ways resembled the "grand hysterics" that so fascinated Charcot and Freud during the late nineteenth century. Charcot was a showman of sorts in his Parisian hospital and famously conducted public demonstrations of suggestible patients before packed audiences. He diagnosed them as classic exemplars of the emerging, broader-based concept of hysteria, a diagnosis Freud also emphasized.

Like Lily, Charcot's patients displayed symptoms of exhibitionism, which they personally misinterpreted as neurological rather than psychiatric in nature. Strikingly out of touch with their own psychological motives, the patients misunderstood their conditions as *physical* illnesses. Lily, on the other hand, mistook her perplexing and painful feelings as a *spiritual* disorder.

More technically speaking, patients like Charcot's and Lily were only rarely suffering from a true psychosis or formal delusion. Their minimal insight exits on a continuum. These individuals are mostly befuddled. Some may have a modicum of self-awareness about their condition, while others have no clue at all. By and large, they are rarely consciously pretending in their extravagant disturbances. There are disturbed patients who merely pretend to suffer from various dramatic psychological or medical conditions, and even individuals who historically have feigned possession. But I believe these latter cases are rare. The possibility of an outright pretense, rather, is a condition better characterized as a "factitious disorder," where a patient makes a conscious effort to mislead others out of various motives, including a desire to be in the spotlight. Lily wasn't lying, nor were Charcot's patients generally lying. They were convinced, at least temporarily, that their presumed states were genuine conditions with which they were involuntarily afflicted.

Some critics later accused Charcot of unwittingly manipulating his subjects. Perhaps Reverend Wayne, unfamiliar with such psychiatric pathology, could also be charged with misguiding his new, highly vulnerable member. But if this were the case, the confusion was surely unintentional on both their parts. It was clear that neither Wayne nor Lily was simply "playacting," though Lily clearly exhibited a great need for attention.

Lily and cases that mirror hers are often featured in short documentaries about alleged possessions. While media production companies are constantly looking to film supposed victims of possessions, genuinely possessed individuals avoid exposure. It's mostly the more exhibitionist false cases who agree to appear on camera, a fair warning to those who too readily accept the exaggerated or odd behavior of people with personality disorders claiming to be possessed or otherwise diabolically afflicted. Like Lily, they are more often than not just trying to imitate the features of what they imagine a possession to be like.

The key requisite in diagnosing individuals like Lily who are only imagining they are demonically attacked is first recognizing and ruling out the rare genuine possession or oppression, or at least being open to their possibility. This knowledge helps one explain to a confused patient why they are not suffering from a demonic attack. The second most helpful requirement to understanding and addressing their real problem is having broad experience with medically and psychiatrically impaired individuals.

A hundred years ago, the Jesuit priest Joseph de Tonquédec, a Parisian philosopher and exorcist, concluded, "Some of the faithful and certain [clerics] . . . take the opposite stand and also end in error, because of their ignorance of mental and nervous pathology and their failure to follow the guidelines given. As a result, they attribute to the devil certain disturbances that are purely natural in origin."

Three decades later, Dr. Jean Lhermitte gave many examples of neurological conditions mistaken for possessions, although neither he nor Tonquédec seem to have come across many genuine cases of possessions themselves. That limitation is not surprising, because Tonquédec operated in a limited geographical pastoral area and Lhermitte worked primarily with a clinical population in which such conditions are rare. Still, the priest and doctor illustrate an essential point: physicians and exorcists are working to the same end of helping suffering individuals. Not all exorcists need to know everything about medicine, and not all physicians need to believe in the reality of demonic conditions to assist exorcists. What they must be willing to do, however, is to approach their respective tasks of discernment with a spirit of humility and collaboration.

Even doctors and health professionals who have little to no familiarity with possessions or any belief in the demonic can be of indispensable service. They have the professional expertise to know whether a case fits a medically recognizable syndrome or not. They best assist by assuring that no medical pathology explains the phenomena in question, leaving open the possibility that something potentially paranormal might be happening. This critical role on their part can save all parties an enormous amount of time and effort by ruling out from the start conditions that only *mimic* diabolic conditions.

The tendency for demonic states to imitate medical conditions is the critical point here—and, in my view, is no accident. In contrast to cases of genuine possessions or oppressions, an even wider variety exists of what some call "pseudo-possessions." I prefer to call them "counterfeit possessions," because this term underlines how evil spirits can *consciously* mimic genuine illnesses or disorders to disguise or mask their presence. Such counterfeit cases are often confused with psychiatric disorders because their symptoms, including trances and altered states of consciousness, often overlap. Evil spirits try to stimulate further confusion by adding other less dramatic symptoms, most notably states of pain, generalized trembling, and other manifestations.

Demons are not stupid, and they love to confuse people, perhaps particularly members of the clergy and medical professions. What better way than to disguise their nefarious activities as a human malady?

But interestingly, and this is a crucial point, evil spirits do not seem able to "get it exactly right." Their power to only *imitate* medical conditions remains flawed, and hence their manifestations are **not** a *truly* accurate imitation of an actual medical or psychiatric disorder.

A notorious, widely thought counterfeit possession of the late medieval era involved a Frenchwoman named Martha Brossier. Her father, sensing a good product like an early-day P. T. Barnum, paraded her around as she submitted to public exorcisms. Sometimes the crowds numbered in the thousands. The consulting physician, a rather smug Dr. Michel Marescot, and other examiners set up some simple traps to detect her fraud, which they claimed to do easily. She confused, for instance, the first lines of Virgil's Latin poem the *Aeneid* with a supposed religious message. The shrewd doctor summarized his view in a famous pithy statement, "Nothing demonic, much fiction, little illness" (*nilhil a daemone, multa ficta, a morbo pauca*). Still, disputes about Mademoiselle Brossier continued for years, in part due to high-level squabbling about the political and religious implications of her case. She died in poverty, last heard of still performing in Milan years later.

To state the obvious again, physical and psychological impairments are different from spiritual ailments instigated by demons. Medically ill patients do not suffer from paranormal features and rarely have in their backgrounds the kind of factors that lead to such attacks. To make any proper diagnosis, medical and demonic alike, one must investigate overall patterns and search for the appearance of a definitive *constellation* of featured symptoms.

• • •

A good illustration of this point involved a man I treated on one of my inpatient units who was diagnosed as a severe schizophrenic. The thirty-five-year-old patient, whom I will call Paul, was a textbook case of schizophrenia, which features psychotic symptoms such as hallucinations, delusions, and a specific pattern of disordered thinking. Paul exhibited prominently these three features and was in and out of the psychiatric system for years. He was exceptionally bright and came from an ambitious family of means. Family members told me they all had high hopes for him as a young man, and his deterioration during his twenties had been devastating to watch. Schizophrenics who come from such privileged backgrounds often feel worse about themselves because they become demoralized after their earlier life of high expectations.

A good example of what experienced psychiatric services call a "revolving door" patient, Paul had been hospitalized about thirty times in his life. He would be admitted in a grossly psychotic state and then invariably quickly recover during his inpatient stays, though sometimes only after going to court to be medicated against his will. Much improved, he would then be discharged, only to be readmitted a few months later because he invariably would stop his medication and de-

teriorate. Whenever Paul decompensated, he always ascribed his recurring outbreaks of auditory hallucinations to evil spirits, even after
multiple attempts to persuade him otherwise. He told me once that
during episodes of increased stress he would get extremely paranoid
about demons, convinced that the spirits had invaded him.

Unlike the coherent messages Sara experienced, Paul always claimed
he heard these malevolent voices directly in his ears. "Where else would
I hear them?" he often asked. He also questioned the staff endlessly
about whether or not they could hear the voices. When the doctors or
nurses denied hearing anything, Paul accused them of lying to him. He
also had a common experience of psychotic patients of a heightened
sensitivity to nearby sounds. If someone closed a door down the unit
hall, he'd react sharply, as if the noise targeted him personally. Every
one of these features of his classic auditory hallucinations were dissim-
ilar to Sara's "messages."

Paul had no idea of any of the work I was doing in this area, but he
seemed to trust the unit personnel and routinely confided in me and
the staff. Upon admission, he would plaintively insist that what he
really needed was an exorcism. About once a year he would petition
the unit nurses to speak to the hospital chaplain of his own faith. The
chaplain, a rabbi, was a kindly and highly educated man familiar with
psychiatric pathology. He always tried to reassure Paul that the voices
he heard were the result of an illness, not a possession. Paul still identified as Jewish and was on friendly terms with some of his old high
school classmates who described themselves as Messianic Jews. They
often visited him on the unit, seemingly encouraging his belief that
his real problem was diabolic. In any case, it was good, old-fashioned
medication, not deliverance prayers or the Roman Ritual, that always
helped Paul. Only after his antipsychotic medication took hold and relieved his disturbing symptoms would Paul admit that the voices must
have been the result of "his mind playing tricks" on him, rather than
the supposed evil spirits.

This sort of auditory hallucination is quite common in psychotic patients, not only schizophrenics. While patients may believe an evil spirit is talking to them or trying to take over their bodies, it is equally likely that patients might think that government agents, aliens, or even other family members might be communicating with them, rather than spirits. Still, just because psychotic individuals believe they are possessed or under attack by foreign agents doesn't mean they are, of course. It is the doctor's job to diagnose a natural cause, rather than a demonic one, and treat the natural disorder appropriately with medication.

Physicians have long known that schizophrenia has a strong biological and brain-based component. It presents itself in many ways and presumably has multiple underlying causes, including genetic factors. Throughout my career, I have sometimes had to bluntly tell suffering patients and families, "No, the patient is ill, and there is no 'demon of schizophrenia.'"

• • •

Another patient I came across when I was working on the unit devoted to patients with long-term personality disorders at Cornell–New York Hospital also believed her major problems were caused by evil spirits. The unit program used many of the theories and treatment techniques of Dr. Otto Kernberg. Sadly, such intensive treatment programs, which were often effective with extremely challenging cases, are largely a thing of the past.

Priscilla was a twenty-five-year-old woman diagnosed with borderline personality disorder. Originally from Missouri, she had been sent to us by her brother, a sophisticated financial professional who felt he had to get his sister away from what he considered an unhealthy and unbalanced religious home environment. To his disbelief, the family blamed Priscilla's emotional problems on demonic attacks.

Patients with personality disorders more broadly are marred by long-standing, rigid, and maladaptive styles of coping or reacting. A seriously troubled subgroup is known as "borderline" patients. By definition, these individuals are unstable and often self-destructive, frequently filled with deep-seated anger. Tragically, patients with personality disorders have high rates of suicide. A large subset of borderline patients may suffer from a variety of posttraumatic symptoms, as many have been abused. We confirmed in our own research on our unit population how common both sexual and physical abuse were in their backgrounds, and even more prominently what we strictly defined as severe "emotional mistreatment."

For many years, Priscilla had been sexually abused by her uncle, who lived in the home until his eventual suicide. He was often left alone with her. Her parents, oblivious to the long-standing abuse, refused to believe Priscilla when she told them about it and never accepted that this regular abuse was a major contributing factor to her problems.

During periods of heightened distress, the more fragile borderline individuals may be prone to become transiently psychotic. Perhaps for that reason, a few of these patients may come to believe they are being demonically attacked, at least to varying degrees, especially during periods of high stress. But in my experience, the most salient factors involve their nonpsychotic but still deep-seated and fragile psychological states of mind. Common among psychoanalytic clinicians is the frequent observation that many borderline patients assume that their inner *feelings* of rage and destructiveness (often, though not always, secondary to abuse) make them think they are "evil" to their core. Not well-integrated in their psychological makeup, they may even ascribe this "bad side" of themselves, as they often phrase it, to some sort of tenuously experienced "foreign" entity. That is, they are attempting to "externalize" their inner destructive feelings. In discussing their inner worlds with many of them, I've heard more than a few patients explicitly refer to a "monster" living inside them, or an "evil *thing*." It is not a stretch for them to personify this feeling of "badness," especially if they are brought up in a certain type of religious subculture that emphasizes the ubiquity of evil spirits.

This was all very much the case with Priscilla. The perception of being beset by an evil spirit can be powerful in such patients. Their "badness" is felt somehow to be outside their control, while still contained "within" their personality structure. This psychologically defensive maneuver may minimize their considerable guilt, shame, and horror of their behavior and past traumas via externalizing the responsibility for such negative feelings. They can, however, mature out of this self-perception, often with effective psychotherapy and other psychological aids. But, caught in a facilitating subculture, such as Priscilla's religious family, they may simply never receive the psychological help they need and be subject instead to all sorts of spiritual ministrations, including sometimes misguided "deliverances."

In Priscilla's case, the social worker struggled to persuade her parents that her problems, which included cutting herself and chronically thinking about killing herself, were psychological in nature rather than evil and demonic. I was not her therapist, but Priscilla regularly confided in me as her hospital psychiatrist that she had come to believe she must be a horrible human, "a spawn of Satan," as she put it. She regarded herself as the worst of sinners, despite a warm-heartedness and honesty evident to all.

Over the years, I have encountered scores of borderline patients who thought the same thing. Such patients frequently share an abusive background similar to Priscilla's, which compounds their struggles.

Patients with another common personality disorder—the antisocial or sociopathic type—similarly feel "evil" inside, but they actually go on to *perform* evil deeds. Rather than being disturbed by these feelings of malevolence inside them, they seem to embrace them and then rationalize their manipulative or criminal behavior. While they may commonly blame their problems on their upbringing or "society," they are more comfortable with their characteristic feelings of sadism and rage, which is why they do not tend to personify these impulses like borderline patients sometimes do. Perhaps to their credit, patients with borderline personality disorder are more troubled and conflicted about such "darker" feelings or destructive impulses than those with outright criminal or antisocial personalities.

Individuals with antisocial features certainly do not see themselves as possessed or oppressed. Nor are they. I cannot emphasize strongly enough that being a destructive or malign person does not automatically mean being a possessed person. This misconception is contrary to an occasional public perception in the face of a truly evil person, such as a serial killer, about whom the lay public may speculate, "I wonder what *possessed* him."

One antisocial patient, a rare one on our unit since we normally excluded them, had a long record of incarceration in upstate New York. He told me that it was not unusual for some prison inmates to casually engage in devil worship. He and his fellow inmates used satanic symbols and makeshift rituals to imitate what they regarded as diabolic practices. He admitted it was mostly an attempt to take advantage of prison rules to have some free time to conduct "religious" ceremonies, a "right" they'd insist to the warden was constitutionally protected. Again, though, he was not possessed, nor did he demonstrate any overt signs of any other demonic attack, however cruel and seemingly "diabolic" his actions were.

I have also often worked closely with obsessional individuals, another common group of the personality disordered whom clinicians frequently encounter and treat. (The closely related obsessive-compulsive disorder is a partially separate, more biologically based condition.) Like borderline personality types, they are often highly conscientious individuals who are greatly troubled by feelings of violence and inner destructiveness. Similarly, sacrilegious and blasphemous thoughts frequently disturb them.

In pronounced states, they may feel like harming, even killing, individuals they love, including children. They may also be filled with images of disfiguring or performing other inappropriate actions toward religious objects, statues, or icons. Such thoughts horrify them. I once treated a man with unsettling and obviously compulsive thoughts of murdering his son. While obsessional individuals may believe they are the targets of a demonic assault, they are suffering from a common psychiatric condition.

• • •

Lily represented still another category of psychiatric patients who mistakenly believe they are possessed or otherwise attacked by evil spirits. These patients are generally characterized as having a severe "histrionic" personality. Some may also be prone to dissociation, a defensive maneuver to ward off painful emotions and memories. While Lily clearly exhibited a histrionic personality, I did not believe that she truly dissociated, though her periodic episodes were marked by irrational and overt "out of touch" behaviors.

In the past, such patients were loosely classified as "hysterics." Histrionic and the closely related dissociative patients display overactive imaginations and strikingly poor insight or self-awareness. These individuals also desperately seek the love and attention that they otherwise miss in their unhappy lives. To come to believe that they are being attacked by unseen forces may paradoxically give them an otherwise lacking sense of excitement or self-importance.

Again, Lily proved a good example of all these traits. She sought out attention on her own, but she also picked up subtle signs from her group prompting her to "play the part," as we noted. Other such histrionic individuals may be less in control of themselves and more actively manipulated by others. Highly suggestible to begin with, these patients readily try to please others and may believe (or just play along with) the role thrust upon them. In the face of exploitive or ignorant spiritual advisers or charlatans, they can readily be persuaded to assume the desired persona.

In the more severe types of dissociating individuals, patients may even manufacture or "elaborate" what are termed separate "ego states," or what has more commonly come to be known as different "personalities," or "alters." Patients with these features were originally said to be suffering from multiple personality disorder; in more recent years, the condition has been more properly termed "dissociative identity disorder" (DID). It was overdiagnosed during the 1970s and 1980s following the release of the 1976 TV miniseries *Sybil* (or exposure to the earlier 1957 movie *The Three Faces of Eve*). For a brief time after I left my position on the borderline unit, two-thirds of the patients were admitted with a diagnosis of DID. About a year later, that craze had passed, and the unit admitted no one so diagnosed. During the course of my career I have probably encountered about a hundred cases of DID. It remains a controversial diagnosis. Better recognized today as a fluid condition with several possible causes, DID may even be wholly fabricated or expressive of a frankly delusional frame of mind. At times, DID may be caused by the treatment itself, being what physicians call "iatrogenic."

By and large, these patients only rarely interpret their conditions as diabolically induced, but a few do. Unfortunately, poorly trained therapists and counselors of religious backgrounds have sometimes latched on to these cases and interpreted any mention of a more "evil" alter as an evil spirit. One case stands out in my clinical experience. A Hispanic-American woman from the Bronx grew up in a heavily Pentecostal family that was preoccupied with sexual sins and strong beliefs in evil spirits. She came to interpret one of her alters as a demon.

On the other hand, in my clinical work I have never known any DID patients to demonstrate paranormal features, as a true case of possession does, or to act in ways that would not easily be understood by a skilled mental health professional as anything other than an example of severe psychological problems, regardless of the patient's cultural or religious background.

Still, because of those cases where the patient comes to describe his or her alter as devilish or even as an evil spirit, DID has probably become *the* disorder most faddishly mistaken today by the naïve and credulous as falsely constituting a mistaken possession.

Conversely, some secular students of possession are too quick to dismiss every instance of documented possessions and diabolic attacks throughout history as merely instances of poorly recognized DID or other instances of dissociation. Anthropologists often aver that alleged cases of possession throughout history and in undeveloped countries to this day must have reflected this diagnosis. Dr. Arthur Kleinman, a Harvard psychiatrist with training in anthropology, argued this position in 1990:

> In North America today dissociation often takes the form of multiple personality disorder. In a society like India, the sense of self is more fluid and socially rather than individually centered; communal religious idioms of distress are more culturally legitimate than egocentric psychological ones. As a result, dissociation appears not as multiple personality, but in the form of possession by demons, which is usually regarded as pathological, or possession by gods, which is usually considered socially acceptable. Thus, cultural context determines the form of mental states and influences definitions of normality and abnormality.

This culturally determined view of possession, however, reemphasizes the observation that many of the same people who write about these phenomena have never seen a *genuine* case. In their writing, they never mention typical and distinctively dramatic features of a true demonic attack, such as speaking foreign languages or possessing hidden knowledge, an omission that undermines their argument.

One can see, however, how even well-meaning clergy members, let alone ignorant hucksters, could mistake or, worse, intentionally mislabel a vulnerable case of DID as demonic possession. I have the impression that these sorts of patients often have been exploited by some ministers and their superstitious and thrill-seeking congregants. I once watched a televangelist parade a confused young woman before a massive audience for his weekly broadcast. She appeared vulnerable and was obviously in a dissociated state of some sort. The poor woman appeared sincere and played the part well, but I had the distinct impression of witnessing a case of DID. Most of these patients aren't compensated for displaying themselves as possessed before large assemblies. But a few people who appear possessed *are* promised help—if they successfully act the part. A prominent preacher who had his own television program asked one woman I consulted to pay him five thousand dollars for an "exorcism." "Or," she told me, "I could agree to be on his program and have the exorcism free of charge." She had the good sense to decline the offer.

The real danger for individuals who have psychological illnesses that are mistaken for demonic attacks is that such people may not be educated to accept that they have psychiatric difficulties. They may expend major energy looking for a simple or magical answer to their complex difficulties, such as via an exorcism or deliverance. I have encountered quite a few people who went to extreme lengths to avoid psychiatric help for years—running from one priest or minister to another, wasting everyone's time, mostly their own.

It may seem farfetched to think that anyone in these various diagnostic groups could come to believe they are assaulted by evil spirits. But so much depends upon not only their possible pathology, but also their cultural environment. We now live in an age where too many individuals in positions of power and influence are prone to entertain the possibility that everyday problems and illnesses are caused by evil spirits. Frank Hammond, for instance, a late-twentieth-century minister and prolific writer and purveyor of videos, attributed to demonic attack schizophrenia as well as common illnesses, such as headaches and stomach pains, and everyday problems, such as gossiping and resentment. He and his wife, Ida Mae, published in 1973 the book *Pigs in the Parlor: A Practical Guide to Deliverance*. It is still in print and has sold more than 1.5 million copies. They recommended prayers against evil spirits for all sorts of similar problems.

While most spiritual ministers are usually less naïve in their beliefs, less careful adherents of various religious traditions can make serious, even tragic mistakes. To rid themselves of illusory demons, some patients defer sensible medical therapies, as we have seen, or undergo drastic procedures. For instance, a man who had been told by his clergyman that his pain was caused by demons was later diagnosed with an inoperable cancer.

Specific neurological conditions have been, and sometimes continue to be, mistaken as preternatural by conveying the impression that a person's consciousness is usurped by outside influences. A prime example is Tourette's syndrome, which is characterized by odd physical tics and outbursts of sometimes blasphemous sentiments. I have seen many such cases and admit how easily such a presentation historically must have confused onlookers as the expression of either a crazed or demonized individual until Tourette's came to be understood as a neurological disorder in the late 1800s.

Similarly, epileptic or seizure disorders have too often in history been attributed to the actions of the devil rather than disturbances of nerve cell activity in the brain. These include grand mal seizures and "absence states" (previously called petit mal attacks) and more "focal" jerks or severe twitches to localized areas of the body. Complicated variants of such focal conditions, such as temporal lobe epilepsy, present with highly varied and exceedingly odd symptoms, including hallucinations; a heightened sense of smell; unprovoked fear, anger, or joy; and even a sense of déjà vu. Because of these bizarre symptoms and the patient's inability to recall what may occur during the seizure, this condition especially may confuse onlookers. In *The Exorcist*, Regan was originally presumed to have this type of seizure disorder.

I once saw a case where a woman presented with severe trembling in her arms and hands that was seemingly outside of her control. Her fundamentalist Muslim family, who had been advised by their imam to consult a physician, was convinced that she was experiencing demonic attack by jinn (called "genies" in the West). When I identified her evident severe anxiety, I prescribed minor tranquilizers and serotonin antidepressant drugs, which improved her tremors. Only then was her family willing to dismiss the notion that diabolic spirits were involved.

Another case entailed a man who had a more severe presentation of uncontrollable shaking all over his body. Though he requested an exorcism, psychological (cognitive) therapy alone improved his shaking as he learned simple relaxation techniques. Such instances of alleged seizures are often psychogenic, and in his case, his anxiety condition resolved rapidly.

On the other hand, another man with tremors also presented unequivocal signs of a genuine oppression and other paranormal features. He also admitted to a history of past involvement with the occult. In a reverse of the previous examples, he and his family believed that he was suffering from seizures, but the condition was unlike any seizure any of his neurological consultants had ever seen. Medical testing, including lab findings, an MRI, and an EEG, were all negative. These periodic attacks followed no anatomical or other organic logic and did not seem to me to be induced by anxiety. Eventually, they responded to spiritual ministrations alone, and he became free of all features of his original state.

I also directly witnessed an even more dramatic example of an episode of a massive convulsive-like state in an unequivocally possessed woman. She and her friend, who brought her to me and a colleague, reported many typical signs of a genuine possession, including her spontaneously speaking foreign languages that she had never studied, hidden knowledge, and a levitation, which her friend had witnessed. As I examined her, this woman suddenly fell to the floor and writhed in a completely inexplicable way for about three minutes. It resembled no previous seizure either of us had ever seen; it was certainly involuntary, and she lost consciousness. But then the state resolved just as suddenly, and she appeared to have no ill aftereffects. She had never had such an attack before and never experienced it again. She later underwent a successful series of exorcisms, and all these features disappeared.

The experience of many exorcists is that possessed individuals may indeed shake or exhibit odd tremors. Fortunately, careful descriptions of the more common biological states leading to such symptoms tend to be of a different nature than these possessed counterfeits, at least to an experienced modern physician and as verified by modern testing. In a true seizure disorder, the underlying brain dysfunction tends to show up on an EEG or MRI, in contrast to the clean test results in demonized individuals.

Two complex cases that I heard about proved instructive for me about the diagnosing of seizures in more obvious demonic states. Both cases underscored the critical advisability of ensuring not only diagnostic expertise, but also appropriate medical supervision in dealing with demonized individuals.

The first was the highly publicized and notorious case of Anneliese Michel, a young German woman who died in 1976 following a series of exorcisms. Her story has been featured in several movies and television programs, including the 2005 film *The Exorcism of Emily Rose*. As a child, Anneliese suffered from what was said to be genuine seizures and depression. She was diagnosed with what her doctors called epileptic psychosis, specifically temporal lobe epilepsy, as a teenager. Later, others speculated that she suffered from a more straightforward psychotic depression or DID. Eventually, she exhibited an extreme aversion to sacred objects and reportedly a few other of the classic signs of possession, so she and her family appealed to Catholic clergy for an exorcism.

She also experienced alleged messages telling her to fast. She believed these messages came directly from the Virgin Mary. Others, however, were convinced that they came from demons who wanted to hurt Anneliese, or that they were psychotic in nature. Whatever the cause, after a series of more than sixty exorcisms over ten months, she died of starvation and dehydration, having refused all medical supervision during her many exorcism sessions.

Though rare, the possibility always exists that a combination of medical and demonic disorders is present in an afflicted person. This may have been the case with Anneliese, though on the basis of the historical accounts, it has remained unclear to me. Her case certainly underscores the point that an individual undergoing a diabolic attack may simultaneously require ongoing medical supervision, especially if the afflicted is suffering from an accompanying medical vulnerability. Some possessed victims may fall into depression, and some individuals under the duress of their situation may become suicidal.

A court case found the two priest-exorcists ministering to Anneliese guilty of negligent homicide. They were sentenced to six months in prison, though the charges were later suspended on appeal. Troubled by the legal verdict, the Catholic church in Germany, many of whose members were skeptical of the possession to begin with, became reluctant to authorize more exorcisms for years.

Anneliese and her family had held controversial beliefs about the cause of her suffering. They were openly critical of what they saw as dangerous trends within the modern church, and Anneliese thought her fasts were an "atonement" for a wayward church. These factors, too, probably complicated a sober resolution of her condition as there were few experts, medical or clerical, they trusted.

Although many details of the case remain debated to this day, what should not have been in dispute is the need in her case for close collaboration between her exorcists and physicians. The priests maintained that it was impossible to persuade either the victim or her family to submit to such oversight. I have argued that this was clearly a dire situation when the family's wishes should have been overruled. Anneliese should have been put in a hospital against her will whenever she stopped eating; a medical expert at the priests' trial testified similarly.

I once consulted remotely on a case of a demonically attacked man who also refused to eat. Like Anneliese, George had previously been diagnosed with a seizure disorder. He shook oddly and without any obvious diagnostically sound pattern. Its description to me made no medical sense, and he already had a negative CT scan and EEG.

Unlike Anneliese, however, George had a long history of occult involvement and exhibited a number of preternatural signs, including hidden knowledge of other people. For instance, his wife verified that he knew accurately the troubled histories of people he had never met. He also experienced anatomically inexplicable pains whenever he tried to pray. I was convinced from extensive reports I'd received from other doctors that he was not psychotic. The Protestant minister dealing with him told me he thought he was unquestionably oppressed.

When I spoke to him and his wife via Skype, the man claimed that his refusal to eat was, like Anneliese's vow, an act of religious obligation, imposed by God himself, with the purported aim of securing his liberation from the devil. He was strikingly stubborn about the point, as had been Anneliese. His wife was afraid that he was going to die, and his minister was also overwhelmed and desperate, thinking he had no recourse because his congregant was so obstinate.

I believed George had become convinced that he was receiving messages, similar to Sara's, and these messages were not auditory. With much reluctance, he had previously agreed to take medication, which proved ineffective. Since George was convinced these were preternatural or supernatural communications, I advised him to entertain the possibility—just as Sara had—that these false messages were coming from a demonic source. Since he had previously experimented with occult studies and paranormal experiences, he listened to me but eventually became convinced that the messages were in fact divine in nature.

Of more immediate concern to me, however, were the reports I'd received that George was becoming dehydrated—the most pressing danger in cases of severe fasts. I tried to persuade George's minister that George was in the middle of a medical emergency, but he stated, "Well, if he goes into the hospital, we can't liberate him."

I replied, "A dead man isn't going to be spiritually helped."

As I advised, his family sent George to the hospital, where he was properly rehydrated and fed. Only that intervention saved the emaciated man's life, eventually allowing further spiritual assistance after he was discharged.

These types of situations all underscore the critical role physicians and other health professionals can play in helping exorcists and those involved in deliverance ministries. Throughout history, doctors have been expected to monitor victims' physical health as well as to diagnose *natural* causes or rule them out before exorcists can proceed with their *spiritual* work. The Roman Ritual is explicit on this point. Even in medieval times, sometimes maligned for being superstitious about demonic activity and disease states, people respected doctors' opinions and did not jump to supernatural explanations. In fact, the formal philosophical distinction between "natural" and "supernatural" causes reaches back to that time. (Though some modern scholars have criticized its sharp dichotomy, this differentiation works well for the purposes in this area.) In the thirteenth century, the Catholic theologian Thomas Aquinas warned clerics not to jump to a supernatural cause when a purely natural one sufficed. He and like-minded thinkers were aware of the separate existence of mental pathologies and spiritual ailments; Aquinas even ascribed "madness" primarily to biological factors, a seemingly "modern" viewpoint and one surprising only to the historically naïve.

Speaking of the ideal exorcist, the Roman Ritual calls for someone not only "outstanding in knowledge" but also with personal qualities such as maturity and holiness. Overly emotional or poorly educated ministers or priests, just like ill-informed doctors or lawyers, don't make good judges of complex situations, such as demonic states, that require patience, caution, and sober judgment. Some astute and experienced exorcists are knowledgeable enough to discern diabolic attacks largely on their own. Still, they are advised to seek a medical professional's opinion whenever any doubt or other medical needs arise—a sacred role passed down in my profession for centuries.

CHAPTER SEVEN

CATHERINE—MOTHER, HOUSEWIFE, AND POSSESSED

Her Series of Exorcisms and What the Rituals Are Really Like

Shortly after my encounter with Lily, Father Jacques asked me to visit a woman with him in West Virginia, which he and I did regularly over a few years. During our drives there, we spoke at length. Hoping to learn as much as I could, I peppered him with questions about the genuine cases of possessions he had encountered over the years, which he described to me in detail. In between these tales, he also told me about the many false cases of possession he had come across, like Lily's.

I felt an added urgency to learn from Father Jacques whatever I could because his health was in obvious decline. I was worried about my friend and repeatedly told him to take care of himself. A private man, he nevertheless told me that he had some heart problems, confiding in me that his physician advised him to watch his diet and exercise more. Despite his health problems, however, Father Jacques remained committed to caring for the men and women suffering at the hands of our various demonic foes, including Catherine in West Virginia, whose prolonged possessions continued to vex and concern him.

Catherine's case was one of the more intractable possessions I've come across, and she had been working for many months with Father Jacques by the time he invited me to meet her. Father Jacques thought it would be good for my instruction to see a prolonged series of exorcisms with the same person. I had already witnessed quite a few rituals by then, but most of the cases he or Father A. worked on had been swiftly resolved.

Catherine lives with her husband, Carl, and their children in a rural town in northern West Virginia. Over the years, I have visited her at her home on twelve or thirteen occasions. Like Catherine, her small town has seen better times. Many of the town's buildings are in severe disrepair or abandoned. Dust collects over everything. Catherine's modest house is near the center of town, a short walk down a gravelly side path. The sparse backyard extends to a small wooded area, where brittle bushes struggle to stay alive.

Whenever we visited, Carl always greeted us at the front door. An unassuming, down-to-earth man, he maintained an equanimity and patience about his wife's condition despite the terrible circumstances. Unfailingly polite, he welcomed us into his home and was effusive in his gratitude when we departed.

Their home is warm, lived-in, and comfortable, with sturdy wooden furniture. Family pictures fill the tables and walls, most of which were taken years ago when their children were younger and Catherine was happier and healthier-looking.

On my first visit, the smell of roast pork greeted us.

"Catherine has been in a bad state," Carl said with a serious look on his face. "It was a tough night for her."

He reminded Father Jacques how strongly Catherine reacted before an exorcism session—a common response, I learned, in many victims. This good husband, I realized, was trying to protect his wife from any undue stress. He hadn't told her Father Jacques was coming—or that he was bringing a psychiatrist along to help him evaluate her case—and yet Catherine knew the details of our trip, down to the rough time of our arrival. "The things my wife knows!" Carl always repeated to us.

According to Carl, as soon as she became aware that we were coming, Catherine had fallen into a typical funk. Her alertness seemed diminished, and she grew distracted and preoccupied with the impending session, which she found so difficult to bear. Based on their previous experiences, Carl and Catherine were both convinced the demons would step up their attack on her because they hated these rituals and were trying to stimulate her fears and reluctance to allow them.

Carl also told us that Catherine's ears were "killing" her, a common complaint. She said evil spirits were taunting her. That morning, after preparing the roast for our arrival, she had gone back to bed.

I was taking all this in when Father Jacques began to explain the plan for the day. First, he wanted to celebrate Mass in their home, explaining to me that it was a good idea to start any scheduled ritual with one. Though he predicted that Catherine would not be able to participate in the ceremony, he was certain she would nevertheless benefit from it. After the Mass, the local parish priest would conduct the exorcism. Father Jacques would assist.

While Father Jacques prepared the family's home for Mass, he asked me to sit down privately with Catherine. Carl called for her to come down from the bedroom. After a few minutes, she ambled down the stairs, mouthing a soft and glum hello, before collapsing on a well-worn sofa. She slumped over, entirely unengaged, with a faraway look in her eyes. When Carl asked whether she'd be willing to meet with me for a few minutes, she nodded unenthusiastically and, seemingly out of habit, trudged over to a cubby hole in the back of the house, which doubled as a small office.

I introduced myself and asked how she was feeling.

"Not good at all," she responded in a flat tone. I could tell she knew that I was assessing her mental state. She started answering my questions without any difficulty.

I had already learned that she had no prior history of mental illness. Father Jacques told me that Catherine had been complaining about the presence of "attacking spirits," in her own words. She often claimed she could see such spirits, which took the form of dark, shadowy shapes. Like Sara, Catherine also claimed she received messages "mentally," which strangely caused her great pain, especially in her ears. According to Father Jacques, the couple had first visited their local general practitioner, a sober believer himself in her possession, who referred her to an ear, nose, and throat specialist. That doctor also could find no physical explanation for her intermittent ear pains.

As we had moved to the back room, she had cupped her ears with her hands. She looked devastated. "They hurt *bad*," she groaned.

While her hearing worked perfectly fine during normal conversations, Catherine could not hear anything of a *religious* nature. She could not hear words or phrases in any way related to spiritual practices and beliefs, which made it impossible to have any discussion with her of a *pastoral* nature. If her priest asked her, for example, "Have you been able to pray, Catherine?" she would reply, "Able to do *what*?" Or, in response to a question like "Have you been to church and received the Eucharist?" she would invariably answer, "Have I been *where*? Received *what*?"

Catherine was experiencing a *selective* and quite specific loss in her hearing. In addition to the ear, nose, and throat specialist, she had seen both a psychologist, who had concluded that there was no psychological explanation for these symptoms, and an audiologist, who likewise had been unable to discern any problem.

I already knew much of her background history, but I wanted to gather some more details. Mainly, though, I concentrated on getting a sense of her current mood and cognitive state as I tried to look for any pathology to assess her general motivation. Before meeting Catherine, I had originally suggested to Father Jacques that she might be suffering from a psychotic depression. As I was interviewing her, however, I became more and more convinced that the array of bizarre and paranormal symptoms could in no way be accounted for by any psychiatric diagnosis, though her air of pessimism and gloom did strike me as having a depressive cast.

"I can see you seem pretty depressed and pessimistic," I offered.

"Yes, I am."

I then switched to a more informal style of conversing with her and asked whether she'd been cooking earlier that morning. She nodded. She said she'd gotten the groceries the day before to prepare for our visit. Knowing she might be blocked from answering or even being able to hear questions about any deeper issues, I tried to intersperse neutral questions with others of a more spiritual nature. I wanted us to chat in a more relaxed way. Since I had seen a pickup in the yard, I asked her whether she drove it. She said she did, regularly. I asked about her children, the house, the recent weather, anything to put her at ease. Like any mother, she brightened while discussing her kids. At that point, I was convinced she was perfectly capable of hearing.

"Have you given up trusting in God's help?" I asked.

"Trusting *what*?" she replied quizzically.

"Have you been able to pray or confide in your pastor?"

Again, she seemed unable to comprehend. "Able to do what? I don't understand," she stammered. "To confide in *who*?"

I asked a few other similar questions and realized I was witnessing the same kind of selective hearing Father Jacques and Carl had described.

A few months and several visits later, with permission from Father Jacques and the family, I took along a psychiatric colleague. We interviewed Catherine together. Again, she made the same sort of dry answers to any neutral inquiries and had the same stupefied look in response to any religiously oriented ones.

We had cooked up the idea of ending the conversation by asking her to respond to written questions on pieces of paper. She clearly understood we were testing her, though I didn't think she knew why. She responded well to about six or seven written queries, such as "What has your day been like?" or "How are your children?" But then we showed her the last two sheets of paper: "Have you been trying to pray to God?" and "Are you going to attend the Mass later and receive the Eucharist?"

She looked at me quizzically. "Dr. Gallagher," she said, "why are you showing me these blank pieces of paper?"

During our visits, I never found evidence of any hysterical conversion reaction or the like, nor did I or anyone else suspect Catherine of guile or playacting. Her loss of hearing was so specific that it seemed implausible to suspect anything other than demonic activity, a hypothesis supported by my experiences and from my research. Blocking one or more of someone's physical senses or speech is a demonic effect frequently reported in possession cases. A demonized man once told me that evil spirits had deprived him of his hearing and his vision.

Similar cases appear throughout history. For instance, in the mid-1800s, Theobald and Joseph Bruner, two brothers from Illfurth, France, were both possessed, according to numerous witnesses and contemporaneous parish records. Like Catherine, the older Theobald became deaf during the course of his possession, though in his case he fully lost his hearing for long periods. The brothers also entangled themselves in impossible contortions. While possessed, both brothers spoke fluently multiple unstudied foreign languages, including Latin, Greek, French, Italian, and Spanish. When Theobald was finally delivered of his possessing evil spirit, these features disappeared, and he immediately regained his hearing.

What made Catherine's "deafness" especially relevant to her demonized state was the evident motivation of the evil spirits to deprive her of her ability to communicate with others in any pastorally supportive manner, a cruel strategy from the demonic realm. Because Catherine couldn't hear the spiritual advice of her priest, her family, or anyone else, she couldn't be consoled. There is no doubt she was being prevented from receiving that support. How could she receive help to work on her own dire situation, so integral a part of so many cases of serious demonic attack?

Catherine was happily living as a mother and homemaker before she was possessed. She was a valued member of her community. There was nothing to suggest to the citizens of her small town that there was any likelihood this pleasant neighbor, raised on a local farm, would come to suffer a dramatic possession.

But she eventually admitted that for a period as a young woman she and two female friends had formed a small "witches' coven," and the three of them had pledged some sort of loyalty to the devil. Though Catherine had long ago left and renounced the group, evil spirits were evidently not done with her. Her behavior had been, in her words, "no lark." At the time she took her involvement in this "devil group," as she came to call it, fairly seriously. She had participated with her peers in what she and her friends understood to be diabolic rites.

During one ceremony, they all thought they'd made contact with Satan himself. She also reported that they had offered several aborted fetuses to the group for ritual use. Presumably, the fetuses had come from that small band of young women, a delicate piece of information I was reluctant to ask about. Due to her shame, I doubt she would have answered the question, or been able to do so in any case. As with some of Julia's grimmer stories, I was repulsed, but I was accustomed, particularly as a psychiatrist, to remaining nonjudgmental and focused on Catherine's sad story and her present condition.

Another idea the family entertained about why Catherine might be possessed was that her mother's aunt was said to have been an avowed witch back in Poland, where that family originated. I never learned any more particulars of this evident guess. Just as Manny's parents had speculated, people in Catherine's life wondered whether she were paying the price for some kind of familial issue or curse. As noted earlier, I am always somewhat skeptical of these remote hypotheses, especially when a more obvious and contemporary historical factor involves the individual directly. It would be hard to know whether the speculation about her great-aunt had any plausibility, but Catherine's reported contract with Satan certainly did.

This brief and foolish period in Catherine's life weighed on her constantly, and she was still guilt-ridden and despairing. She saw herself as having committed unforgivable acts. She felt she could do nothing to lift the pain or bring about her liberation. In my view, she feared her fate would be to suffer perhaps eternally as the demonic world engulfed her.

Catherine's problems first surfaced with the not uncommon features of a preliminary oppression and then progressed to a full-fledged possession. At the outset she seemed to be beaten up by spirits, a clear example of the vexation or external oppression that Maria and Stan had suffered, although their cases never progressed to a possession. That's because, presumably, neither had engaged in such nefarious conduct, as Catherine claimed she had.

When the pain and other manifestations, including the emergence of the characteristic trance states, continued to increase, Carl and Catherine requested their local priest to perform an exorcism. Eventually, this priest had gotten in touch with Father Jacques to solicit his advice. Jacques had been assisting at a number of sessions with Catherine before he invited me to join them as a witness.

After my initial talk with Catherine, I told Father Jacques that she had been cooperative with me as best she could be and that she had also experienced her hearing difficulty with me. Father Jacques then got ready for the exorcism session.

• • •

I am often asked what exorcisms are like, but this is an impossible question to answer because each case presents different circumstances and has different needs. Yes, there is a basic structure to the Catholic Rite of Major Exorcism, but as Father A. used to tell me, "No two possessions are alike, and no two exorcisms are alike either."

At the same time, different Christian denominations and different religions practice different rituals. Subcultural differences, including the extent of public acceptance of the controversial possibility of a demonic attack, also influence the way things are done.

In addition to the specific features of a particular possession, the different personalities of the priest-exorcists and the spirit or spirits involved dictate events. I would say, however, that Catherine's possession and her exorcisms have been somewhat typical for Roman Catholic exorcisms, though her series of exorcisms have been more extended than most, without dramatic success yet.

Despite the mandatory use of the Roman Ritual, even Catholic exorcisms may vary greatly. The manner in which the priest-exorcist chooses to combine the set prayers with spontaneous dialogue is always somewhat singular, for instance. Catholic prayers of exorcism are classified as either "deprecatory," asking for God's help, or "imprecatory," commanding the devil to leave. Though the formal rite combines both, only ordained priests can recite imprecatory prayers.

Historically, most attempts to exorcise malignant spirits have been plainer affairs than the Catholic ones of recent centuries. The Roman Catholic Church and the Orthodox Church have elaborated the most formal rituals and procedures for exorcisms. Older than even the Catholic rituals, the set rites of the Orthodox Church were established by Basil the Great, a fourth-century bishop and church father from Asia Minor, or modern Turkey. Rules about who can address and command demons in a ritual are different between the Catholic and Orthodox Churches, but both almost always confine any real dialogue to the chief or assistant exorcist.

If conducted at all, exorcisms within mainline Protestant traditions similarly adhere closely to traditional rules, though formal prayers are not standardized. The Episcopal *Book of Occasional Services* includes provisions for exorcisms, but these provisions offer no specific prayers or "office" of exorcist.

The Church of England's 1974 influential York Report called for careful medical evaluations ahead of formal exorcisms, stating in no uncertain terms that proposals for exorcisms must be "consonant with sound philosophical, psychological, theological, and liturgical principles"—a stringent requirement shared by the Catholic and Orthodox Churches. Similarly, as in the Catholic tradition, formal exorcisms among Anglicans must be approved by the local bishop.

In the 1970s, the Methodist Church in the United States released an official statement about the topic, also advising a cautious and cleric-oriented approach, and the Lutheran tradition follows similar practices. Exorcisms by many evangelical ministers, conducted now around the world, have a much more egalitarian flavor. These ceremonies or prayer sessions may simply be called "deliverance prayers" and are used for a broader range of demonic assaults, primarily oppressions.

In the past thirty years or so, Catholic priests and laity are reciting "deliverance" prayers as well, though that terminology is sometimes avoided recently. The Catholic tradition draws a sharper distinction between formal exorcisms of possessions, which are authorized only by bishops, and these less official prayers aimed at cases that fall short of a full possession. In fact, the Catholic Church has no real formal doctrines or canon laws regarding deliverance ministries per se, as opposed to its formal exorcism procedures and its defined and closely defended dogmas about the reality of Satan and demons.

I once discussed with a young man his successful deliverance from an unequivocal possession. He had joined a nondenominational Christian church, though previously he had been heavily involved with occult practices for years. Recognizing the seriousness of his situation, seven of the church's evangelical ministers came together to pray over him in a lengthy session. He described a much more informal ritual where any of the participants, including several laypeople, could take turns praying over him for several hours, laying their hands on him as he sat in the middle of a large circle.

Members of less traditional Christian congregations, such as some Pentecostal and Assembly of God churches, are even more free-wheeling in their practices. They address demons collectively, either with groups of the faithful speaking in tongues or by having their leaders perform such ceremonies in front of large assemblies, which are sometimes televised. These groups as a whole may call out direct commands and insults to the presumed attacking spirits.

Such activity would normally be strictly forbidden in Roman Catholic circles, although I was once invited to attend an authorized Catholic exorcism where just such practices occurred. Enthused laypeople were shouting at the demons and seconding the priests' commands. I wondered whether I had wandered into the wrong church. This more loosely organized session, which is more common within charismatic communities, was the exception among Catholics, because such behavior is not officially sanctioned by any Catholic bishop as part of the church's formal Rite of Major Exorcism.

More lay-led and spontaneous prayer initiatives among Christians to combat evil spirits claim to hearken back to what some proponents believe were the earliest practices of Christians, though other scholars dispute such assertions. These groups may cite the historical precedent that the early church did not seem to appoint official exorcists, arguing that any good, faithful Christian was empowered by God to cast out demons. By the third century, the organized Catholic Church seems to have become more sensitive to possible excesses and abuses among overzealous lay faithful in these matters, and its hierarchy decided to confine the role of exorcists to clerics. Still, sometimes that general rule was waived, apparently, as saintly figures were at times asked to conduct such ceremonies.

As we have seen, in his practice, Father A. preferred to employ the Roman Ritual in Latin, specifically the older text from 1614, although he believed others were free to do it differently. In Catherine's exorcisms and those I've witnessed during the past fifteen years in the United States, the priest has invariably recited the rite in English and specifically employed the revised 1998 version. However, Father Gabriele Amorth, the second president of the International Association of Exorcists (AIE), held the controversial view that the newer ritual's lesser stress on commands was less effective than the more traditional approach to exorcism.

Those rare Catholic priests around the world who still seek permission to use the Latin text may maintain that they find the Latin starker and more beautiful. They also feel that its use precludes any possibility of suggestibility, as only the demon, not the victim, can understand what is being said.

The various evil spirits also show differing personality characteristics and degrees of intelligence, to an extent that will lend different flavors to how specific exorcisms play out. The traditional teaching is that, as spirits and fallen angels, demons are quite intelligent. But like humans, this intelligence varies greatly from demon to demon.

Once, as a priest recited the Apostle's Creed in Latin, to be discussed later, I heard the demon speak with sarcasm and despairing intelligence. Within the voice, I detected a distinct personality. Most exorcists prefer not to have the demon "show off" through such diatribes or ad hominem attacks via a mocking commentary or personal attack. In some cases, a distinct impression of low intelligence is given, although it is hard to know whether that is a ruse or simply a mark of narrow mentality on the evil spirit's part. Rather than engage in "chatting," or posing abstruse questions, the priest persists to attempt to force the demon to answer the key and oft-repeated questions, "What is your name, and when are you leaving?"

Sometimes, when the demon pontificates about broader theological themes, which can happen, such conversation may be an attempt to distract and mislead. As noted, I once heard an evil spirit argue that Satan recently had "changed his mind" and was now seeking a reconciliation with God. Other times, however, demons may offer surprisingly sophisticated admissions of profound religious truths, though one always must be cautious in how one interprets such utterances.

The famous 1928 case from Earling, Iowa, previously cited, is a dramatic example of a possessing spirit spouting nonsense. A formerly devout woman known to be possessed was brought to Earling to be exorcised by the German Catholic priest Father Theophilus Riesinger. The exorcisms proved eventful: the woman levitated to the ceiling, uttered typical demonic ravings, and grew enraged in the presence of holy objects and blessed water. A pamphlet documenting all these events was widely published. The demonic spirit claimed that the "anti-Christ" had already been born in Palestine and would appear in 1952. He was supposedly an unimpressive human who was, however, "possessed" by Judas Iscariot. According to witnesses, the alleged voice of Judas was heard repeatedly throughout the exorcisms.

Possessing spirits always try to spread confusion among us poor mortals. Messages in various cases I've witnessed have involved false predictions of the end of the world, a popular theme among religious cranks and false visionaries. The firm theological understanding is that demons do not know the future. All one can be sure of is that these demons habitually lie, although at times they do seem compelled to make honest statements. Another common strategy is for the evil spirit to claim to be a single demon and give only one name or boast to be many evil spirits, or deities or dead souls.

Some demons seem more arrogant than others; a few seem visibly more frightened or tentative in their speech. In some rituals, the demon exhibits a strong sense of entitlement, maybe the chief personality feature held in common among demons. In these regards, they resemble human beings with certain personality disorders, with a similar variability in presentation. These various traits do not reflect the human victim's own hidden attitudes in any manner.

Strange to say, some demons have been known to claim outright "legal" rights over the possessed and can even scold the exorcist for not respecting the proper authorities. It's as if, since they themselves feel "under authority" from their superiors, which is probably the case, the demons expect the same from others. An Italian exorcist once told me that a demon asked him whether he had, indeed, obtained the bishop's permission to perform the exorcism. "You must, you know," the demon told him.

The different spiritual traditions that speculate about possessions contend that various purposes can be served by these lengthy trials. One exorcist told me a remarkable story about a demon who seemed to *want* to leave. When the priest asked what was preventing it from departing, the evil spirit responded, "Your stupid boss [referring to

God] won't let me." Like all sorts of evil, which God doesn't *cause* but "*allows*" for his mysterious reasons, some providential purpose beyond human understanding was presumably at work.

• • •

In Catherine's exorcism, many of these same features were apparent. To prepare for the ritual, Carl drew the heavy shades of his family's living room and covered the tinted glass on the front door. Privacy was paramount, and only a select few knew about Catherine's possession. Most Catholic exorcists prefer to conduct these sessions in a church setting, often in a room where the Eucharist is present. But sometimes, busy church buildings cannot ensure the desired privacy, or the victim is unwilling or unable to go into a church. Because Catherine couldn't tolerate being in a church, all of her exorcisms occurred in her home.

Over a makeshift altar with two candles and a crucifix set on a white sheet, Father Jacques started celebrating Mass in the dining room. Stupefied and in pain, Catherine immediately retreated to the far corner of the room, as far away from the altar and Eucharist as the house allowed. Her pain increased throughout the liturgy, and she seemed to slip in and out of consciousness. Experts sometimes recognize this partially dazed condition as a distinct and periodically recurring phase, like the full trance state, which similarly comes and goes. Neither state is predictable, though an exorcism tends to elicit both. In the dazed state, a person exhibits diminished control of his or her faculties, though not as much as during the full trance when a person's consciousness completely submerges beneath the presence of the possessing entity.

Soon afterward, the parish priest arrived. Accustomed to performing the Rite of Major Exorcism, Father B. proceeded in a workman-like manner. After assessing Catherine, Father B. presented her with a waiver to sign—a requirement for exorcism sessions in the United States. The waiver makes clear that the victim is *voluntarily* undergoing a *spiritual* procedure. Catherine roused herself to sign it. Whatever her fears or misgivings, she clearly wanted the procedure to proceed. (A Spanish exorcist once told me that in his estimation this insistence on legal protectiveness promoted less than a fully pastorally congenial atmosphere. "Well," I told him, "you must not yet have encountered the American legal profession.")

Robed as a member of a religious order, Father B. donned a white surplice over his habit for the ceremony, with a long purple stole around his neck stretching down his flanks, as stipulated. He carried a large gold crucifix and had holy water at the ready, both of which he employed at the start and often during the ceremony. When he commanded the evil spirit, he held the crucifix against Catherine's forehead.

Eight people were present for this session, including Catherine's sister. A nurse was on hand to monitor Catherine's physiological condition during the taxing rituals. When a demonic spirit appears under the influence of the commanding prayers of the exorcism, the victim invariably tries to lash out physically in order to inflict bodily harm on the exorcist and his attendants, or to escape from the scene. To prevent both possibilities, we sat Catherine on her living room couch, which allowed Carl and others to hold her down.

Proper selection of assistants and participants is important. The chief exorcist decides who should attend and who should not. Catholic exorcists prefer that the laypeople assisting be sensible and believing individuals, although a few priests in my experience have not been so insistent. Anyone with major life problems, emotional or otherwise, might be excluded. During an early exorcism I witnessed in New England, a lay assistant developed serious emotional problems afterward. Children are not allowed to attend the rituals, and sometimes even close friends or relatives may be excluded if they do not possess the necessary objectivity or equanimity.

Father B. started the session by reading from the revised Roman Ritual word for word, reciting an invocation asking for divine assistance: "Holy God, who among your other wonders, deign to command, put the demons to flight. . . . Strengthened by your power, may I attack with confidence the evil spirit who torments this creature of yours . . . O God . . . let not the evil spirit dwell here, and let every snare of the evil foe come to nothing."

Father B. followed this blessing with the litany of saints and a Gospel reading. Father Jacques and the lay attendees, including myself, gave the responses expected. He then addressed the demon directly. He asked the demon for its name and when it would leave, the two key questions repeatedly posed during most exorcisms. Both queries are thought important as part of the effort to exert a commanding authority over the evil spirit. Catherine's demon often said its name was something that sounded like "Scalias," though in later sessions, the demon claimed a different name.

Between further set prayers, Father B. interspersed commands for the demon to depart, the second of the two most essential tasks. Beyond these questions and commands, the exorcist rarely engages in much back-and-forth with the demon. Throughout the ordeal, Father B. remained sober in his questioning. Like all good exorcists, he and Father Jacques discouraged any comments motivated by idle curiosity and sudden outbursts of frustration.

Ten minutes into the session, Catherine transitioned from her dazed state to the full trance state. That's when the demon started surfacing overtly. Now under the demon's full control, she became more agitated, struggling strenuously against all those holding her. I could see Carl and the others tightening their grips, straining against Catherine's efforts to break free.

Father B. again asked the demon when it was leaving.

A petulant voice replied, "Never."

Father B. then ordered it to leave Catherine alone.

The same voice answered, "Or what?" and forced a smirk to form across Catherine's face. "We will not go," it said. "*You* leave. We're going nowhere and *you'll* be *sorry!*"

The demon implied—during this session and subsequent sessions I attended—that it was entitled to possess Catherine. "She allowed us in," it reminded Father B. "She gave herself to us, and she can never be set free."

The voice taunted the priest when he challenged this bond, often with an annoying, supercilious expression. Whining, the demon complained that Catherine "had made a *promise to us*," hinting that she had entered into a kind of "marriage" with it and now the demon was entitled to its due.

There was a recognizable personality there (perhaps more than one) of an arrogant and giggling torturer. To make itself difficult to hear, the demon often whispered, although if I listened closely, I could make out constant boasts and antagonism, which were interspersed with vile and blasphemous sentiments, sarcastically mocking the priest and his prayers. The demon's voice pattern changed over the course of the session. The general manner, however, was of an obstinate bully, an immature and pompous adversary.

Mostly the demon spoke in English, but at one point, I detected some ancient Greek. At a later session it also interspersed a vague, Asian-sounding language and was able to contort Catherine's face, especially her eyes, into a distinctly far Eastern facial expression.

Despite being physically restrained, Catherine was clearly trying to escape the scene, attempting (unsuccessfully) to strike and kick those holding her down. Father B. was the demon's primary target, however, verbally and physically. If we hadn't kept Catherine's lower limbs secure that day, Father B. would have been kicked on numerous occasions. The entity also repeatedly tried to bite or scratch people nearest Catherine. Interestingly, she sometimes seemed to be prevented from doing so without anyone grabbing her hands or face. Many participants believed they escaped injury because of the commands of the exorcist to the demon not to harm anyone in the room. I had that experience myself several times during later rituals, when I assumed a position to restrain her and her face stopped within an inch of my arm as she moved to bite me.

The Rite of Major Exorcism generally takes about an hour, but different exorcists choose differing lengths for these sessions or may repeat the prayers more than once. On this day, the battle lasted for about ninety minutes. Catherine's exorcisms were true physical ordeals; how she was able to sustain this effort was remarkable. The duration exhausted Carl and the others who fought equally long in their roles as protectors. During a later session, I was asked to help hold Catherine, and by the end of the ritual, she had resisted so vigorously that we were nearly spent. I once heard about a case of a petite woman who easily raised her leg with a 250-pound man clinging to her, lifting him straight off the floor.

I have attended some exorcisms that lasted three hours or longer. If the sessions are too long and frequent and seem unproductive, the attendees may grow discouraged, and some exorcists feel these lengthy sessions are not a productive use of time. The need for extended sessions may suggest that the time for deliverance is not yet opportune or permitted by divine favor.

For some possessions I have witnessed, one or two exorcisms result in the resolution of the demonic assault. Catherine's were obviously not so efficacious. This is not to say that the exorcism prayers "failed." Most experienced Christian exorcists contend that no prayers for liberation and certainly no formal exorcisms are a waste of time. All such prayers and rituals are of inherent value. Just because a prayer is not immediately answered (or sometimes does not seem answered at all) does not mean that it was of no merit. Prayers, as Father Jacques always reminded me, are answered in "God's due time and manner."

After the ritual, Catherine slowly emerged from her condition, demonstrating the dazed state again for a short time. As we began to converse with her, she complained anew about her ears aching. Slowly, she surfaced more fully, the pain went away, and she became active, if a bit subdued in manner.

Eventually, she got up from the sofa and, astonishingly, turned to hostessing. She was quiet and slow in movement, but she was trying hard to make us all feel at home. She found some comfort, I sensed, in heading to the kitchen and heating up the food she had prepared for our visit.

As a busy doctor with a family of my own, I was often eager after the ritual to hit the road and start the long ride home. But I always lingered to enjoy Catherine's good food and delicious pies. It helped us all relax after the intense ritual, as we all ate and conversed for a while. I would then see Catherine's pleasant side, as she seemed to enjoy the banter at that stage.

After this first ritual, like many possessed individuals, Catherine went on to lead a *partially* normal life for another period of time, a fact that continues to amaze me. She hardly thrives, but she is not totally dysfunctional either. On good days now, she can help out at the parish complex. She doesn't—or "can't," as she puts it—go into the church itself, which still causes her physical pain.

To this day, her exorcisms continue, and Catherine and Carl still believe each session has its benefits, though they are short-lived. Her loved ones persist in hoping the rituals will weaken the demonic stranglehold sufficiently so that someday she can return to her normal self.

CHAPTER EIGHT

THE SERIOUS INVESTIGATOR

My concerns about Father Jacques's declining health were well-founded.

My family went on a vacation to Vermont, so I was out of communication with my office for a week and a half. When I checked the messages on my voicemail, I found two from Father Jacques. His first let me know he wasn't feeling well and he was going to check himself into a hospital near where he lived. He sounded tired but not in great distress. He had a respiratory ailment that he originally hadn't taken very seriously, his usual habit with health concerns. But this time the infection had gotten progressively worse and he spiked a fever.

The second message was more alarming. His voice sounded weaker and more desperate. Things weren't going well at the hospital, and he was now more directly soliciting my opinion, asking that I call him as soon as I got home. I got the sense that he wanted me to have him transferred to the academic medical center where I worked. This follow-up message had been left about two days before our return. I immediately called the hospital and tried to reach him in his room, but the attending nurse told me he was on a respirator and couldn't talk.

Immediately, I drove to the hospital, where the nurses on duty informed me that his prognosis wasn't good. They also told me that a relative had requested a DNR (do not resuscitate) order, which I questioned. I had several times told Jacques that if he wanted me to have the proper authority in such situations, he'd have to make me his health proxy. Characteristically, he had never followed through on that suggestion. I felt helpless, and even more so when I visited him bedside and witnessed his sad, but still inquiring eyes. He seemed to want to tell me something, but he couldn't. I had as bad a feeling as when I had last talked face-to-face with Julia.

My misgivings proved prescient. Father Jacques died twelve hours later of septic shock.

Sometimes we don't realize how important someone is in our lives until we lose that person. Such were my feelings at the time. Though our lives were very different, Father Jacques and I had become close colleagues on so many cases involving tortured individuals in a rare field of endeavor. This had fostered a stronger bond of friendship than I think I had realized before his sudden death.

I knew that he had taken me under his wing, and I realized in retrospect, I think, how he had seemed happy to have been able to share so much of his massive experience and, yes, wisdom with a younger professional colleague. I think he was proud, too, that I had been grateful to have absorbed so much from him, such that he'd become assured of my own level of expertise. And just when I had developed that confidence of my own, he was gone—so unexpectedly. I considered him my early stalwart guide through a strange world, where good and evil are locked in an ongoing battle. All these years later, I still greatly miss him.

At Jacques's funeral, I met Lorraine Warren, a noted if somewhat controversial "paranormal investigator." With her husband, Ed, she became a centerpiece of *The Conjuring* series of films, which were based on their experiences. The blockbuster franchise has earned more than $1 billion at the box office, a testament to the public's insatiable interest in this topic around the world. Before Father Jacques passed away, he and Father A. had discussed some of the couple's cases with me, giving me sober and detailed-filled accounts that the movies had little interest in capturing. Lorraine was a well-spoken and gracious woman. She knew how close I had been to Father Jacques and remarked about how he had been "always generous of his time." This sentiment echoed what I heard from many people. Several people remarked to me that Father Jacques was the "kindest man they ever met." Not a bad legacy for a life.

After Jacques died, I sometimes kept Father A. informed about my work in this field, but I saw and talked to him much less frequently than I had done with Jacques. His reflections remained valuable, but I was at the point where I'd begun to realize I was on my own. In the service of whatever I could contribute to others, I needed to keep learning but had to rely much more on my wits and my own experience. Luckily, I felt I had absorbed enough from these two good priests to be able to serve that role responsibly and confidently.

Despite our infrequent personal meetings, I appreciated that Father A. had become more than just a colleague. But unfortunately, he also died a few years later. An ex-Marine, he had been an imposing presence, at six and a half feet. He had a no-nonsense manner, but he had a big heart.

These two priests were sometimes criticized in their unique vocations as busy exorcists. I once saw Father Jacques on *Nightline* eviscerate, to the delight of Ted Koppel, in his phlegmatic way a skeptical fellow Catholic priest on the subject of exorcisms. Father A. worked more privately and was more temperamentally combative. But he was also more threatened by Satanists themselves. Not surprisingly, the often sleazy but scattered devil-worshippers despised him, and, in my opinion, demons hated him too.

Like Father Jacques, various cult members had long tried to intimidate Father A. The local police, who were fond of this good man and frequently consulted him whenever they encountered cultists, warned him to be careful. As a former Marine, he was a licensed gun owner and carried a small revolver in his pocket, but he once admitted to me that he never intended to use it. Years later, when he confirmed many details of Julia's dramatic possession to the media, I wondered whether the cult would still pursue him for his speaking out so publicly, although I also questioned whether the group still even existed by then. Despite being the most fearless person I ever met, I never knew whether one day Father A. might have been tempted to pull out that pistol.

A little-known fact was that Father A. was one of the key founders of the International Association of Exorcists in the early 1990s. Father Jacques and I often traveled together to Rome to attend the association's biennial meetings. The group became a vehicle for me to expand my recognition of what was happening internationally in the field. Many truly scholarly lectures were fascinating to me. The AIE, whose statutes were approved by the Catholic Church in 2014, represents one of the most sophisticated of the church's efforts to guide and train more exorcists and direct such work in prudent directions. The Vatican does not track international or countrywide exorcisms, but in my experience—and according to priests for whom I continue to consult—demand for sanctioned exorcism is on the rise in many areas. Included in this trend are multiple requests for the professional guidance of psychiatrists.

The United States is home to about one hundred "stable" exorcists—that is, those who have been designated by bishops to combat demonic activity on a semiregular basis. This number is up from just twelve a decade and a half ago, according to Rev. Vincent Lampert, an experienced Indianapolis-based priest-exorcist who is also active in the AIE. (He says he receives about twenty inquiries per week—double the number from when his bishop appointed him in 2005.) The Catholic Church has responded by offering greater resources for clergy members who wish to address the problem. In 2010, for instance, the US Conference of Catholic Bishops organized a meeting in Baltimore for interested clergy. There are also a couple of ongoing, independently run training groups in the United States.

Most AIE members are constantly called upon to help as demand for such assistance has grown so markedly. Some experts think that trend has been stimulated by a growing decline in traditional religious practice, especially in Europe and now in North America, too. Others point to a purported marked increase in occultism of various sorts in many developed countries. Still other commentators find the trend to blame the demonic for people's problems to be exaggerated.

Such debates are perennial, but one must be careful not to overgeneralize about the practices of specific countries to worldwide trends. Variability remains the rule. Nonetheless, there remain large areas of the world where efforts to combat evil spirits have been endemic for ages and where people tend to regard Western skepticism about that reality as naïve and ethnocentric.

One chronicler of such trends was the French conservative theologian Father René Laurentin, who was another early officer of the AIE—a sort of semiofficial scribe. Now deceased, he was a prolific writer. He and I enjoyed many interesting discussions, though I didn't always agree with some of his views about specific "private revelations," as alleged holy apparitions are called. His 1995 book *Le Démon: Mythe ou réalitié?* was based on AIE lectures, where he furiously scribbled notes. This book—specifically its defense of the reality of devils and the efficacy of exorcisms—caused a sensation in France.

Many exorcists now publicly acknowledge their participation in the AIE. Physicians have been involved from the beginning. I have addressed the association's international meetings about relevant psychiatric issues and the need for rigorous discernments. The group broadly accepts the premise that medical caution is always warranted, particularly in confusing cases.

Since its founding, the AIE has also provided a forum for scholarly discussion of possession and the careful procedures of the exorcism ministry. Its first president was Father Jeremy Davies, an English priest and psychiatrist, who was succeeded by Father Gabriele Amorth, who became the association's undoubtedly most prominent, if sometimes controversial, president.

Father Amorth once told me that he used medical doctors to help him assess complex cases whenever needed. But he thought many

European and American priests were much too hesitant in performing exorcisms. I wasn't surprised by his admission, because he had performed so many—he claimed to have performed about sixty-three thousand exorcism rituals. Described by some of his critics as an ecclesiastical bull in a china shop, Father Amorth was especially critical of bishops who would not authorize exorcisms. He accused them of a serious dereliction of their duties, which did not endear him to some members of the church hierarchy.

In defense of the number of exorcisms some European priests are said to have performed, many foreign priests use the term "exorcism" where American priests would call what they are doing "prayers of liberation"—a difference of usage that softens that high number. More recently, many priests have started calling their modified set of prayers for serious cases that fall short of formal possessions "minor exorcisms," while consciously eschewing the term "deliverance" altogether.

I have expressed some reservations about how many of the ritual prayers Father Amorth sometimes performed—a respectful if understandable concern for a physician, given the risk of inadvertently encouraging potential psychiatric cases to mistakenly believe their difficulties are spiritually induced. But Father Amorth was an intelligent and educated man who took care to consult physicians when necessary. He told me once that he simply felt there was little downside in using the prayers liberally.

Father Amorth died in 2016 yet still became embroiled in controversy. The Hollywood director and screenwriter William Friedkin, who directed *The Exorcist*, recounted how he had been trying for years to make a documentary about one of Amorth's most striking cases, which Amorth eventually allowed him to observe and film. The movie, *The Devil and Father Amorth*, was released in late 2018. It ends on an ambiguous note. Despite a premature celebration of the liberation of the movie's subject among the large group of witnesses present for the exorcism (another debated aspect of Amorth's procedures), the movie's ending revealed the tortured woman reverting back into her possessed state. It was unfortunate that such a case was chosen because it left the impression of an inefficacious exorcism (or a bogus case) when I knew well that Father Amorth had conducted many successful exorcisms.

Despite the controversies, I found Father Amorth a generous and thoughtful man who had a good sense of humor, especially about himself. He once commented that his successes as an exorcist (and he had many) may have been the result of his being "homelier than Satan himself."

Through the AIE I came to know another fine priest, Father Giancarlo Gramolazzo, who succeeded Amorth as the association's third president. He appointed me to the governing board for a time. I think he appreciated that a professor of psychiatry was involved and understood the aims of the organization, especially in combating simplistic errors about false cases.

Father Gramolazzo died in 2010. The AIE is now in the capable hands of Father Francesco Bamonte, an experienced exorcist and a true scholar and able administrator during its recent growth. I could cite numerous other priests and laymen associated with the group, including its American priest representative, Father Roberto Cruz, who replaced Father Jacques. He has done a wonderful job building a model program in the United States, with inclusion of both professionally sound expertise in the discernment process and ample supports for unfortunate victims.

Some AIE members prefer to remain out of the limelight, although a few now have been willing to speak out or write about cases publicly. Father Benigno Palilla, for instance, has described multiple examples of modern possessions and exorcisms in his 2018 book *Rescued from Satan: 14 People Recount Their Journey from Demonic Possession to Liberation*.

After one AIE convocation, I met an American journalist living in Rome, Matt Baglio, who wrote the 2009 book *The Rite: The Making of a Modern Exorcist*. He interviewed me over dinner in Rome, wanting my opinion as a psychiatrist about my professional evaluations of possible possessions. The book is about the real-life training of the US priest

Father Gary Thomas to become an exorcist. Father Thomas, who is now a busy pastor in California, was amazingly open with Baglio in sharing his personal history and emotions as he underwent his training. The 2011 movie, also called *The Rite*, was loosely based on the book; but it is an example of Hollywood's ludicrous mangling of the theme of exorcism. The experienced Italian priests about whom Baglio wrote are a well-educated and dedicated group of men; neither they nor Father Thomas, whom I know, are anything like either the troubled trainee priest or the elder, eccentric exorcist portrayed by Anthony Hopkins in the movie.

Around the world, multiple efforts are being made to ensure safe and sensible exorcism procedures and to describe for the public these formerly secretive matters fully and openly. Among Catholics there are now more official exorcists than ever before—a trend fully supported by recent popes, including the "progressive" Pope Francis. Official exorcists among Catholics are exclusively priests. Lay participants sometimes assume quasi-exorcist roles, but too active a role has met with official disapproval.

Protestants, especially evangelical Protestants, have also given increasingly serious and detailed attention to instructing exorcists and ensuring sound practices. Their efforts at training new exorcists tend to be more informal and often involve mostly apprenticeships and the inclusion of laymen. Official associations of professional Protestant Christian mental health experts have also been made available for consultation.

CHAPTER NINE

THE HISTORY OF BELIEFS IN EVIL SPIRITS, THE EMERGENCE OF THE IDEA OF THE PARANORMAL, AND INFESTATIONS

Throughout history, personal and cultural preoccupations with states of possession and the fear of evil spirits have waxed and waned, a cycle of fascination and uninterest that will likely continue in perpetuity. Nevertheless, these are truly perennial beliefs over the ages.

In a remarkable display of scholarship, Erika Bourguignon, a prominent modern anthropologist, unearthed documented accounts of possession in about three-quarters of 488 cultures she surveyed. Considering that the absence of evidence is not the evidence of absence, belief in possessions in primitive, prehistoric cultures was nearly ubiquitous; certainly, the belief in evil spirits was. And, as Bourguignon's work shows, such beliefs appear in probably nearly every era and nearly every culture in recorded history too. To underline this point: there has, it seems, never been a time in human history, or prehistory either, when beliefs in evil spirits or specific efforts to combat or exorcise them were not present within specific cultures or subcultures, however these evil spirits or acts of exorcisms were understood.

The same is true today in modern times.

The great nonevent of the twentieth century, according to many commentators, was the "nondisappearance" of traditional religion. Other critics have labeled the present era as the "return of the devil." Enlightenment thinkers and, later, the atheist philosophers of the nineteenth century argued that religion represented an infantile stage of human development. Freud thought so, too. Many predicted that by the end of the twentieth century, traditional religions with beliefs in supernatural beings, including angels and demons, would die out.

They were wrong, spectacularly so.

Far from becoming extinct, a concern with spirituality retains a strong hold on most humans. And most striking is the widespread retention, even growth, of beliefs in devils and evil spirits, including Satan. The United States in particular continues to have high levels of traditional religious practice. Most Americans still identify as Christian; an overwhelming percentage believe in God and surprisingly high numbers accept the idea of the devil.

Whereas parts of the world have simultaneously witnessed a process of secularization, especially in Europe and now more than in the past among younger people in America too, strong signs remain that in many regions, modern historical religions are reviving or replacing pagan beliefs to a striking degree. For instance, one hundred years ago, many African countries were heavily pagan or Islamic, and only about 10 percent Christian. Today, throughout the continent, 50 percent profess the Christian faith and most of the remainder are Muslims. All across Africa, and in many areas of Asia and South America, a robust faith in evil spirits has prevailed. One reason for the growth in Christianity is that many developing cultures have embraced Pentecostalism, the fastest-growing Christian denomination in the world. Parallel to this growth is the persisting belief in demons and practices aimed at combating them, which has continued to swell in the past few decades throughout developed and developing countries alike around the world.

My interest in the history of this subject matter and the variety of past and present belief systems about evil spirits was not merely academic. Globalization, coupled with patterns of immigration, has brought about such a mixing of cultures in this country and throughout the world that I found it impossible to help afflicted people without a thorough understanding of and a deeply respectful appreciation for different cultural identities and different faith practices. I continue to apply the lessons I learned to help bring about positive, lasting changes for people from a multitude of backgrounds and diverse faiths.

My immersion in such studies came in handy, for instance, when a Vietnamese couple brought their son, who had recently been diagnosed as mentally ill, to my office for a consultation. The mother and father were both well-educated and career professionals, but neither agreed with their son's conventional diagnosis. Steve was their youngest child; his older siblings were all married and pursuing satisfying careers. When I met with Steve, he was twenty-three years old—a talented, good-looking, and intelligent young man with excellent social skills. His mood was normal and his thinking coherent. Like Sara, he did not appear to be mentally ill, despite reporting bizarre symptoms, which led me to believe he was suffering from a possible combination of internal and external oppression.

How did a mentally sound young man from the suburbs of Connecticut fall victim to such a demonic attack? As the father explained, he himself grew up as an ethnic minority in his native Vietnam, describing his ancestral background as pagan. The couple converted to evangelical Christianity, but they worried that their family's pagan lineage was related to, or the cause of, their son's difficulties in some unspecified way.

Steve had been brought up in his parents' faith and attended their church until he was sixteen. At that point, like many teenagers, he started to question his family's faith. In many other ways, as well, he had rebelled against what he saw as a too conservative and conventional upbringing. Like a lot of inquisitive young people, he started to look for an alternate belief system to fill the vacuum. He eventually began to practice what some scholars label "neoshamanism," a term based on a traditional concept, shamanism, now broadly employed by anthropologists and scholars to describe a set of beliefs and methods of seeking visions and of healing historically associated with many native cultures around the world. Surviving indigenous cultures throughout the Americas, Africa, eastern and mainland Southeast Asia, and Siberia still value shamanic traditions, many of which continue to influence the belief systems of a surprising number of people in modern nations. South Korea, for instance, has more shamans than psychotherapists.

Shamanism is a set of practices from differing spiritual heritages that involves a practitioner (called a shaman) entering an altered state of consciousness to interact with a world of spirits. The shaman is viewed as an intermediary with that spirit realm, especially in facilitating healing. What sets neoshamanism apart from the historical practice of shamanism is its stripping away of vital cultural contexts and some associated valued spiritual beliefs, which is why it is often criticized as a distortion of traditional shamanism and an inappropriate form of cultural appropriation.

Curious about such indigenous practices, Steve started associating with local neoshamanic adherents in and around New York City, of which there are surprisingly many. He combined his interest in neoshamanism with Wiccan and other neopagan tenets. According to Steve, he initially went through a wide range of paranormal states; eventually, however, he became disillusioned with the movements and turned away from this shamanic period.

Unfortunately, the spirit world was not done with him. Even after he broke off his relationship with devotees of such esoteric practices, he continued to experience visions of spirits and other seemingly paranormal images. Many were downright weird—images of crude beings in the shape of dark shadows, or as Steve described them, "blobs."

And, like Stan and Maria had reported, Steve told me that these spirits turned hostile and violent, physically striking his head. To be clear, he wasn't experiencing headaches; he felt literal blows to his head, though he did not bruise, as Maria had, nor show any signs of scratching or other marks, as Stan had. Our demonic foes vary their strategies and methods, once again to be maximally confusing and disorienting to curious students.

Like Maria and Stan and countless others, Steve gave no evidence of any psychiatric problems. His symptoms did not respond at all to medication, he had no thought disorder per se, and the context for his strange condition was clearly defined by a phase of serious occult involvement. All the criteria for a genuine diabolic attack were occurring—another striking case of a simultaneous internal and external oppression, that is, involving both internal images and so-called physical vexations by evil spirits, or demons, as Steve came to believe on his own.

After I ruled out any psychological or physical ailment, Steve returned to Christianity and started to work with a local priest to help him in a process of liberation. I am happy to report he is vastly improved, though he has not yet been fully liberated from his demonic oppressors.

Strange paranormal experiences, associated with a variety of spiritual or esoteric traditions, are unusual but hardly as rare as most people today believe. Many "seekers" attempt to experience what can be termed either the paranormal or the spirit world, depending on one's interpretive framework. I have directly spoken to many of these self-styled explorers, who often get in "over their heads," as one regretful woman described her surprising outcome.

Steve's suffering was similar to what many people undergo who have been curious to elicit pseudo-mystical or esoteric states of mind; they too often get trapped in a world beyond their imagining. They struggle to understand how their troublesome symptoms came about or why they won't go away. One woman I met had traveled to South America to spend time with an indigenous shamanic healer. She has been afflicted with spirits ever since. Stan's story was similar, and he eventually interpreted his spiritual oppressor as explicitly satanic. No biological explanation will ever suffice to explain these bizarre phenomena. And if one thinks these stories, so often associated with New Age searchers and the like, are always benign or uncommon, one doesn't know much history or much about spiritual life.

Still, if you assume that the best historian of the spiritual states of oppressions and possessions was an exorcist or a theologian, or even a traditional Christian believer, you would be wrong. The classic work of states of oppression and possession throughout world history was written almost a hundred years ago by Traugott K. Oesterreich, a professor from the German town of Tübingen. An agnostic German polymath, Oesterreich became an early believer in parapsychology, a field that also secretly fascinated Freud. The wealth of detail in the voluminous 1966 translation of his work from 1921, *Possession: Demoniacal and Other, Among Primitive Races, in Antiquity, the Middle Ages, and Modern Times*, is unmatched. (Author William Peter Blatty read it before writing *The Exorcist*, deriving a lot of his background material for his fictitious account.)

Like Freud, who wrote in 1923 a famous short monograph on the subject of possession, which he called a "demonological neurosis," and like many other secular intellectuals of that period, Oesterreich originally considered parapsychological states as emotional disturbances or illnesses, interpreting such conditions as psychiatric in nature. He categorized the trances and aggressive behaviors of possessions as resulting from dissociative states related to inner hostility projected outward as a personification of evil, or as compulsions. Like Freud, he originally interpreted possession cases diagnostically as hysteria, severe neurosis, and psychosis. However, Oesterreich never could explain how such mentally disordered individuals could levitate, possess arcane knowledge, speak or understand foreign languages, or experience many of the other features he cited in the myriad historical cases. Mystified by such observations, he changed his mind. He came to feel the mysterious phenomena to be so inexplicable that he concluded that states of possession must go beyond the natural and material world to reflect "spiritist" (his word) or paranormal realities.

And so, in his magnum opus, Oesterreich concedes that his earlier, more exclusive focus on mental pathology was mistaken and noted that "researchers of scientific standing consider such explanations as unsatisfactory . . . and regard the 'spiritistic' hypothesis as valid." Oesterreich included thousands of accounts of and references to such cases, showing over and over how both anthropologists and historical chroniclers have found ample evidence that these odd states have always existed. Not surprisingly, Oesterreich again and again gives historical citations of many of the phenomena described in this book. For instance, he chronicles voluntary and involuntary possessions and how pagan rituals over the ages typically solicited spirits, thought to be benign, as spirit guides and helpers. But these episodes often turned out badly. Sometimes—as we witnessed in the case of Speedy, the MS-13 member who was expected to solicit hidden knowledge from the spirit world to achieve the group's evil purposes—these "voluntary" requests backfire and supplicants conclude they were the true victims.

Oesterreich cites hundreds of examples of involuntary possessions across cultures that are remarkably similar to many of the cases for which I have consulted. These include cases involving animist beliefs in Africa, where spirit forces possessed humans, who were then reported to speak various unknown languages or reveal pieces of hidden knowledge. He describes historical Hindu possessions, presumed to occur by the activity of gods and "lesser powers," but that this thoroughly agnostic scholar remarks bring us "perilously close to belief in demons." He also gives examples from multiple pagan and non-Western sources of recent history, as well as reports of possession cases that are broadly similar to cases presented in the Christian and Jewish sources he cites, too. He includes accounts within texts from all of the world's religions.

Some poorly informed modern critics of the reality of states of possession and oppression claim that only credulous members of traditional religious subcultures experience such states. Nothing could be further from the truth, as historical and contemporary accounts regularly attest. In my experience, people with no real religious background who turn to occult practices are among the most frequently attacked by spirits. And because they lack solid spiritual foundations, or "spiritual armor," they are *more* mystified about what is happening to them, which makes their liberation from demonic oppressors that much more difficult to achieve. In their desire to have paranormal experiences, they are among those most naïve about a spirit world.

Regardless of time or place, throughout history and diverse secular as well as religious cultures people continue to document the existence of a rich and active spirit world and the very real predatory activity of evil spirits and demons. I witness this continuous and complex diversity of demonic or spirit-related expressions today in people who seek my advice from all over the world.

● ● ●

From the dawn of history, ancient cultures clearly believed that the spirit world, however defined, was often hardly benign. A multiplicity of beliefs about spirits existed, regularly conceptualized as gods, "intermediary" spirits, dead souls, fallen heroes, past rulers, or deceased family members, to name a few commonly found concepts. The Greek term *daimones*, from which we derive the term "demons," referred originally to more benign nature spirits and later became a broader concept, for instance as employed by Plato as a sort of creative inner spirit. Eventually the term came to be used in the Septuagint to translate the Hebrew words *shedim* and *si'irim* and was later adopted in Christian literature to refer to evil spirits.

The first society to have written records was the Sumerian. From the beginning, the cuneiform writing of ancient Sumer (present-day Iraq) referred to demons as *gid-dim*. The Sumerians were conquered by the Assyrians, who developed out of the regional polytheism a belief in a supreme god, Ashur. Along with Ashur existed a series of minor gods, often described as diabolic.

The Exorcist starts off with the elderly priest Lankester Merrin excavating an Assyrian site in Iraq. He unearths a figure of the Assyrian demon Pazuzu, who eventually possesses Regan. The Assyrians had elaborate exorcism techniques, including fumigation, incantations, charms, and, it seems, drugs. Like exorcists today, the Assyrian priestly caste sought the name of the demon during the earliest reported rites of exorcism. Later, Babylonian and Persian ideas about religion also contributed to developing notions of demonology and probably influenced captive Jewish populations. On the other hand, since "spirit experiences" of different sorts, and especially possessions, have been found independently among so many cultures, these beliefs frequently seem better understood as spontaneous and "transcultural."

The dualistic Persian religion Zoroastrianism emphasized a cosmic realm of competing "powers," one side good, the other evil. This dramatic historical background in the Middle East is important in appreciating the disputes early Hebrew tribes had with surrounding cultures before the Christian era, and the variety of opinions about "demons" and their origins that later developed into the notions common to Christianity and Islam.

In a historical development unique in history until then, for which their ancient texts still receive too little credit, for centuries the central Hebraic tradition, with its singular focus on a high ethical and monotheistic system of thought, resisted what was seen as occult contamination from neighboring pagan cultures and religions. Protecting their genuinely elevated understanding of God (as well as depreciating dualistic notions) seemed to entail a general ignoring of interest in other lesser spirits.

The word "paganism" itself (originally a term of opprobrium) is often used too loosely, as it encompasses a wide variety of beliefs and practices. And many of these other belief systems have had noble elements too, of course. Many pagan practices, as a sort of state religion, have especially extolled human virtues such as public-spiritedness, honesty, and martial courage. What we think of as "Eastern" and often esoteric notions of spirituality have characteristically highlighted genuine compassion and selflessness.

One common element of traditional, popular paganism, though, has been prayers and sacrifices offered to a panoply of spirits. "Paganism," in its broader sense, including as a common accompaniment to certain advanced world religions, that is, has historically almost always been intertwined with an overall worldview suffused with superstitions about gods and goddesses (hardly without blemish themselves) as well as about outright malign spirits, however conceived. Within specific more typically pagan cultures, including the biblical Canaanites and Philistines, for example, a broad belief existed about the need to propitiate these forces, essentially to "bribe" them, even with evils like human sacrifices. Such latter practices, most prevalent in the baser, "darker" cultures of history, have unfortunately not been uncommon.

The Hebrew Bible, or Tanakh, pulled no punches in opposing and condemning such "occultism" (another complex term) and idol worship as part of what Hebrews rightly thought was an evil variant of spirit beliefs. The book of Deuteronomy, for instance, calls "a consulter with familiar spirits, or a wizard, or a necromancer" (someone who summons dead souls to foretell the future) an "abomination unto the Lord" (Deut. 18:11–12, kjv). Mosaic law, as codified in Leviticus, prescribes the death penalty for such practices (though such punishments seem rarely to have been carried out).

This antipathy for neighbors who engaged in occult practices, as well as worse, such as the ritual killing of women and children, does much to explain the bellicose condemnation by the ancient Hebrews of their rivals (not that they never performed such practices too). Ancient Romans and Greeks, too, came to condemn human sacrifice as barbaric. The Romans, for instance, fought several wars with the North African Carthaginians, who are now widely believed to have conducted human sacrifices and were regarded by Romans as debased.

Nonetheless, almost all of the ancient world, including the Israelites, carried out ritual sacrifices commonly, at least of animals as well as of humans. Even when in the Old World such atrocities were largely abolished, for many centuries afterward these abominations continued in the "New World," especially among the Mayans, Aztecs, and Incas; the latter society would drug young girls, then freeze and mummify them. Clear evidence for child sacrifices has also been discovered in large areas of what has come to be known as the Mesoamerican cultures, including parts of what is now the continental United States. Excavations from the Greater Pyramid of Tenochtitlán, which is now Mexico City, have unearthed the remains of numerous children ritually sacrificed to appease their "gods." The fingernails of some of the children were torn off to appease these spirit deities. Similar human sacrifices have been unearthed at the pre-Columbian Teotihuacán site, considered the "birthplace of the gods." These various ancient societies surely considered such rituals as being efficacious, in much the same way Julia believed her cult's own grisly ceremonies elicited favors for her from Satan.

Of course, the ancient Israelites were often chided by their own prophetic figures as backsliding into idolatry and unfaithfulness to their unique sense of a covenant with Yahweh. But overall, the Jewish Bible itself reflects little preoccupation with demonology and occultism, using modern technology.

While the typically pagan atmosphere of magic and its attendant preoccupation with evil spirits is largely absent from the Jewish texts, a few scattered biblical references do attest to underlying beliefs in less benign personal forces in the spiritual cosmos. Select passages allude to darker, intermediate spirits, sometimes referred to as "destroying angels" or "evil messengers," but they may do God's bidding and be perceived as agents of his avenging will.

The role of evil spirits took on a more prominent emphasis in

Jewish texts during the so-called intertestamental period (from about 420 BCE to 30 CE), particularly in sectarian Jewish movements just before the Christian era. Writings from this period are included in the biblical canon by some groups and not others. The book of Wisdom, which was written by an Alexandrian Jew two or three centuries before the birth of Christ, includes a clear warning: "For God formed us to be imperishable . . . / But by the envy of the devil, death entered the world" (Wis. 2:23–24, NABRE). The book of Jubilees and the book of Enoch both recount strange tales of fallen angels. Enoch was highly influential in first-century Jewish popular belief. The Essenes, a near-monastic Jewish sect, also placed a significant emphasis on the cosmic nature of the battle between God and the angels against Satan and his minions. Several references to evil spirits exist in then contemporary Jewish texts, now called the Dead Sea Scrolls, found during the past century at Qumran in today's West Bank in Israel. Many examples of later rabbinic acceptance of the notion of evil spirits followed. And finally, more populist Jewish beliefs about spirits—such as "dybbuks" (thought to be dead souls)—persisted even into the modern era in some subcultural branches of worldwide Judaism.

This trend toward more emphasis on demonic forces was accelerated in the early Christian biblical texts. By the time of the life of Jesus of Nazareth, a demonological preoccupation marked many Mediterranean cultures and, scholars agree, proliferated in the immediate centuries thereafter, whether reflecting pagan, Jewish, or Christian ways of thinking.

Not everyone believed in evil spirits and diabolic possessions. The Sadducees, for instance, did not. Yet as the New Testament literature emerged, significant segments of then-contemporary Judaism certainly did. The book of Acts references "itinerant Jewish exorcists," as does the first-century Jewish historian Josephus.

While the New Testament is not without scholarly controversy, needless to state, scholars agree that Jesus explicitly tied his messianic role to the overthrow of the reign of Satan, the "prince of this world" (John 12:31). The New Testament refers approximately three hundred times to the devil, though these references employ a variety of terms to describe Satan and his realm. There was at the time scant systemic teaching in the New Testament in this area. Still, three of the four Gospels recount the famous story of Jesus's temptation by Satan in the desert. Jesus even opens his public ministry by casting a demon out of a possessed man in the synagogue at Capernaum, a clear indication of his authority over both the spiritual and physical worlds. Later, in another Gospel story, a demon or "unclean spirit" addresses Jesus, asking him, "What have you to do with us, Jesus of Nazareth? Have you come to destroy us?" (Mark 1:24, ESV). Jesus then rebukes and casts out the spirit.

There are seven episodes in the four Gospels about specific cases of possession. The common pattern consists of the demon's challenge, Jesus's command for the spirit to leave, and the evil spirit's rapid exit. Despite claims by some modern commentators, there is no suggestion that Jesus was speaking metaphorically, nor is there any evidence that he simply borrowed the beliefs of the time. Careful historians, whether Christian or secular, widely agree that the historical Jesus was renowned as an exorcist. And yet he frequently condemned other contemporary superstitions, including the idea that sickness was caused by either personal sins or the sins of one's parents. "Curing the sick" was also always put in a separate category in the Gospel literature to "driving out demons."

Are these accounts credible? Having studied them for many years, I find them to be sound, though complex, source materials. Also, I find them trustworthy in describing otherwise hard-to-believe details about possessions, since I myself have witnessed similar phenomena and a wide success of such practices continuing to this day.

The New Testament certainly suggests that Jesus spoke about this subject with unparalleled confidence and authority. Eventually, he enlisted his disciples to cast out demons as well, a prerogative he associated with an ushering in of the long awaited "kingdom of God," presumed by his followers to have been foretold in the book of Daniel. This belief had a strong influence on the then-contemporary debates about the coming of the Messiah, involving claims, Christians believe, by Jesus himself that driving away demons was a sign of his messianic status as the "Son of Man" and an early indicator of the eventual arrival of God's kingdom.

Ever since, Christian churches have mandated that carrying out Jesus's command to drive out evil spirits is important to their missions. This work required protracted efforts by Jesus's followers, but with great success, to such an extent that the early church used their triumphs as proof of their religion's superiority against the less-effective efforts of pagan priests (much in the way Moses claimed a superior power from Yahweh's assistance compared to that of the Egyptian priest-magicians).

At the same time, rabbinical Judaism slowly moved away from some of the earlier Jewish sources that accepted the idea of a cosmological battle between Satan and his devils with God. Demonology eventually did not hold any central role in official rabbinical teachings, though, as noted, populist beliefs in attacks by demons or at least mischievous deceased souls long persisted.

This development toward Jewish skepticism was a gradual one, according to both Jewish and secular historians. For instance, the Jewish historian Josephus, in his *Jewish Antiquities*, mentions a Jewish exorcist operating "for the utility and salvation of others." In the fourth century the Christian bishop Athanasius attests to exorcisms still being conducted by Jews with the use of readings from the Hebrew Bible. The Halakhah, the body of Jewish religious laws, still accepted the reality of demons. Observance of the law was regarded as the best preventative against their influence, as it is in some Jewish sects to this day.

Many medieval Jewish philosophers also did not question the existence of evil spirits, with a notable exception being the physician and philosopher Maimonides. Later on, the mystical Kabbalists revived ideas expressed in the noncanonical book of Enoch and other early Jewish writings about demons, though with the most frequent emphasis again upon the role of dead, wandering souls. These dybbuks in

Jewish folklore to this day can be benign or malicious and are said to inhabit a human host to work out some purpose. Still in the modern world some rabbis in the Kabbalist tradition continue to do exorcisms. I have spoken to some individuals of Jewish backgrounds who have described such rituals done on their behalf. More mainstream Jews criticize much of these Kabbalist practices or those of other heterodox groups and dismiss their significance. But some Orthodox Jews believe in demonic activity of sorts, though they may interpret the demonic as so intermingled with humans' evil inclinations (*yetzer hara*) that it becomes difficult to disentangle the two realms. Nevertheless, there cannot be said to be any "unified" or official Jewish position; one prominent rabbi told me he was personally agnostic about the issue and felt that attitude was the most sensible position for Jews to take.

After the decline of the Roman Empire, another cultural force came to dominate the Middle and Near East and eventually much of the southern and western Mediterranean: Islam. The prophet Muhammad was born at Mecca in 571. At the time of his life, there was widespread belief in djinn, or jinn (genies), and they are mentioned in the Qur'an. Key Islamic texts also feature terms for angels and demons and promoted an active belief in both; jinn were conceived as creatures intermediate in nature between angels (and fallen angels) and humans. In the Qur'an (72:11) a jinni is reported to say that "some of us are good and some not." Terminology in these matters over the centuries has been historically complex, but both Islamic and non-Islamic scholarship confirm the common Islamic differentiation of spirits into angels, jinn, and demons (*shayatin*); all three could affect humans, and jinn and demons could both possess individuals.

Belief in demons among devout Muslims continues to be the rule today. Although most educated Muslims I know believe that medical maladies should be ruled out before one jumps to the notion of a diabolic attack, they accept possession as fact. Still, in my experience, most Islamic clergy, like most of their Christian counterparts, warn of the dangers of an overuse of exorcism and believe, as I do, that suspected demonic attacks are most often psychological disturbances and not an assault from a spirit world.

Over the centuries, all three monotheistic faiths—Christianity, Judaism, and Islam—have ritualized their more formal attempts at exorcism. Though they employ materials such as holy water and oils, the notion of exorcisms among these religions took a more "spiritual" turn than in most other religious traditions. The key idea that developed in all three of these faiths is that primarily *spiritual* means should be used to combat and drive out the possessing or harassing entities because they are spiritual enemies—they are spirits, not material beings.

Christianity is a religion of a "theoretical," or "theological," approach. Its principal intellectual focus is less on commentary or juridical rulings about its practices, as is the case within Orthodox Judaism and traditional Islam, than on systematizing its beliefs in creedal formulas and catechisms. Not surprisingly, therefore, the most elaborate "theology" of the demonic realm has been found in Christianity. An orthodox doctrinal teaching developed about the rebellion of Satan and other demons and this realm's ongoing efforts to harass and tempt humans. Exorcisms continued to be conducted throughout the Catholic world over the centuries. During certain periods, authorization for exorcism was granted rather infrequently. In recent decades, however, Catholic exorcisms have experienced a revival, as we have seen.

The Protestant world came to rely less on formal exorcisms, but the reformers remained convinced of the strong influence of the devil and the stark reality of his overt attacks. Martin Luther is said to have been preoccupied with Satan and demons, who, he thought, materialized frequently. He regularly recounted his own experiences with demonic appearances. A black mark on the wall of a room in Wartburg, Germany, is said to be where he tossed an inkpot at an alleged demonic intruder.

While even some conservative mainstream Protestant churches have in the past few decades become more interested in the reality of the demonic, the so-called enthusiast movements within modern Christianity are the most preoccupied with such attacks, including Catholic charismatics. Those promoting efforts to help afflicted people usually call themselves "deliverance ministries." This trend, with its plusses and minuses, is not least evident in the United States, though it is accurate to say that there was never a period in US history when belief in both God and devils was in any manner an unusual viewpoint.

• • •

Many past periods of human history have been suffused with evils such as slavery, treating women like chattel, constant and often brutal wars, and even human sacrifices. Few people today truly wish to return to the beliefs and some of the practices of such times—including propitiation of the sometimes capricious or malevolent gods and goddesses; anxieties about the mischievous sprites of antiquity; pervasive fears of the mysterious, dark forces of the ancient world—all of which seemed to contribute to these abuses.

But some do.

Traditional pagan beliefs—broadly defined as we noted already and not discounting their virtues—persist in some long-standing cultures. But today, some modern practitioners describe themselves as "neopagans," adopting a mishmash of pagan notions, attempting to eschew any of the old abuses, but retaining typically pagan spirit beliefs.

As many scholars argue, a *return* to paganism is a very different matter from the original systems of thought. In my view, these "neopagan" variants are rarely a rational path nor a simple reversion to cultures that in their day knew no alternatives. Modern regression to such beliefs often seems to arise primarily out of a personal rebellion against monotheistic religions, along with some of their moral codes and demanding creedal systems. Julia, for instance, celebrated her so-called pagan notions as an explicit rejection of the stricter morality of Christianity.

Weird experiences and motives still prompt some people toward such cruder forms of neopaganism, however, which historically have often promoted paranormal experiences and what most people now consider "occult" (from the Latin "occultus," or hidden). And adherents of the "newer" paganisms, and other curiosity seekers, are drawn to phenomena that have never quite vanished.

But in my experience, the occult and the paranormal are also never too far away. An assortment of neopagan ideas and acts—fortune-telling, clairvoyance, communication with the dead, and even rare ritual animal sacrifice—may seem at first blush as intriguing and novel. But the mishmash of ideas characterizing neopagan movements—often little different from so-called New Age notions—is not really new at all. And these practices have consistently been condemned as foolish by the major world religions for millennia.

Even *The New Yorker* magazine published an article in 2019 on the current interest in astrology, a traditional pseudo-scientific and New Age–y belief. A subsequent letter to the editor noted the article's curious omission of any recognition "that astrology is nonsense." The letter writer observed how disturbing it is that "an increasing number of Americans make life decisions based on such a belief system." The annual Chapman University Survey of American Fears found in 2018 that 25 percent of Americans believe in astrology, 41 percent think that aliens have visited the earth in the past (and 35 percent believe they have done so recently), and more than three-quarters give credence to at least one or more defined paranormal notion (such as the existence of Bigfoot, haunting spirits, and telekinesis).

Much of Hollywood seems to believe in a smattering of such views from the spate of movies and celebrities espousing New Age notions. A good example of the genre is the 1999 movie *The Sixth Sense*, starring Bruce Willis as a psychologist eventually revealed to be a ghost. One wag remarked that when people cease to believe in sound religious teachings, they don't come to believe in "nothing"; they come to believe in "everything."

Recent times confirm this saying precisely. In the United States and Europe, belief in New Age ideas is growing. Myriad television shows and books about the paranormal flood the media, a good indication of how this topic continues to fascinate. That interest includes consulting psychics, perhaps the most common way in which an ordinary citizen experiences paranormal "professionals." Almost every city around the world has storefronts advertising fortune-tellers and psychics, and they also advertise through other media and across the internet.

The vague guesses or cold-reading techniques employed by many "psychics" may draw a lot of people in, but some are genuinely tapping into the realm of diabolic sources of knowledge that are characteristic of the activities and abilities of demons.

A young woman doctor I knew told me that a fortune-teller she had visited had revealed remarkably accurate information about her past. The "psychic" knew many private details of the history of one of her deceased parents. The young woman became "hooked"; but then she became devastated when the psychic told her that she would never find a husband. I told her that there was no way anyone, including any fortune-teller, or any spirit for that matter, could possibly know the future for sure, let alone that sort of life outcome for her. She was thankful for my advice, and within a few years she married.

No psychic can tell the future because evil spirits cannot tell the future either. They can, however, sometimes make good, educated predictions based on the hidden knowledge we have seen displayed by demons in cases of possession. Of course, they are often wrong, too.

Some paranormal practitioners have even set themselves up as paid exorcists, a scandal recently publicized in France and spreading to Hollywood. California and Manhattan have their share of neoshamanic practitioners who perform "cleansings" and self-styled exorcisms. In my experience, they are ineffectual and often make a difficult situation eventually, if not immediately, worse.

Older style pagan exorcisms have hardly disappeared either. For instance, a shaman from Siberia was arrested in September 2019 after walking about seventeen hundred miles toward Moscow to exorcise Vladimir Putin and drive "demonic" forces out of the Kremlin. With much fanfare, including a YouTube video streamed more than a million times, he invited people sympathetic to his goal to accompany him on his mission. To exorcise Putin, he proposed a public bonfire in Red Square with fermented mare's milk and horse's hair to be burned to the accompaniment of the banging of a leather drum. He predicted this pagan ritual would help Putin "come to his senses and quietly resign."

There's a similar proliferation of witchcraft. Julia is an extreme example, but many lesser figures—some frivolous and culturally critical, others quite repellant—can be found across cultures today. Despite appropriate historical warnings about how innocent women can be caught up in witch hysterias, interest in practicing the "craft" continues to grow in popularity. Such appeal is often justified as an attraction to "white," as opposed to harmful "black," magic. But these practices cannot be so neatly compartmentalized; white witchery can ensnare the foolish or naïve, because like its black magic counterpart, it emerges from the same demonic sources. A recent *New York Times* article highlighted a self-identified witch who organized a well-attended 2019 conference for students of witchcraft hosted at New York University. After recording a lesson of her popular podcast about the ancient craft, she showed off her home altar—overlaid with a statue of the goddess Diana, candles, crystals, pendants, and a book of spells—in her Park Slope townhouse.

What makes all these neopagan topics so interesting to the public today is that many people now question the traditional religious explanation for such phenomena, which they believe to be too doctrinal and rigid; but they cannot dismiss such phenomena as nonexistent either, because they have simply heard too many believable stories. Stuck between what they regard as two unsatisfying views, they embark on their own search for the truth. The more enquiring ones may immerse themselves in these pursuits, get in over their heads, and then desperately search for whoever they think may help them. Often, in distress, they come to me.

Many thoughtful and intellectual observers of all these phenomena have tried to study them "scientifically" as naturalistic subjects. Like

Oesterreich, some come to see that such events have a genuine basis in reality. Recognizing that such things have been documented throughout history, they struggle to understand them. In the past couple of centuries, these seekers have mostly lit upon one of two major explanatory frameworks. The first, adopted by secularists and dogmatic materialists such as Freud, pathologizes these experiences and sees victims as being sick. This quick dismissal, however, neglects the careful diagnostic distinctions required to distinguish between illness and demonic or preternatural activity.

The second framework labels these experiences as "paranormal"—a term that may sound scientific but essentially explains nothing. Oesterreich called this a "label without meaning," and he, among others, became a chief proponent of the field of "parapsychology," which was conceived as a kind of alternative or supplement to the mainstream field.

Along with the word "paranormal," the loose term "parapsychology" was coined in the modern era to explain these so-called psychic phenomena and the "gaps" in our scientific explanations of the likes of possessions, hauntings, and ghost stories. Of course, this realm of study never advances because, as spiritual phenomena, these experiences can't be subjected to traditional scientific and experimental scrutiny. And yet the pseudoscience of parapsychology marches on. I was consulted by a physician recently who confessed his desire to find a university where he could become an "expert in parapsychology"! I quickly disabused him of the idea.

In the face of the skeptic's ridicule, earnest students of "spirit communication" or supposed communication with the dead often seek out more and more evidence. Their putative "neutral" study of such phenomena is relatively recent in history. Past eras took the realm of spirits, however variously conceived, for granted. But as materialism emerged as a distinct philosophy and then became more prevalent in the 1800s, many secular intellectuals had to grapple with the residue of these odd "nonmaterialist" episodes that past eras—pagan and religious alike—

had understood to be supernatural or demonic in nature. Accounts of all these phenomena fill both popular and academic texts, including the voluminous records of the Society for Psychical Research, founded in both England and the United States in the late nineteenth century.

For all his commitment to materialism, Freud was also fascinated with these phenomena, along with one of his closest colleagues, Sándor Ferenczi. Freud and Ferenczi believed in telepathy, a term also coined in the late 1800s, which the two men in their private letters to each other called "thought transference." According to some of his biographers, the Swiss psychiatrist Carl Jung was a sort of occultist himself; he was certainly seriously interested in such matters, including esoteric beliefs such as Gnosticism, alchemy, and Renaissance magic. He hated his pastor father and orthodox Christianity, an antagonism he shared with Freud.

These men and other luminaries of the day paid close attention to the establishment of the Society for Psychical Research, which attempted to study "spirit" experiences as a new science. Its first conference occurred in London in 1882. An American branch was founded a few years later and included William James, the great Harvard psychologist and philosopher of "pragmatism," who was intrigued by various sorts of religious experiences and wrote the classic 1902 book *The Varieties of Religious Experience*. Many prominent academics joined the English society, including the Nobel laureate Charles Richet. Perhaps the most interesting member was Alfred Russel Wallace, who, like Charles Darwin, conceived of the theory of evolution through natural selection. He started out as a materialist but eventually decided that "spirit" existed as a separate realm apart from the material world.

The Society for Psychical Research still exists, with branches in at least twelve other countries. One of the society's chief objects of study came to be called "spiritualism," which was a hugely popular movement during the nineteenth century and into the twentieth, with millions of American and European devotees. At its height, at the turn of the twentieth century, spiritualism probably had around ten million adherents on both sides of the Atlantic. People looked to spiritualist ideas in the hope of gaining a window into nonmaterialist realities. As traditional religious belief waned, some were grasping for evidence of survival after death. Its popularity was said to have originated from newspaper descriptions of the table "rappings" of deceased spirits reported by the notorious Fox sisters from upstate New York during the mid-1850s. After many years of acting as mediums and making money from tours and lectures, Margaretta, Kate, and Leah Fox were eventually exposed as frauds. They were shunned by the growing spiritualist movement, and shortly all three of them died in poverty.

The spiritualist movement lingers to this day. In early 2020 two New York theatrical productions centered on spiritualist themes. In particular, Brazil, with its mixed traditions of spiritual syncretism, remains a special haven for contemporary variants of spiritualist practices. A famous nineteenth-century proponent and founder of "Spiritism" (a variant of spiritualism that strongly emphasizes reincarnation) named Allan Kardec is still a cult figure in Brazil, especially in middle-class urban centers.

A growing number of spiritualists have also arisen again in the United States, though they do not always use that term to describe themselves. An acquaintance of mine who proudly does call himself a spiritualist argues that as a medium he can facilitate contacting dead souls to communicate with mortals through the telepathic-like channeling of the spirit world. He maintains that he tries to be rigorous in his work, but he complains that mainstream science ignores such efforts—as well it should, I tell him. I give my acquaintance some credit for perspicacity in one respect: he has the smarts to recognize that unfortunately, many of these spirit contacts seem to become hostile and antagonistic. Indeed, some "spirit communications" are decidedly nasty, coming as they do from demons.

In my role as consultant, I have interacted with adherents of all of these varied spiritual traditions. Knowledge of this complex history has proved invaluable. It has been crucial in my being able to help the many people over the years who have come to me to better understand their often-naïve immersion in paranormal pursuits. This endeavor can prove to be outright dangerous if done without any appreciation of the true nature of some of the spiritual forces one is playing with. In their own ways, Stan and Steve both learned this painful lesson the hard way, before their eventual liberations.

• • •

There remains a final type of demonic attack, what Christian thinkers have traditionally called "infestations," from the Latin *infestare*, "to attack or disturb." Defined as spirit activity, infestations are not attacks on people directly but on specific locales and objects. Possessions, oppressions, and infestations comprise what are together labeled the "extraordinary demonic assaults"—as opposed to widespread beliefs in temptations, or "ordinary diabolic influences." Throughout history, infestations have been regularly associated with hauntings and have been believed to stem from evil spirits or, more commonly perhaps, dead souls.

A possessed woman whose condition I knew well told me that religious objects, such as crosses, would break apart or become twisted in her presence. A rosary on a shelf in her living room once split apart, and the beads scattered across the room. One night, her dresser tipped over while she was sleeping; its heavy drawers landed on her. Inexplicably, her bed shook at times, not unlike the incident portrayed in *The Exorcist*. Her adult children corroborated every detail and even showed me pictures of the broken items.

Ghosts, poltergeists, dark shadows. Things that go bump in the night. Sacred objects breaking or religious pictures falling to the floor. Unexplained noises, screams, tables rising and then collapsing, bedroom chests tipping onto victims. All are best seen as infestations, which have been reported in all ages. Advertised as "not for the faint of heart," Hobo Hill in Jefferson City, Missouri, is among the most visited of hundreds of reportedly "haunted houses" in America. As a money-making tourist "attraction," rentals start at $275 a night, "sleeps eight" as noted in their brochures. Multiple guests have reported not only the humdrum dark figures and creaking floorboards, but also, perhaps tellingly, a distinct smell of sulfur.

Such hauntings and other paranormal manifestations are fodder for endless documentaries and interminable analyses by a parade of pseudo-experts on cable channels and across the internet.

Sometimes the term "infestation" is also applied to spirit attacks on animals. The night when our cats went berserk before I met Julia could be called a fleeting infestation. Reports of spirit influence have long been associated with cats; we all recognize the stereotype of the witch dressed in black and her black cat—sometimes called a "familiar" in occult circles. The term "familiar spirit" can also describe a demon that feigns befriending or even being in love with a human.

Standard collections of ghost tales, not quite so popular today, but never an extinct literary genre, perhaps provide the classic examples of infestations. A cottage industry has also grown up refuting their existence, but accounts of hauntings and spirit sightings will never go completely out of favor. The Jesuit scholar of this genre, Herbert Thurston, believed that "the enormous amount of evidence available" concerning infestations is "hardly appreciated." He also pointed out that "it is often hard to see how simple people, who plainly know nothing of the existence of other similar phenomena, should describe over and over again just the same peculiar happenings that are attested elsewhere by eyewitnesses of the highest credit."

The same observation can also be made about oppressions and possessions. Thurston believed the diabolic explanation of their genesis to be the most plausible, especially in the most severe and destructive cases.

Witnesses to these frequently terrifying infestations rarely visit a doctor. They often importune their local clergy to bless their home, and sometimes they get good results. I most commonly hear such stories in the context of evaluating individuals whose more pressing concerns involve possessions or oppressions. But there have been exceptions when an infestation has been the exclusive complaint offered for my opinion. Of course, some people are overly sensitive or superstitious and misinterpret peculiar noises or, say, drafts or vague shadows in their homes as spirit-induced. But hardly everyone.

About ten years ago, a woman came to me who gave no indication of any features of a possession or oppression, but she was certainly experiencing an infestation in her house. She mainly complained of "nuisances." A few objects, like saltshakers and kitchen utensils, moved around her kitchen table, and she heard unexplainable noises. She appeared quite mentally normal, and several of her adult children verified all the details, stressing that they had directly witnessed some of these strange doings as well. She also reported hearing odd speech patterns at times, again mostly in the kitchen. They resembled, she said, the whimpering sounds of someone in distress, though it proved hard for her to pick out the words. Other family members heard these sounds on several occasions, though they tended to occur most often when the woman was alone.

Was it her imagination, or was she mentally ill or hypersensitive? She gave no inkling of any suggestibility or any personal distress or past symptoms. And why did the others in her residence experience the very same matters, albeit to a lesser degree? She was never physically attacked in any way, but one could certainly describe the experiences as an intended harassment of her. I came to think of them as a minor attack upon her, though not technically a true oppression. I told her as much, and she agreed that it appeared to be something demonic. Her own theory was that she was being bothered because she recently had been having a "deeper religious conversion experience," as she put it. After years of neglecting her faith, she had been going to Mass daily, and she guessed that evil spirits didn't care much for this development. Almost in passing, she mentioned how as a teenager, she had fooled around with her friends with a Ouija board and Tarot cards. But she wasn't sure whether these practices had any relevance to her current difficulties.

This proved a typical example of how our demonic foes, if unable to seriously attack us, still are capable of making nuisances of themselves. As regards this woman, their deeper hope may have been simply to disquiet her, perhaps to the point of so distressing or preoccupying her that she might turn away from her newfound religious practices. But these experiences, as it turned out, had the opposite effect. She intensified her spiritual involvement, sought out the advice of her local priest, and had the house blessed. Soon thereafter her odd experiences disappeared.

A more serious infestation happened in the house of another individual who traveled all the way to New York from Kansas to consult me. This young man described himself as a "natural medium" and reported that he had been seeing spirits since age five and had exhibited other paranormal powers, including being fed bits of information he had no other way of knowing. He did not regard himself as being especially "attacked"; however, he did report an incident during which scratches appeared on his body and another in which he was actively "pushed by a spirit"—a not so unusual occurrence, one most commonly ascribed to some sort of vengeful entity of an undetermined nature.

Mostly, though, he believed he was unusually "gifted." His parents, he said, had always known of what they, too, saw as his "abilities," but they had no idea how to advise or caution him over the years of his otherwise fairly normal upbringing. A robust guy, he had played high school football, had friends, and was on his way to college. He complained, though, of one disturbing trend. He was finding himself becoming more and more preoccupied by all the apparitions he was seeing in his bedroom and basement; this was interfering with his life, and so he wondered what, if anything, he should do about it.

He was afraid that these spirit experiences, which he attributed mostly to deceased humans, might get too distracting for him to concentrate on his studies. When I talked to his parents by phone, they verified everything that he had told me. They confirmed that they and their daughter had also seen dark spirits in their home. They all had occasionally heard strange, inexplicable noises, too, though nowhere near as frequently as their son.

Interestingly, they all had their own theories about the cause of these episodes. They had learned that the house they had bought many years earlier had previously been owned by a defrocked Protestant minister and his family. Neighbors eventually confided in them that this cleric had lost his Christian beliefs and turned to the worship of Satan. There was a strong suspicion, they said, that out of zeal for his newfound adherence to devil worship, this man had killed his young daughter in a ritual sacrifice right in the house.

I am well aware of the exaggerations and cultural hysteria surrounding such accounts, but this was a plausible rationale for an infestation, and the family members seemed sober and sane reporters. I was able to assure them that despite their son's immersion in paranormal experiences since his youth, he appeared to me to be completely free of any frank mental disorder, except perhaps for some posttraumatic stress symptoms. Since they were nominally Christian, I advised them to consult a local member of the clergy and have the house blessed.

To their surprise, the blessings by an experienced evangelical minister proved much more effective than they anticipated. Not only did such episodes cease in their house, but their son returned to his religious faith and practices. He was, however, disappointed that he lost his ability to see spirits and discern remote events. This is also what Julia had feared, which was one of the many complicated reasons she never fully committed to her exorcisms. Months later, the young man told me that he had never felt better and that his improvement in mood and attitude with fewer distractions was worth the price of his lost aptitude as a "natural medium."

A few spiritual experts I know do believe that deceased humans might be able to produce such effects—even a possession or at least the haunting of a house. Many credible people have always maintained that they have seen visions of dead relatives or saints and the like, but these do not appear as "ghosts." Some early Christian thinkers posited that deceased souls, who in their view were damned, could wander the earth seeking revenge on their enemies as ghosts and possibly possess an individual.

The major objection to this view is just how frequently observers who have witnessed cases where spirits claim to be dead humans testify that the spirits are later forced to admit they've lied and are really demons. The key lesson from Sara's oppression may be the very sequence of how the evil spirits presented themselves. Only after initial claims to her to be either angels or dead souls did the demons unequivocally admit to being demons. And only after that admission were they successfully driven out.

This common observation among exorcists led one spiritual writer to express the opinion that paranormal events of *all* sorts should always be presumed to be diabolic until proved otherwise—an elusive goal to be sure. Yet I agree with that opinion. No one has ever, or likely will ever, provide any proof that humans after death have any such abilities. We also know that demons lie and can disguise themselves by assuming an astonishing variety of different forms. Why not expect they are doing the same by playing upon humans' fears of ghosts and the like? In any case, I clearly think the burden of proof is on anyone trying to challenge the time-honored view among most religious experts that the strange abilities of the demonic world are aimed at misleading and terrifying us, including through the wide variety of infestations reported throughout history.

CHAPTER TEN

ALICE

*A Case of a Successful Exorcism and a Further
Word About Causes and Solutions*

Soon after my discussion with my medium acquaintance and the case of the youthful "natural medium," a woman from the West Coast came to see me for an evaluation. Her case featured all three elements of a history of spiritualism, a clear diabolic infestation, and a full possession.

Alice walked into my office with her earnest and thoughtful exorcist-priest. I couldn't have been more surprised. She was a divorced, professional woman who resided in California with her teenaged daughter. Unlike many of the cases I've seen, nothing about her stylish appearance suggested any level of distress, let alone any indication that she was possessed by a demon.

From the moment she started talking, she proved articulate, expressive, and sophisticated in manner. When I probed her about relationships, she talked about her closeness with members of her family and her active friendships. She had worked her way out of a small town in Central America, earned her doctorate here in the United States, and in more recent years had developed a successful career.

It wasn't immediately apparent why she was in my office.

Alice wasn't done with the surprises. When she began to feel attacked, she researched her own symptoms, which according to her friends included periodic and protracted trancelike states and disappearances from her home for extended periods. As troubling as this was, Alice had no recollection of these experiences. Through a process of elimination and some deeper research, she came to believe she was possessed, because no other explanation made sense. More specifically, she believed she was possessed because her mother had raised her within circles of the occult. Alice's mother was once a prominent spiritualist healer, a practitioner of *espiritismo*. She had hoped her daughter would take her place because, according to Alice, she believed Alice was to be "the carrier of her gifts."

Alice said that at one point her mother "assigned" her a spirit and that she was "consecrated" to the spirit world on several occasions, including before her birth. Despite exposure as a child and young teen "to secret séances," as she put it, she resisted her mother's efforts. As a young adult, she reported several perilous encounters with members of satanic or spiritualist groups. Either ashamed by or ignorant of the details of these brief encounters, she left it at that, and I never heard the complete story, if there even was one. All Alice told me was that she was able to escape from the worst dangers, including the threat of rape from members of this occult band. Having survived this more dangerous period of her life, Alice continued on the path of personal growth and professional success. She described how as a young adult she felt on her way to becoming a fulfilled and successful professional.

During her thirties, however, problems surfaced. She started to experience demonic oppression, receiving the same beatings from invisible spirits that Maria, Stan, and Steve had all endured. The beatings resulted in numerous bruises and scratches. At one point, an unseen force pushed her against a door. Her own friends reported to me their feelings of bafflement and helplessness in being unable to take any action against such invisible assaults.

In Alice's case, the demons were not content with just oppressing her. They wanted to invade her body and take full control of it. As her case unfolded, Alice began to report classical signs of possession. In her trances, a demonic voice emerged. She also underwent a periodic personality change. This self-contained woman who kept a firm control of herself started to act out in erratic and risky ways. When people tried to help her, she grew violent, attacking them on more than one occasion. Alice told me that she felt drawn against her will to a local gathering of self-styled witches and Satanists. She would emerge from a trance, appalled at where she found herself and what she was in the middle of doing. Alice also described signs of an infestation. She reported that religious objects fell apart in her presence, and holy pictures and crucifixes, which were hung throughout her house, regularly fell off the walls.

Remarkably, most other times, she functioned satisfactorily, even at a high level. One could argue that her condition represented a less severe, though still genuine possession. This was another indication that for periods demons may "lay low," while acting in full control during other periods. Alice, however, maintained that these hiatuses, during which she was still able to perform her work, suggested her generally strong mental and spiritual health. I didn't disagree. It was a remarkable fact that apparently no one in her office noticed anything was wrong with her. She was never eccentric at her job.

Alice made a strong case for her belief that she was possessed. Several clergy and a number of psychological experts corroborated her point of view. I gathered several written reports from other licensed professionals, including one from an experienced psychiatrist in San Francisco. They all unanimously documented their assessments of her sanity. They independently reported to me that in their opinion only a paranormal cause could explain their findings in an otherwise stable individual, though they told me they didn't know enough about possessions to maintain that possibility. Alice and her priest mostly wanted me to confirm that a possession was in fact what she was experiencing.

Subsequently, the first major exorcism, authorized after our lengthy meeting, lasted several hours, though it didn't seem to change much for Alice. The demon inside her bellowed out characteristic and clichéd expressions of bravado, hate, and rage toward anything religious—a typical performance of our demonic foes.

To help herself, Alice redoubled her efforts with prayers and intensified her devotional life. Another lengthier "marathon" exorcism, which extended over two days, proved effective. The demon was clearly subdued. Like many successful exorcisms, the ending seemed anticlimactic: the demon left with more of a whimper than a bang, with no fireworks closing things out, as sometimes can happen. Alice emerged with a peaceful look on her face. All sensed the ending was positive.

Rapidly, for cases of this sort, her condition had resolved.

Alice now regards herself as fully liberated from all demonic attack. I stayed in touch with her, and today she is a highly functioning woman again, satisfied with her life and work. She shows no signs of lingering consequences from her assault by demonic spirits. The people who helped Alice believed that her own motivation and redoubled spiritual efforts contributed greatly to the rapid success of the exorcisms. From the start, this resilient woman displayed a powerful desire to return fully to her earlier practice of a devout life. Valiantly, she persisted in praying and spending time in church to ensure she stayed free of demonic influence. Her exorcist had worked hard to encourage her in this spiritual fight and felt she greatly aided his efforts.

• • •

Why are some people targeted by demons and not others? Are women more targeted than men? Criminals over those never in legal trouble? What are the common factors involved?

Most exorcists report an equal occurrence of males seeking exorcisms, but females are probably more open to being helped, which is also the case in the mental health field. This may be why some exorcists believe females are more commonly attacked. That perception persists, although it has always seemed to me a bit biased against women to believe that.

Although most of the cases I've discussed in detail have had obvious causes, admittedly there are always questions of why some individuals rather than others, who may have little apparent differences in their backgrounds, become victims of demonic assaults. As is generally the case in dealing with spiritual matters, we are often left with something of a mystery. Ultimately, such a question cannot be answered. It is hardly coincidental, of course, that the possessions I've presented in this book occurred in individuals with "satanic" or at least serious and explicit occult involvement in their personal histories. All had either turned, or "been turned," to evil. In most serious possessions, one sees these scenarios again and again.

Sometimes people only reluctantly admit such involvement. Stan was a good example of how at times one has to pry such information out of someone. Similarly, a Chinese-American woman a few years back told me that she was being harassed by spirits; but only after many meetings, like Stan, did she finally acknowledge her strong immersion for years in various pagan and occult practices. When I asked her why she hadn't told me about this background originally, she admitted that she had found it highly embarrassing to talk about and had often been judged harshly by her community before coming to the United States.

Undoubtedly, the main reason people become possessed is because they have such histories.

To complicate the discussions, however, Alice proved to be a major exception to that rule. She had apparently never immersed herself directly in Satanism, the occult, or evil. Rather, her mother, as a practitioner of *espiritismo*, had *assigned* her a spirit and was thus presumably the main factor instrumental in the development of her daughter's affliction. Many people find it difficult to believe that demonic attacks may occur even to those who seem blameless, such as Manny and Sara. A few very holy or saintly people may also become attacked, like Maria, though rarely to the point of a full-fledged possession. Here the demonic strategy (and there always is one, I had learned well from Father Jacques) seems to be pure revenge, or at least obstructing a person's good works.

This claim that even fine, religious folk can become attacked is something many people often deny. For instance, a woman from Georgia who had signs of a minor oppression consulted me. She was experiencing being pushed and scratched by demons. Her mother witnessed these phenomena and verified that these features of an external oppression unquestionably occurred. Strangely to me, however, the mother seemed to have little sympathy for her daughter's condition. She even blamed her for it. The daughter, by then in her mid-twenties, was psychologically intact, had a good job, and socialized with many friends. But she was extremely upset because her religious congregation, and even her father, who was a pastor, were shaming her and considering expelling her from their midst. They thought that she must be "un-Christian" in some serious way because she was being attacked by evil spirits. This belief is analogous to how some societies have shunned and persecuted anyone thought harboring a demonic spirit.

I found her to be a lovely young lady who was generally striving to live a worthwhile and spiritually informed life. She had had a few, trivial experiences with her girlfriends as a teenager playing with a Ouija board but had done nothing since that period of a similar nature or been involved in any other occult practices.

Here seemed another case where demons were harassing a good person, including by making her fellow Christians reject her. This lack of support among coreligionists is often painful and confusing to good people who become victimized, as they feel judged and are sometimes treated harshly by their fellows. Once again, these individuals can be victimized because they serve as exemplary models to others and may be seen, perhaps, as "the enemy" par excellence by demons. But because good people especially often tend to place higher moral demands upon themselves, or more than others of lesser striving, and because few people truly meet all the moral ideals they try to live up to, these victims may often come to believe, in their sincere humility, that they must "deserve" such harassment.

I've also come to hear about (and this factor is admittedly extremely rare) devout souls who, under unusual circumstances, have even offered themselves up for demons to attack as a kind of penance or sacrificial substitution for others' welfare. These motives help explain some truly saintly and at least temporarily possessed individuals. Such "offerings," though well-intentioned, tend to be discouraged by the church as imprudent and potentially self-destructive, just as early Christian leaders tried to dissuade martyrs from recklessly flinging themselves in the path of the Roman authorities during times of persecution.

One older woman I met told me she had made just such an "offering" to evil spirits in service as a spiritual "sacrifice" for "family members and the church as a whole." Anneliese Michel may have done the same thing. But this woman had come to regret her decision as she said the spirits took her at her word, and she suffered pains for several years that left her practically incapacitated. She felt demons had cruelly taken advantage of her resolution to serve as a "victim for others" and believed her impulsive decision had been prideful. She eventually concluded that her action was "probably contrary to what our Lord ultimately would have really wanted." I agreed with her.

The example of Alice also illustrates the most crucial point about achieving relief from these troubling states. It is a theme I have repeatedly emphasized, but it nevertheless bears deeper discussion. Those with a smattering of knowledge about exorcisms are tempted to regard them as magical ceremonies or a series of mysterious incantations—as voodoo of a benign sort. If only the right phrases (or correct use, say, of blessed salt and holy water) are employed, all will be well. I call this the "St. George driving out the dragon" model of liberating the beleaguered soul. Similar to physically or mentally ill patients, victims of possession and oppression want the "magic bullet," the "quick pill," the ritual formula that will make everything better with little effort on their part. This is a natural human wish, but a shortsighted one.

Patients with chronic diseases don't get better in a moment; most illnesses require time and effort to recover. And so generally do demonic assaults.

Movies purporting to represent exorcisms reinforce the stereotypical view of such rituals. If only the holiest minister or the precisely correct set of prayers is mustered, all will be fine. Individuals who come to realize they may be under demonic attack are frightened and desperate. They frequently turn to inappropriate or ineffectual sources of assistance before they go to an exorcist or a knowledgeable evaluator. Some are advised by acquaintances to seek the assistance of indigenous healers or allegedly helpful "psychics." Though well-meaning, many of these unorthodox practitioners prove unhelpful, or even harmful. Some of them are mercenary and manipulative. Some may be serious occultists themselves. Still others, calling themselves "parapsychologists" or even "demonologists," may be in over their heads. I have known a number of cases where someone self-described as a parapsychologist or psychic healer met an individual in distress and the situation deteriorated, perhaps after a brief respite.

A common feature is that these practitioners often charge a fee, sometimes a hefty one. One woman I know practically bankrupted herself by visiting regularly with a person she called her "psychic healer." Some ministers or televangelists in this country have also been known to expect a lucrative payment or the euphemistic "donation." As a physician, I generally consult upon these cases pro bono, and I am not, of course, directly offering spiritual assistance or spiritual advice. I recommend to victims of demonic assault that they find someone truly committed and spiritually advanced to help them out, and I advise that they be extremely leery of anyone who charges them money. Pastoral help should be a vocation, not a business.

As in the mental health field, quick solutions are rare. Father Amorth used to say that "spiritual help, such as serious prayer and the confession of one's sins, are often more valuable than exorcisms." Similarly, his successor as president of the International Association of Exorcists, Father

Gramolazzo, told me once that "90 percent of what helps possessed individuals occurs outside the exorcism rituals."

The most experienced exorcists know this truth and make it very clear. Their ritual prayers are not magic charms. The most important aspect of the course of action recommended to afflicted individuals is their own spiritual development and effort. This advice in no way "blames the victim," nor does it diminish the value of exorcisms in loosening the hold of evil spirits. The encouragement, however, to oppressed and possessed people to pray when able, to cultivate the virtues, and to avoid and repent of their faults can be paramount. Exorcism, even in its most elaborate forms, is no substitute for the value of the victim's own role in resisting the devil's actions. An exorcism has been described as part of a "journey." Here, as elsewhere in the spiritual life, there are few hard-and-fast rules.

Many Protestant commentators have pointed out that the exorcisms done by Jesus in the Gospels seem pretty simple and straightforward affairs, concise commands free of elaborate formulas. But no one else in history had such quick and frequent purported successes, in my view, as the Gospel figure of Jesus reportedly had, believe that claim or not.

And this is not to say that more formalized prayers do not have merit. Beyond a broad acknowledgment that prayers and other traditional means, such as fasting, can be efficacious, there is a high variability in rates of success. We know that the efforts of individual victims are often instrumental in the success of a case of possession, but here as elsewhere it is hard to generalize or predict individual results. Exorcisms seem to "weaken" the demonic hold so individuals can then develop the inner resources to fight on their own—usually by more ordinary spiritual means.

Exorcisms, at any rate, are not a form of *bargaining*, that is, ritualized formulas or promises for an assured result. Deliverance from a possessed state is not a product, not something one can buy from a purported expert or ensure by just the right words and methodology. It is a strange unfolding of a plan beyond our comprehension, though one with presumed providential meaning.

What we do know is that we are *not* dealing with ancient notions of a *transaction* in this spiritual endeavor. Religious scholars have characterized the mindset of some ancient religious and pagan ceremonies—a mindset by no means absent from our modern world—to be one of an exchange or "appeasement" of the gods or of an amorphous spirit world. This transaction was conceived as a mutual bargaining and obligation between parties—in the words of the Latin expression *do ut des* (I give [to you] so that you may give [to me])—whether the party was conceived as benign or darker in nature.

The rapid success of Alice shows a completely different moral universe. The exorcism ritual seemed an important *part* of her deliverance, but Alice's own personal spiritual battle against the forces ensnaring her was evidently crucial. Indeed, most of the people who assisted in her liberation concluded that her efforts were the more critical component of her rapid, successful outcome.

PART THREE

CONSULTANT AND SCHOLAR

The Advocacy and Cautions of a Physician

There are two equal and opposite errors into which our race can fall about the devils. One is to disbelieve in their existence. The other is to believe, and to feel an excessive and unhealthy interest in them. They themselves are equally pleased by both errors and hail a materialist or a magician with the same delight.

—C. S. LEWIS, *THE SCREWTAPE LETTERS*

CHAPTER ELEVEN

BARBARA AND THE WIDER SATANIC PANIC

True vs. False Memories

In the past decade or so, I've been more frequently consulted than ever because I have become more willing to speak out and to be interviewed by the media. I also teach a course on this subject. With some lingering reluctance, I decided that I should take on such roles more openly.

I had long been confident in my ability to understand what works and what doesn't in freeing people from demonic assaults. I wanted to be of whatever help I could to the suffering people who were increasingly contacting me—to the point where I had to set some limits, given time constraints. Since I was now being approached by people from all over the world, I became further convinced that even if these serious conditions remained rare, still in the *aggregate* we were hardly talking about a trivial number of cases, as I had already known from the historical record.

But many other individuals besides victims also solicited my opinion. And increasingly, I became more willing to respond publicly. For instance, aware obviously of the great public interest, *The Washington*

Post, CNN, several US network and foreign news services, and many websites and podcasts, among other media outlets, were approaching me for my views.

Certain groups of people were preoccupied with the subject, while others simply discounted the whole business as superstitious nonsense. These diverse audiences had widely differing attitudes and questions. But I knew well that an obsession with the subject was as short-sighted as a smug dismissal.

More skeptical people were either unconvinced or undecided about whether this whole subject had any scientific credibility. Others, whom I call the genuine seekers—not a few suffering themselves after a history of precarious paranormal pursuits—wanted a better idea of where to turn for guidance and direct help. The more sober-minded among them sincerely sought to understand how these beliefs made broader sense.

Still others—the more traditional believers—wanted to get a better perspective on this complex field with its legitimate controversies and its many exaggerations and misconceptions. They probably intuitively agreed with the warnings C. S. Lewis made in the epigraph above but wanted someone to help them sort out the complex truth amidst the noise and nonsense.

And finally, those prone to seeing demons everywhere with excessive fearfulness and credulity came to me, too, mostly to relieve their anxieties and overreactions. They also deserved a respectful response.

The importance of keeping a balanced, humane, and scientific perspective when dealing with all these kinds of people is critical, and challenging. The extremes on both sides of the issue must be avoided, especially the hysteria of seeing Satanists and possessions everywhere, even dredging up false memories about them; the harm wreaked by the exploiters and abusers of victims or those only thought to be so; and the common misdiagnosis of possession cases and other scientific misconceptions.

The tragic story of Barbara and her intractable possession highlights the thorny issues of false memories and of the wider satanic panic at the time she became possessed. Barbara's case encapsulated aspects of many of these concerns of the diverse audiences importuning me. I have sometimes called her the "poster child" of a typical "cult" victim as well as of someone harshly subjected to the paranormal properly understood.

Her long-standing case, which I came to know well, provided clear evidence for each of the following: a demonstration of all three types of extraordinary demonic attacks—infestation, oppression, and possession; obvious evidence for the true underlying nature of the so-called paranormal; and a credible example of the sort of Satanism that is still not uncommonly doubted in certain circles and is grossly exaggerated in others.

This final case proves another point, I think. Adding more and more examples of possession will not persuade some people, however impressive the evidence. And some will never be convinced even if they were to speak directly to the individuals highlighted in this book. It is too frightening to some people, too challenging to others, perhaps too incomprehensible to still others. Many simply prefer not to face these disturbing and, what has by now come to seem to me, obvious realities.

● ● ●

Congregants of Barbara's small Lutheran church in her rural Indiana community questioned why the church hall doors were locked one day. Inside the nondescript hall a tall, hefty young man gathered with a few fellow parishioners. Truth be told, they were excited because they were trying to help a woman who was under severe demonic assault.

At the center of their prayer group was a nervous-looking woman and her attentive German-American husband. This man, an immigrant as a boy but now a successful small-town contractor, was himself distressed. He had long observed his wife's suffering with a growing sense of powerlessness. He and Barbara had agreed to put her in the hands of this intense deacon whose air of confidence belied his youth.

Despite the seriousness of the occasion, the deacon tried to foster an atmosphere of bonhomie. He had read about what demonized individuals were like, and though this was his first serious encounter with someone who might be possessed, he relished the role and challenge. *What could go wrong?* he wondered. He was a fit young man, and the woman's husband was large-framed and strong. He doubted any resistance would come from this pale, slight woman who had been pleasant and cooperative, if terribly anxious, in their previous short interview. He hadn't felt it necessary to consult any doctors or more experienced clergy, convinced, from his private reading and brief interview with this woman, that he, as a true spiritual warrior, could handle things.

How difficult could this be with the good Lord on my side? he was thinking. He didn't call what he was doing an "exorcism." That was Catholic terminology, and he thought the Catholic Church's ritualized manner of working was too formal. For him, a mix of less stylized prayers and entreaties by all the assembled in a more spontaneous manner should do the trick. Christian "optimism" pervaded the air in the large gathering place.

He began the prayers, but things did not go according to plan.

He was only a bit surprised by how quickly this woman went into a trance and the demon's voice emerged. This was the goal, after all, and he had known, from the husband's report, that this was possibly a dramatic possession. The vehemence of the evil spirit's hostility and level of its agitation, though, were stunning. The deacon's attempt at appearing unfazed did not last long.

Almost before he had begun his commands to the demon in the name of our Lord, the woman pounced. And she came after *him.* She picked him up and threw him across half the room. His body hit the wall, hard. He groaned. Everyone in the church stared at him and the woman in horror.

The session was clearly over. Taken aback and mortified, the deacon admitted that he should have been more cautious. The group had not taken the precaution of restraining Barbara during such prayer sessions,

as is more standard with more severe possessions and more knowledgeable ministers. Barbara remembered nothing. When she came out of
the trance after the incident, she was ashamed when she learned what
she had done. All reassured her that she wasn't to blame.

Experience with such matters counts. She and her husband decided
to turn elsewhere.

By the time Barbara was brought to my office, the reality of her
possessed condition seemed no longer in doubt. She was accompanied
by her husband and an agreeable and experienced priest, who was less
naïve than her earnest deacon had been. He told me that his bishop had
insisted on a psychiatric evaluation and he'd had trouble finding a local
doctor who would agree to assess her.

Barbara, her husband, and the priest had long been convinced that
she was possessed. I was told that in her possessed states she understood
foreign languages that she had never studied, including Russian. Another classic sign was that she proved knowledgeable about the lives
of those assisting the exorcism. They also told me about the enormous strength she had exhibited when she threw the deacon across the
church hall.

Barbara was a middle-aged woman who had the air of someone
younger. She had a soft voice and a large tattoo of a tiger on her upper
arm. She had no psychiatric history. She had been a devout child,
brought up a Protestant. She had a relatively happy upbringing until, she
recounted, she was nine years old. At that age, her parents' marriage was
coming apart, and for solace she turned to a neighboring couple, who
befriended her and seemed generous with their time and attention. Barbara soon noticed, however, that the two, who were considerably older
than her parents, practiced "black arts rituals," as she put it. At one such
rite she was "dedicated" to Satan and, according to Barbara, was *given
a demon.*

When Barbara was fourteen, her parents moved and she lost contact
with this couple. In our first interview, she described a fairly normal
teenage and young adult life thereafter. She was involved in various

Lutheran church activities, which she enjoyed. By her account, she was again content and at peace.

In her later twenties, however, she felt herself becoming antagonistic to religious practice. Then she experienced what she described as a near constant assault by occult powers—pains, voices, constant threats and commands, with worse threatened to come if she didn't "obey." In addition, people were telling her that she was entering trance states without her awareness. The trances would last for half an hour or so, and others would sense a "presence" there, though it did not speak out. When Barbara emerged from this state, she remembered nothing.

Barbara also reported being physically attacked via scratches and blows to her body without any visible presence manifesting itself. Suddenly she would become "black and blue," though neither she nor anyone else present could or stop the apparent attacker. As with Maria's husband, Barbara's spouse insisted that he directly saw these marks "appear out of the blue" on many occasions. Naturally, he was horrified.

These episodes usually occurred at night but could also happen during the day. At other times, Barbara had been thrown to the ground or pushed up against others by what she called "unseen forces." A number of witnesses claimed to have seen such events and to have been mystified and unable to help her.

Barbara acknowledged that her manner of coping had not always been ideal. She long struggled to resist what she felt were demonic suggestions and wishes—not an unusual trial for those possessed. But sometimes she succumbed, because, she said, "I suffered greatly if I didn't agree to what the spirits wanted and didn't obey them."

Consequently, Barbara frequented cemeteries, when she felt so commanded, compelled in her view by the spirits to sit amidst the graves. "I just hung out there," she told me, afraid of further attacks. Hanging out at cemeteries among the dead, a strange and depressing habit, has the feel of a gothic novel, but it was all too real in Barbara's case. Similarly, in the New Testament Jesus drives out a demon who gives his name as "Legion," of a man who comes to meet him running, it's reported, from his usual "abode at tombs." Like Barbara, as well, he could not be subdued and would even smash the shackles with which the local populace tried to restrain him.

Further paranormal disturbances in Barbara's home were also frequent and in almost the exact same way they occurred in Alice's infestations. Religious objects would break apart or fall off the wall spontaneously. A rosary on a shelf in her living room split apart one day. Her dresser tipped over; her bed would shake.

All of these features, which involved so many of the classic signs of an oppression and then a possession and an infestation, were persuasive enough for the diocesan bishop to authorize a formal exorcism. During these rituals five or six people were required to hold her, as she struggled for hours during the sessions to free herself. During each one, the purported demonic entities again openly displayed a typical arrogant stubbornness. In responding to commands to leave, the alleged spirit said, "I will never leave."

During the rituals, the entity's ability to either speak or understand foreign languages was evident. The best example of this sign of demonic activity that I encountered with Barbara was an exchange between the exorcist and the demonic voice during an evening ritual witnessed by seven people. The exorcist decided to add to his prayers the Latin version of the Apostles' Creed. To the opening words "*Credo in Deum Patrem omnipotentem*" (I believe in God, the Father Almighty), the demon replied (albeit in English, as often happens), "Well, I don't!" To the phrase, "*descendit ad inferos*" (he descended into hell), the demon said in English, "And he's still there." To "*tertia die resurrexit a mortuis*" (on the third day he arose from the dead), the response was, "No, he didn't." To the ending clause of the prayer, "*Credo in . . . vitam aeternam*" (I believe . . . in life everlasting), the demon's voice expressed with weary emotion, "There is no life."

The sad tone or, more accurately, the despair with which these last words were intoned might have elicited a modicum of sympathy if one did not realize that the demon was not only refusing to leave its hapless victim, but seemed invested in torturing her as much as possible in the interim.

Barbara had had no higher education and was not brought up Catholic. As noted, she had never studied any foreign language, let alone Latin, and was astonished to be told afterward that she had understood and commented upon this Latin prayer.

Many exorcists demand that the demons declare their names in order to know by whose "authority" the possession is occurring. One often obtains the "generic" names of traditional demons or dead individuals from history, such as Judas Iscariot in the Earling case, a sensationalist ploy. The demons may represent their presence as single or multiple—often as what seems a ludicrously massive number. Some claim to be particularly powerful demons, like Beelzebub. Julia worshipped Asmodeus, a demon traditionally associated with lust. I pay little attention to these boasts and frequent lies, although most exorcists feel the revelation of a particular name to be an integral part of the eventual process of liberation. When Barbara's entity spoke, it resisted efforts to identify itself. "No, *you* tell me *your* name," it said several times in response to the priest's entreaty.

The evil spirit(s) possessing Barbara remained obstinate to the end, and she continued to struggle for the rest of her life. Before she could be delivered, she passed away. Some inquirers have suggested that she must be with the evil spirits in Hell. But no one could possibly know that. The standard teaching is that even possessed humans may sincerely strive to do the right thing under tremendous duress, as Barbara clearly did. While she evidently proved powerless to fight fully and successfully her demonic foe, in any case, only God can judge anyone. One hopes she eventually found a peace in the afterlife she never experienced during so many years of her affliction.

● ● ●

I had been exposed to a few patients who alluded to their involvement in overt diabolic activities even before I was pulled into this field, but I had mostly discounted their stories. As a busy psychiatrist experienced with a wide range of patients, I had generally discovered that these individuals were psychotic or suggestible and suffering from what at the time were being called "false memories."

Right before I was first asked to assess these kinds of suspected demonic cases, there was an understandable skepticism among more experienced clinicians, especially during the 1980s and early 1990s, when stories of satanic cultists abducting children seemed to pop up regularly in tabloids and nightly news reports. There was a widespread exaggeration, even hysteria, about a then-growing number of reports of Satanists in the country. Highly organized satanic groups that commit egregious crimes are undoubtedly rare in the United States. That doesn't mean there aren't a certain number of hidden though self-styled Satanists who may engage in petty crimes—such as defacing churches and the like. I am directly aware of such actions, and many police have since verified them to me in private conversations. Also, we seem to have our share of groups—such as the Church of Satan—that openly claim to worship Satan.

On the other hand, unquestionably there has been a popular uproar regarding the supposed ubiquity of highly influential and gruesome activities by some Satanists, including claims of their abducting children. Such fears linger in some quarters, though to a much lesser degree, including most notoriously the assertion of kidnappings leading to so-called satanic ritual abuse. The latter even has its own acronym, SRA, and calls to mind the allegations of ritual murder against Jewish communities during the Middle Ages, often with just as little credible evidence.

The most prominent charge of SRA occurred in the 1980s at the Virginia McMartin preschool in Manhattan Beach, California. The couple who ran the daycare program there were accused of bizarre diabolic ceremonies and grisly sexual mistreatment of their young clients. The allegations included secret chambers under the school where satanic rites were conducted, and children were said to have been molested and photographed naked. Such photos were never found. The trial became the longest running and most expensive in US history, and ended without a single conviction.

Naïve believers in widespread child abductions and ritualized sexual abuse by Satanists caused well-documented damage to innocent people. One evangelical author, Michael Warnke, simply made up such tales for his 1972 book *The Satan Seller*, though major news outlets widely quoted him for a time. Poor investigative methods and over-zealous prosecutors fed the frenzy. Many books and monographs documented these travesties. One commentator pointed out that in one year there were more reports of satanic kidnappings in the United States than actual proven youth disappearances *in toto*, many of whom were simply runaways.

To address the question of the magnitude of this putative threat in as scholarly a manner as allowed by such often clandestine groups, Dr. Gail Goodman of the University of California, Davis, directed the largest study of this subject for the National Center on Child Abuse and Neglect. "After scouring the country," she concluded, "we found no evidence for large-scale cults that sexually abuse children." She acknowledged, however, that there was "convincing evidence of lone perpetrators or couples who say they are involved with Satan or use the claim to intimidate victims." Barbara's case was a variant of the latter, though judging from her possession, it was much more than just human intimidation.

Defenders of the reality of at least a few of the SRA stories, however, still challenge any complete minimization of the now widely recognized more outrageous reports about organized Satanism to this day. Lonely voices continue to claim to me their own anecdotal evidence. Mostly, I find their accounts dubious, though a few seem unquestionably genuine, such as Julia's.

A true academic cottage industry of critics and debunkers, especially unbelieving of the more phantasmagorical and lurid accounts of the SRA phenomenon, has continued to speak out. While some innocent, allegedly satanic practitioners were falsely accused, the majority of convictions were decided on narrower grounds of single abuse charges, not the ritual abuse allegations. A number of such perpetrators were indeed abusive though later used an exaggeration of satanic involvement as a smoke screen. The courts seem to have learned from the controversy, and most sensationalist charges have mostly disappeared by now.

Still, each side of the Satanist debates frequently lacked any nuance or real-life experience with such cultists, such as Father Jacques and Father A. had, and myself by now. Those more clandestine groups *are* sometimes criminal; Speedy and Juan were real-life examples of individuals who certainly turned to Satan—and, to their later regret, got real-life results.

In my experience, credible or not, there remains not a trivial number of people who still claim exposure to Satanists and abuse by them. I have had a fair amount of direct clinical experience with people who are outright delusional about the subject.

Equally important as these outright delusions, however, are the cases where so-called false memories were stimulated. Similar to the remarkable story of Lily, who was highly prone to the power of suggestion about herself being directly attacked by an evil spirit (though without any obvious mistaken past memories of any satanic human abuse), other suggestible individuals, seemingly well-intentioned and fully coherent, may remarkably come to believe they recall witnessing or experiencing satanic practices years later when no such thing ever happened. Unfortunately, their stories have been, and still are, too frequently accepted at face value by poorly trained or overly credulous therapists.

How such false memories could be created is illustrated by Raymond, a nineteen-year-old man from the Carolinas. The family wanted to consult me about his long-standing self-destructiveness, a suicidal episode, and a recently diagnosed personality disorder. Raymond gave me his permission to tell his story in the interest of sharing just how one could understand the plausible genesis of such a strikingly bizarre false memory.

Along with the diagnosis of a personality disorder, Raymond had been diagnosed with a mood disorder, suffered from panic attacks, and on occasion abused drugs. On the basis of the information I had already received from his maternal uncle, a cardiologist I knew from Yale, I thought Raymond was overmedicated. The uncle called his sister, Raymond's mother, a religious fanatic who, in his professional opinion, suffered a borderline personality disorder herself. She had wanted the model child. "She didn't get one," he said matter-of-factly. "But my nephew, a good kid, tried for years to be the perfect son." He felt Raymond was essentially rebelling. He added that Raymond's father, his brother-in-law, had been in the Air Force, was frequently overseas, and had rarely been at home during the years the boy was growing up.

When Raymond and his parents visited me, the father seemed stiff and himself depressed. He was pleasant and deferential, but aloof. The mother, also described to me by her brother as an overprotective and "high-strung type," did most of the talking. Meanwhile, Raymond looked morose. He gave an impression of uninterest, but I could tell he was paying close attention to the discussion. Despite his initial demeanor, when the two of us talked alone, he revealed a more likeable quality—a good prognostic sign. He also seemed very bright.

I reviewed his history in depth. At that time, he rarely ventured from his home and mostly watched television all day. He had been a champion swimmer but had recently quit the team. Contrary to his regular summer routine, he hadn't tried to get a job. Though he'd had a past suicidal episode, Raymond swore he wasn't at present suicidal, a claim his parents backed up, calling him "very honest." *Another favorable sign*, I thought, *if true*. But he was still cutting himself, albeit superficially, as I could tell from the faint scars he showed me on both his forearms.

The Westchester Division of New York Hospital was then a center known for treating patients with borderline personality disorder. We attracted such patients from all over the country and gave them excellent treatment. We had even started to contemplate a study comparing the modified psychodynamic techniques for patients with severe personality disorder developed by Dr. Otto Kernberg, who was at that time still clinical director there, with the emerging version of a more cognitive-behavioral approach known as dialectical behavioral therapy, or DBT. DBT's originator, Marsha Linehan, like Kernberg, was a prolific and articulate proponent of her therapeutic approach. She had come to the Westchester Division at one point to explain her recommended methods, and I had received some direct training from her. So I was well-versed in both the more traditional psychodynamic mode of therapy and the newer cognitive-behavioral approaches to treating such patients.

At the end of our visit, I told Raymond and his family that I thought he had some strong borderline features, but other personality traits, too, as well as some neurobiological vulnerabilities that we technically call "axis I disorders." These were Raymond's documented anxiety and depressive tendencies. Since he wasn't presently suicidal and his mood seemed to have been improving slightly in recent weeks, I believed that he could be treated successfully as an outpatient. Having confidence in our tailored borderline inpatient unit, I said that he could be hospitalized at any point in the future, if needed, but that I thought it unnecessary at the time, *provided*, I stressed, that he received the proper treatment back in his home area. Raymond visibly relaxed. I realized how much he had feared his parents were going to hospitalize him against his will.

I wanted to develop a better outpatient plan. I was respectful but confident and a bit forceful in my therapeutic suggestions because Raymond's mother, who seemed the main decision-maker, had already disparaged psychiatry. "Medication is okay," she said, "but I'm not sending him to one of those Freudian types. Sex and blaming the mother is all they want to talk about."

I could see that I had my work cut out for me. I decided to make my psychopharmacological recommendations first. I was taken aback when Raymond's mother told me that she herself was obtaining the prescriptions for her son from their local general practitioner. I told them that the medication changes I suggested could be monitored on an outpatient basis, but they should be prescribed by a psychiatrist instead of the GP. I especially encouraged them to pursue for Raymond a course of psychodynamic long-term therapy, which I felt was the treatment of choice, when he returned home.

A bit to my surprise, his mother jumped at the idea. I wondered whether she had already had someone in mind. I said I regretted that I didn't know any psychiatrists in their area, but I advised Raymond to talk to his uncle, who could perhaps help him find someone at a medical school near them.

If the problems worsened, I told them, they were to call me.

About three months later, Raymond traveled to meet again as scheduled. This time he came by himself—a good sign. He was less stressed, had stopped the cutting, and had become more active, taking a class at a local college.

"I'm functioning better," he said. "I met a woman, who has become a good friend. She cuts herself, too, deeper than what I used to do, but I finally have someone to talk to. That helps."

I decided to discuss the medications first and then turn to how his therapy was going.

"I still get the rages, but you were right," he said, "I was overmedicated. To the max. When the new psychiatrist my uncle got me first saw me, he said, 'Whoa! We've got to lower some of those heavy-duty antipsychotics. You're also on way too many "benzo's" [minor tranquilizers]. So he put me on a different antidepressant, and voilà, the side effects disappeared in a week. He said he agreed with all that you had recommended. He had heard from my uncle what you had suggested."

I asked whether his uncle had also arranged for a competent therapist or whether the psychiatrist was serving in that role, too.

Raymond told me that the psychiatrist told him he "didn't do therapy" but that his mother "chewed him out" when he tried to suggest a psychologist from the medical center. She was obtaining one on her own, she said. He thought this was typical of how Raymond's mother kept control of him, "and everything else," he added. Later, she told the psychiatrist that she would take care of arranging a good "counselor," as she described him.

Later, when I ran an adolescent inpatient unit for a year, I realized his was a common complaint about medication regimens for teenagers in particular. I was appalled by how many teens were on so many psychiatric drugs at a time; Raymond had been on seven.

But at that point I wanted to hear about Raymond's psychotherapy. He said his mother had arranged for him to see someone in the town where they lived. He called the psychotherapist "a guy's guy" and liked him. He described him as warm, unlike his distant father. He was also "cheaper," his mother said.

I asked whether he knew the discipline of this treater.

"Discipline? You mean background? He just calls himself a psychotherapist, I think. Does it matter?"

I certainly did not want to disparage the counselor or therapist, sight unseen. Raymond seemed to be doing better and had connected with the man. I didn't want to rock the boat, but I had my qualms.

It turned out that his mother had arranged that he be treated at a local Veteran's clinic, where the fee was covered by Raymond's father's VA benefits. And it seemed she chose this particular therapist primarily because he was a member of her Bible group at her church. She thought the therapist was a nice man, though she knew nothing more about him.

I was becoming more concerned.

She had insisted Raymond be treated by someone who specialized in treating posttraumatic stress disorder (PTSD). She had long told Raymond that his only "real" problem was that he'd been traumatized and that his father had caused all his problems, due to his absences and the rare but intense volatility the father could express when he was home.

Raymond told me that his parents "used to fight all the time, and they actually smacked each other a few times. No bruises or anything. He never hit me. But she freaks out a lot. I hit her once myself, and she grounded me for a month."

I knew that treating patients with borderline personality was not a ride in the park and that the better trained and skilled the therapist, the better the outcome was likely to be. Like Kernberg, I found that a sensible "dynamic" therapy conducted in a flexible and empathetic way normally worked best for this type of patient.

I again was weighing my words. "Did you later learn anything else about your psychotherapist?—his education or his training?"

Raymond then remembered that he had called himself once a "peer counselor." He told Raymond that he had obtained an online certificate in "trauma studies." He had dropped out of college because he didn't like school, joined the army, and gone to Vietnam. He was primarily at the clinic to treat fellow vets, helping them "process their trauma" and deal with drug problems, as he himself had done.

Again, none of this was reassuring.

"Oh, right," Raymond continued, "he calls himself a 'traumatist,' too. He claims to have been traumatized during the war, and he said he had learned it could lead to a lot of different symptoms, just like mine." Raymond said that the counselor explained to him that trauma is the key to pretty much everyone's problems. He also disclosed that he himself had severe PTSD and still experienced nightmares. Perhaps if Raymond could also "find his trauma," as he said to Raymond, he'd recover rapidly.

Then Raymond paused.

"And now I've found my trauma!" he announced.

I was thinking that for such a highly intelligent young man, Raymond didn't have a clue what he needed. But I reminded myself that he was still young and immature. Also, he had come from an invalidating family that had never helped him identify emotional states, let alone channel his anger appropriately. His mother had also so denigrated psychology that it was hardly surprising he would be lost in the woods here.

But then Raymond really alarmed me.

"He does a little hypnosis with me," he said. "That's when I first recalled the memory that is at the root of my problems." The counselor knew Raymond was preoccupied with the game Dungeons and Dragons and was watching a lot of movies about the devil. He told Raymond that this fascination must stem from some earlier event.

The counselor had started to hypnotize him to see whether he could remember any startling memories about this subject matter. "I think we hit pay dirt," Raymond told me with glee. "A memory *did* come up. It's vague, but the counselor told me it makes a lot of sense. Sure enough, I think I remember one afternoon being at my mother's church. I was six, I'm guessing, because that's when this particular minister would've been there. Anyway, my mother was gossiping with some of the women in the pews and I wandered off and got to the room where this pastor advised people. The door was open a crack. I vaguely remember seeing him taking a baby in some kind of ritual and slitting its throat."

I was aghast, but I kept a straight face. I told Raymond I wanted to hear more.

"At least I *think* that happened. My counselor told me it made perfect sense. Even my mother told me it *probably* happened when I mentioned it to her. Her friends from out West have sent her stories like that, and she's read some book about that stuff. She thinks it's a big problem in this country and is being covered up by the FBI."

I think he realized from my lack of an immediate reaction that I probably didn't give much credit to his story. He asked whether I believed him or whether I thought it sounded unlikely. I felt I should choose my words carefully, but I also decided I had to became more proactive at this point since Raymond was sincerely seeking my professional opinion and had traveled so far.

"Well it sounds a little 'pat,' to my mind," I told him. "It sounds like you're looking for a simple 'solution' to a complex set of problems and have come up with an idea that to me is a bit implausible. I think maybe you should talk it out further with the therapist, and maybe with your father and uncle, too, who might have some thoughts about the memory—you know, to see how likely others believe it to be true, not just your mom."

I suggested that he not "overfocus" on this one, supposed memory so exclusively. He had struggled with a lot of issues, and the causes of difficulties like his were rarely so simply determined. I told him to include in these discussions with the therapist his own doubts about whether this incident truly had happened since I sensed he already had some. "By all means," I added, "you can talk to your counselor about this, but include your own reservations—and then perhaps decide what you want to do with this therapy." I was thinking to myself, *Not the term I would use about what's going on.*

Two weeks later, Raymond called me. He said he had immediately spoken at length to both the counselor and his uncle, whom I knew he had always respected. After reporting his heart-to-heart with his uncle, Raymond said that even the counselor admitted that he wasn't exactly "sure" the incident had really happened, though he still thought it a not-unlikely source of Raymond's problems. "Time will tell,'" he had stated.

"My uncle, however, thought it was all BS," Raymond said. "He told me he knew the minister a little and that he was a really good guy, hardly a 'satanic monster.' He told me the whole charge sounded absurd to him."

Raymond relaxed. "Reading between the lines, I thought you were saying that, too, but I know you wanted me to decide for myself."

I was relieved how rapidly this intelligent young man had come to this sensible conclusion. I asked what he planned to do about it. He replied with more confidence. "I have to agree that the whole thing now seems sort of ridiculous to me. It also made me question the therapist's competence. One other thing convinced me. I remembered something he told me once. I don't think I gave you this specific detail about atrocities he'd referred to. He said the worst thing he ever saw in Vietnam was the brutal death of some young children caused by some soldiers in his platoon. He said he didn't report it at the time and would never get over it. He seemed to feel very guilty, as if he should've stopped it from happening." In short, Raymond rightly believed that the counselor's own war experiences had colored his view of the roots of Raymond's problems and that he had unwittingly helped dredge up the inaccurate "recollections."

• • •

Despite the strangeness of these events, Raymond's story is not so unusual as one might think. The counselor had felt that witnessing such a violent episode involving children was the primary cause of his own distress and PTSD, and so he had projected his ideas onto Raymond for a time, thinking that some such similar trauma *must* have also occurred to him. Coupled with his mother's preoccupation with the allegedly common occurrences of satanic rituals, Raymond's own shame about his mild interest in occult-type games, readings, and movies likely contributed to his gullibility.

The details of Raymond's story include all the elements that so often explain the genesis of such wild and bogus "satanic" tales: subcultural exaggerated fears, contributory family problems, the dubious and misinformed use of hypnosis, a poorly trained and simplistic counselor, and internal reasons like the guilt and confusion Raymond had about his supposed role in the genesis of his complex problems. All these factors contributed to making what might seem a totally weird and almost psychotic belief—in a nonpsychotic but vulnerable young man—all too explainable.

Lest one think this story so singular, another shorter one proved to be similar.

A few years after Raymond's consultations I went to a conference that included discussions about abuse and trauma, as well as supposedly innovative treatment recommendations, many of them questionable to my mind. It also prominently included patient self-reports, with various individuals offering their testimonies. The atmosphere seemed to discourage any questioning of these accounts, which organizers believed would be invalidating and harmful. It wasn't an academic conference, and many of the stories hardly sounded credible to me.

But I was researching false stories of various abusive experiences at the time, so I had an interest in attending this "patient centered" conclave. The meeting included reports from alleged victims who claimed to have undergone strange incidents, including alien abductions. Of course, I didn't believe a word of it. A few patients also reported what I thought were dubious tales of satanic ritual abuse. It seemed to me that some presenters were competing with each other to tell the most sordid and outlandish stories.

The one testimony I remember best was from a young woman. She stood up and recounted her lengthy tale of having been forced to attend, and then having been abused at, a series of elaborate satanic ceremonies. Her supposed "Satanist" father had taken her to them repeatedly—several times a week—from the time she was eight until she was twelve years old.

Not unusually, and in fact predictably for such alleged memories, she insisted that she had totally forgotten these dramatic remembrances for many years afterward. Then, lo and behold, one day her therapist lit upon the idea of hypnotizing her. Almost immediately, this young woman dredged up these supposed recollections of satanic abuse with such gory details that I could sense even the other participants found her story unbelievable. No one said a word, though. But their silence didn't deter the somewhat oblivious woman, who admitted that she carried diagnoses of a severe personality disorder and long-standing substance abuse. She was happy for the first time in years, she concluded, after "her wonderful counselor" had agreed to work with her several years earlier.

Many academics, therapists, and patients appropriately stress the importance of trauma and its ill effects on human psychological development. I had already written a journal article documenting the high rates of abuse in the backgrounds of most of our borderline unit's inpatients. But given my clinical experience with the vagaries of memory and the then-current hysteria about Satanism, I thought the woman's story of abuse was as ludicrous as Raymond's tale about the minister. The facts that Raymond and this woman both claimed to have recollected their Satanist memories under the influence of hypnosis *and* only after many years of having completely forgotten them were red flags.

Hypnosis, a dubious way of trying to help people recall memories, is a common element in many false-memory cases. These recollections have been labeled "repressed memories" by some. But when elicited under such conditions, they have repeatedly been shown to be unreliable, especially after long years of a total lack of recall of such dramatic episodes.

Of course, dubious reporting of false memories may well occur in reports about a wide variety of other events, too. But a serious burden of proof has to be placed upon reports from people who claim to have entirely forgotten the existence of years of such spectacular events, including alleged satanic rituals. Common sense argues that those reconstructed stories seem implausible, until truly proved otherwise.

To help explain the magnitude and lingering persistence of these debates about false memories of satanic actions, we must look more closely at the global views of the mental health field about so-called repressed memories and abuse, and then turn our attention to law enforcement personnel for their perspective on these controversies. It's a complex story, and it shows that not all mental health professionals were without their own biases and that not all prosecutors were as misguided and naïve as they were sometimes portrayed.

The vagaries of human memory and the tendency of certain patients either to exaggerate or to become deluded or suggestible about purported past experiences of abuse led me early on to spend several years studying these issues. As part of my research, I investigated the accuracy of victims' memories of such phenomena as possessions and Satanism, too. Various forms of abuse are not uncommon and are certainly a serious source of psychological harm. Most reports of abuse are probably true, but, unfortunately, a lesser amount are not. The same holds true about accounts of satanic cults and demonic attacks more generally, though in my experience the ratio of false reports to true ones are much higher in these latter cases. In my experience most well-trained mental health practitioners who heard fantastic tales from their patients about ritual abuse did not come away convinced and concluded, just as I did, that these reports were exaggerated, especially the ones involving "recovered memories."

Academic experts in memory have continued to congratulate themselves for recognizing the inaccuracies of human memory (obvious at times) and emphasizing the great power of "suggestion" on vulnerable human minds. But various writers jumped on the bandwagon and appeared to lecture to what they regarded as an ignorant and superstitious public how not to get carried away by *any* claims about the existence of Satanists.

A more nuanced perspective of these complex and often misunderstood controversies requires a short digression concerning the relevant topics of repression and distorted memory. The varied reliability of reports about Satanism, just like those about other traumas, need considerable unpacking with this background in mind.

• • •

The so-called academic memory wars were mostly fought during the 1980s and early 1990s. The polemics reached back into a technical debate of how Freud dealt with human forgetfulness and the distortions of his early patients, a "problem" largely the fault of Freud himself. Like many legitimate debates in the field of psychotherapy, the controversies about repression and memories of abuse originated with him.

Early in his career, Freud offered his findings that eighteen cases of what he called hysteria that he had treated in the early years of his experimentation with hypnosis and psychoanalytic techniques were *all* caused by repressed memories of sexual abuse. His clinical research, he claimed, had revealed that these patients had forgotten their early episodes of abuse. Only under the uncovering method of psychoanalysis, Freud claimed, had they been able to become conscious of these traumas.

He was incorrect, as widely recognized then and now.

For many years, though, many of his followers defended Freud and elaborated a standard explanation for his misguided theorizing. Psychoanalysts and historians alike argued that Freud, during the last decade of the nineteenth century, was energetically searching for his *caput Nile*, that is, in his Latin phrase, the "source of the Nile." His aim had been to find the central causative factor of the often severely neurotic (and probably at times near-psychotic) disorders he was seeing in his practice. At first, Freud believed the "spontaneous" reports of his patients that they had been sexually abused. According to this idealized portrayal by many of those first followers, however, Freud in time became convinced that his patients' overimaginative psyches had created these stories and that such tales were more properly accounted for by deeply determined and long-repressed fantasies, now uncovered by his novel methodology. Sympathetic biographies of Freud, such as those by Ernest Jones (*The Life and Work of Sigmund Freud*, published in the 1950s in three volumes and then in one volume in 1961) and Peter Gay (*Freud: A Life for our Time*, 1988), for instance, offer this view. Gay writes that Freud "for a time" accepted his patients' lurid tales as true but eventually recognized them as being "a collection of fairy tales."

A closer reading of Freud's writings of the 1890s, however, might have made more obvious what was really going on. One can see through his own writings that Freud unwittingly engaged for a time in the same behavior that later became so suspect among the overenthusiastic supporters of "recovered memories," including about satanic rituals, so many decades later. An unbiased reading of Freud's 1896 paper "The Aetiology of Hysteria" suggests that he was leading the witnesses, not the reverse. Freud there notes of his patients that before their analysis they knew nothing about the scenes they were recounting. As a rule, they were "indignant" if he warned them that such scenes might emerge. "Only *the strongest compulsion* [my emphasis] of the treatment could induce them to embark on a reproduction of them," Freud wrote.

After having stated that he had "laboriously forced some piece of knowledge" upon his patients, Freud with his colleague Josef Breuer wrote in another early article, *Studies on Hysteria* (1895), that even as patients came to accept this point, they still insisted that they "can't remember having thought it."

Freud's conclusions appeared obviously driven by his own early theories and methodology. By his own logic, Freud thought he was working with memories that lay at an unconscious level, were subject to strong resistance, and therefore were *not* spontaneously generated. It seems inescapable to conclude that Freud was dredging up what we later called "false memories."

Not surprisingly, Freud's unwarranted generalization was not well-received at the local congress of Viennese physicians where he presented these early ideas. His findings were roundly criticized and disbelieved, and Freud was regarded as monomaniacal in his sexual theorizing. To his credit, Freud learned from his mistakes and changed his views. Rather than accept responsibility for this embarrassing episode and his initial misjudgment, however, he continued to blame his patients.

One sad result of this early chapter in psychoanalytic history was that for many years real-life trauma was somewhat deemphasized as a contributing factor in the development of psychiatric problems. The general feeling among therapists through the middle years of the twentieth century was that abuse and trauma in the background of patients were fairly rare; one text at that time cited the rate of incest as only one in a million children. Even when I started out as a psychiatrist, many senior clinicians largely discounted any significant role for or prevalence of abuse.

The inevitable backlash to this mindset occurred in the 1970s and 1980s. It became obvious to many of us treating more disturbed patients that the rates of various categories of abuse in their backgrounds were enormous. Several diagnostic groups of patients, and especially those with borderline personality disorder, had frequently been sexually, physically, and emotionally abused, a finding now widely accepted. A fuller understanding has also developed of the neurobiological consequences of such histories.

As can happen, however, the pendulum then swung too far in the opposite direction. In some therapeutic circles (and among some poorly trained mental health professionals to this day) uncovering and "healing" the "traumatized" self became the main, sometimes the only, focus of treatment. Some therapists even preferred to call themselves "traumatists," as Raymond's counselor did.

It was at this point that quite a number of psychotherapists seemed subtly or even obviously to be pressuring their patients to retrieve remembrances that did not in fact reflect real past events, just like Freud did, as many now believe. Mostly, these involved reports of abuse. Some therapists became so convinced of the importance of abuse that, like Freud almost a century earlier, they encouraged their patients to search the recesses of their recollections in a belief that they *must* have repressed such memories.

In our published research, we were careful to exclude equivocal memories. We believed that patients who were abused *did* remember the trauma; they did not need therapy to "recover" it, although details may have faded somewhat. I never recall any of my colleague psychiatrists at the four medical colleges with which I have been associated claiming to believe patients who suddenly "recovered" recollections after years of forgetfulness of serious trauma, let alone of ritual abuse.

Another hospitalized patient I knew well claimed to have been tortured by her mother and other members of a satanic group as a child. This was not a recovered memory, she said, but a recollection she had always known. Since she had worked for many years with a psychologist who had hypnotized her and told her that she had multiple personality disorder, however, I was somewhat skeptical of her claim, though she consistently maintained its reality and I could not disprove it, of course.

These clinical vignettes are good reminders not only of the vagaries of memory, but also of the observation that many individuals, like Raymond and his counselor, search desperately for a single but simplistic reason for their troubles. It is easier to believe that there might have been a definitive event that explains their problems rather than a complex mix of vulnerabilities and multiple causes. On the unit for patients with borderline personality disorders, where so many had traumatic histories, I sometimes heard a common refrain from patients with no recall of having been abused. Several told me that they wished that they, too, had such a "good reason for why I am a mess."

In this context, it is understandable why certain patients and counselors came to latch on to outlandish claims about satanic kidnappings and ritual abuse. But distinctions must be made. As I have argued, there are indeed at least a few "Satanists" around, albeit of different stripes and levels of seriousness. Not all of them are dangerous to children and others, but not all of them are sitting around merely playing Dungeons and Dragons either.

In my experience, the reality about the work of some police and prosecutors was always more complex than they were given credit for or as many of the academic experts supposed. As their consultant at times, I have probably learned more over the years from law enforcement about such complaints than from anyone else. For instance, a New York police detective related to me his experience that cults attempt to keep as low a profile as possible, like the Mafia, because some of their activities are criminal. Other observers feel that most cults are small and tend to exist in rural areas. Catherine's earlier involvement in some such "Satanist" practice was undoubtedly of this variety. Their membership is often drawn, this argument runs, from people who are marginalized and disgruntled and are looking for license and a bit of excitement in their sometimes-narrow lives. Reports of the antics of dabblers or of more notorious and sometimes loathsome activities of serious followers of scattered Satanic notions crop up in many newspaper and online articles, though their extent is disputed. Some even conduct more explicit rituals, like Black Masses. In Canada, in the summer of 2019, a rare *public* Black Mass was celebrated near Ottawa's diocesan cathedral to the obvious dismay of the local Catholic community.

In cases of suspected satanic ritual abuse, police and district attorneys were sometimes portrayed unfairly as simple dupes of the exaggerated tales told by children. Although investigative techniques in certain cases with impressionable kids were no doubt overly aggressive and misleading, the legal system eventually worked out a balance. The bigger problem was frequently the opposite one. According to some prosecutors I have spoken to over the years, the problem was less frequently unwarranted exonerations (or prosecutions) of Satanists than missed abuse convictions on narrower grounds. Of those cases that involved accusations of satanic and ritual molestations that made it to the courts, many started out as simple sexual abuse allegations supported by evidence. But soon the charges became magnified—not always because of prosecutorial overzealousness, however. Just as often, according to this perspective, manipulative adult defendants and their clever attorneys used such stories to confuse jurors.

In this common viewpoint among experienced prosecutors, some genuinely guilty defendants quickly realized that the evidence against them was strong. But rather than admit to their wrongdoing, they tried to muddy the waters by admitting to all sorts of bizarre and preposterous charges, such as ritual abuse, in the hopes of creating confusion. In this reading of the controversy, the "memory experts" (at least at times) unwittingly buttressed a calculated defense strategy. In emphasizing the great power of suggestion on vulnerable human minds, the testifying experts sometimes only confused some jurors in their recognition that the children in question had been misled by improper questioning. The defendants and their attorneys then hoped that the jury would conclude that the overall testimony had become so compromised by overblown charges that the more credible original accusations were obfuscated. And so, savvy prosecutors thought these experts were being manipulated.

I don't know how often this revisionist view was the accurate one. The court system is so adversarial in nature that it is difficult for any outside observer to sort out all the facts and contradictory testimonies, and there was no dearth of such disputed cases. I was privy, however, to some inside information about one notorious and publicly reported case on the West Coast in 1988, which always gave me pause.

In this particular case, a former police officer, Paul Ingram, was accused of abusing his children and being a practicing Satanist, along with other prominent members of his community. Ingram initially admitted to the abuse but then began, in the fashion mentioned, to add all sorts of absurd admissions, such as that he, other men, and other members of his family had been participants for years in rapes, orgies, and ritual murders during satanic ceremonies. When his children first corroborated these tales, the case garnered tremendous publicity. Soon the memory experts were testifying that this man was confused and making these confessions only out of some distorted sense of guilt, extreme suggestibility, and a wish to "please authority."

Local law enforcement believed that Ingram only wanted to save his own hide. They confidently concluded that he was in fact guilty of some abuse and that he then lied to the police about the more farcical aspects of his story to throw law enforcement off. In any case, he was successfully prosecuted on the less spectacular charges and went to prison.

I was later directly informed that the ritual abuse accusations were never proved in court but that additional evidence for Ingram's participation with a satanic circle did indeed exist. The charges that Satanism was something of a factor in the case, though rigorously disputed by most commentators, remains indisputable in the minds of at least some of those involved with it, or so they continue to allege to me.

Similar charges, some of them extremely well-substantiated, go back centuries, lending credibility to the possibility of their existence today. In the fifteenth century, for instance, Gilles de Rais, a French nobleman, was put on trial and executed on similar allegations of murdering scores of children in satanic ceremonies. Historians have expressed little doubt that this sordid tale was accurate.

When I travel to Italy, I hear the same stories—and the same controversies. Italy had its own McMartin-type case in 2007 at a school in Rignano Flaminio, a village about twenty miles north of Rome. Six staff members were implicated. In another infamous allegation from 1996, the president of a group called the Bambini di Satana (the Children of Satan) was accused of raping a teenage girl and a two-year-old boy during a satanic ritual. Neither charge resulted in a conviction, and many people challenge the notion that Satanism is quite so widespread in Italy, as some believe and allege.

And so the debates continue on both sides of the Atlantic. I retain some skepticism toward the more sensational charges, yet I have talked over the years to alleged victims of Satanists who swear to me that they were ritually abused and have no difficulty remembering the horrors. They admit, however, that they can offer little proof of their abuse.

The most common history behind most modern Satanists may be one, rather, of either minor crime or a turning to occultism. Legal experts have told me that the "trappings" of satanic cults frequently accompany crime scenes. I once saw, for instance, satanic markings defacing a local seminary—made by pranksters or serious cultists? This seems to be where the experts end in their agreement and anecdotal evidence begins. From my interviews with scattered law enforcement specialists and more believable witnesses, I am convinced that at least a few of the more macabre accounts might be sound.

Of course, modern history provides enough tales of horror and cruelty—from serial killers to Hitler and Pol Pot—to convince nearly everyone with good sense that true evil exists. Evil does not require explicit Satanism to declare itself. Similarly, the past is replete with ghastly tales of human behavior, from ancient practices like mass crucifixions and impaling to the widespread murder of infants through "exposure"; to the terrors of warfare and the all-too-common subjugation of whole peoples by sadistic conquerors; to the unimaginable horrors throughout history of slavery, including slaves serving as commonplace objects of sexual exploitation. Demonic foes alone hardly explain human depravity, as I remind those who try to mislabel this or that serial killer or school shooter as "possessed."

We would all like to believe that our modern Western world has left such shocking beliefs and scenarios behind. But strange and dreadful reports of atrocities, at least occasionally thought to be diabolic in nature, still resurface in every age, including our own. Their perpetrators' motivation toward secrecy has made their detection difficult and estimates of their prevalence problematic. But neither fact gainsays the occasional reality of such atrocities, however much fears about their existence can become overblown.

CHAPTER TWELVE

FINAL CONTROVERSIES

The Abuse of Exorcisms and a Final Note to Critics,
Searchers, and the Media About the Scientific Status
of Possessions and the So-Called Paranormal

Since exorcisms and beliefs in demons will never die out, and human disagreement is so ubiquitous, neither will controversies about the ideal scope, discernment, and training of exorcists and deliverance ministers. Disputes have always surrounded these topics around the world. A sober and balanced perspective is forever in order. An excessive preoccupation with, or ignorant notions and malpractices concerning, exorcisms and the belief in demons will produce only unsound outcomes. Perhaps most worrisome in the contemporary era have been the shoddy discernments. One of my chief roles in recent years has been to try to counter such distortions.

I have not directly encountered abusive episodes by clergy per se because I normally consult only on cases where I know a sensible spiritual adviser is available. If a spiritual adviser is not involved or if a victim asks me for advice, I suggest the names of prudent and knowledgeable religious practitioners I know.

Still, beyond sensible precincts, the incidence and variety of abuses are not trivial. Perhaps most visibly in our media-saturated culture, self-interested healers manipulate innocent victims for exhibition and profit. To considerable publicity, a wide range of self-styled exorcists in France recently did just that; their efforts were as appalling as they were inefficacious in the end. The most public examples of this sort of behavior in the United States come from some televangelists, many of whom have become multimillionaires. Robert Tilton, for instance, took to "shaking" himself on camera and tried to convince people that they too could "shake off" the devil and their infirmities—provided they sent him money in advance. Similarly, the media figure Benny Hinn claimed he could cast out demons just by "blowing" on people, relieving them of their drug addictions by liberating them from the responsible evil spirits with a puff of air. My favorite televangelist, though, was the one who proclaimed that a bunch of congregants were possessed with some fifteen devils, then slapped them on their foreheads as all fifteen devils came tumbling out in a heap.

Even more disturbing, however, are episodes where fake healers or irresponsible ministers physically abuse or harm people, either intentionally or through ignorance. Some disturbed people may take matters into their own hands and use violence against others to attack alleged demonic enemies. This may have been the case, for instance, when the ex-boyfriend of Morgan Freeman's step-granddaughter murdered her in a rage. He claimed he was driving out demons, but upon further examination, he appeared to be suffering from paranoid delusions, perhaps brought on by his use of drugs. As he stabbed the young woman, he claimed that God wanted her to die because she was possessed by the devil. Later, he pleaded innocent by reason of insanity, claiming that ingesting PCP stimulated his paranoia.

Violent and abusive exorcisms have always existed. They happen much more frequently among the ignorant and in more primitive societies. But as modern science and educational opportunities have expanded around the world, physical ordeals aimed at expelling demons, long employed by ancient cultures, are actually markedly decreasing. Nonetheless, they still occur sometimes even in more advanced countries.

As I have already emphasized, the main underlying error is the belief that *spiritual* problems can be helped by *physical* means. Violent or inappropriate physical methods employed to drive out demons are risky and superstitious. Physical methods cannot affect spiritual beings like demons, though things such as holy water or other sacred objects, whose physicality contains a sacramental significance, are hardly dangerous or damaging.

The press and other media outlets have recently documented episodes where so-called exorcisms have physically harmed people around the world. Mental problems can remain untreated and even death can result from people improperly understanding relevant criteria or ignoring suggested practices, particularly when it comes to drawing the proper distinction between illness and possession. Ignorant and greedy practitioners or just desperate families have been involved in such travesties. Most often, superstitious and abusive practices are done on the fly by laypeople; it is even more inexcusable when the offending party is a cleric.

In 2003, during a "deliverance" ceremony, an eight-year-old boy was tragically smothered to death. Following the incident, the officiating minister, Ray Hemphill, was arrested. He had started a fundamentalist storefront church known as the Faith Temple Church of the Apostolic Faith. At his direction, he and participants had laid on top of the boy to restrain him as Hemphill tried to cast out the supposed demon. The boy had been diagnosed on the severe end of the autism spectrum; such people are often nonverbal, communicating in ways that misinformed people might mistake as being "demonic." According to court testimony, many people in the family's church believed the boy to be possessed, and they all believed an exorcism would "cure" him.

In another example, a couple once brought to me their agitated autistic daughter because they thought she might be demonically possessed. I had to disabuse them of that notion emphatically. Autistic patients sometimes present as highly aggressive, as do some organically impaired patients with damage to key inhibitory centers of the brain, especially the frontal lobe. Again, I have often had to tell confused parents that these pathological symptoms hardly indicate that the patient is being controlled by evil spirits. Such individuals, whose caretakers are often desperate to "try anything," are in my experience especially vulnerable to fringe practitioners and wacky theories of causation.

Media interest in possessions and exorcisms has grown exponentially. Examples of cases of "exorcisms" gone wrong are easily found in media accounts around the world and across religions: a twelve-year-old Swiss girl who was beaten to death during a violent exorcism; a twenty-two-year-old woman in New Zealand who was drowned during a ritual to expel an evil Maori spirit; a German woman who was instructed to drink gallons of saltwater during an alleged Islamic ritual of exorcism; a young Muslim woman who was beaten and starved to death after eight days of "efforts" to expel a spirit; a woman in Thailand who was forced by Buddhist monks to drink two large bowls of "holy water" to cleanse her.

It is inevitable that the media cover the trend of more worldwide exorcisms being conducted today than ever before. Along with that comes increased coverage of possible abuses. But despite appropriate and increased media attention, such abuse is, by and large, *not* proportionately growing.

While any abusive practices, of course, should be identified immediately and halted and prosecuted, where appropriate, the need for caution calls, rather, for better training and more enlightened understanding of this complex field.

The argument among critics of exorcism is that such abuses justify doing away with exorcisms altogether. But that's like saying the solution to construction injuries is outlawing new buildings. The solution is more sensible teaching and apprenticeships in this area, not less, not banning the proper practice of exorcism or sweeping legitimate needs under the rug. Many efforts at training more skilled practitioners are under way. Interestingly, however, some of these efforts are opposed by the leaders of various faith traditions, an example of the blind leading the blind.

Ignorance and exaggeration constantly compete with rationality and caution among humans. Perhaps no more strikingly is this true than in this convoluted realm where people become frightened and too little sound guidance is available. Another old Latin phrase is apt: *abusus non tollit usum*—the misuse of something doesn't remove its proper use. Hardly has every self-styled exorcist always shown good judgment. But, again, we don't ban cars because drunken drivers exist. We shouldn't deny the value of exorcisms because of a few ignorant practices—or practitioners.

• • •

Nor should we deny the importance and necessity of promoting scientifically literate and well-trained practitioners of sensible, properly authorized exorcisms. It is far too easy to shoot fish in the barrel of poorly conceived religious practices and beliefs, and our country has had more than its share of such. Of course, a few of the deliverance folk are ignorant and extreme, and some in the "antireligious crowd" are equally so. It's hard to keep a sane and balanced perspective about a consequential, if convoluted, and disturbing subject that has been debated for centuries. Brilliant minds have tried to understand its complexity for millennia, sometimes veering off-kilter, sometimes displaying a very human struggle in the face of a great but confusing cosmic mystery.

Though I regard the study of the paranormal without a spiritual foundation as pseudoscientific, belief in phenomena of a genuinely spiritual or even supposedly paranormal nature is not irrational and shouldn't be treated as such, despite the excesses or limitations of some of those who write about the subject. Nor is it an "antiscientific" position. Civilizations throughout history have been built on solid spiritual foundations; others have been built on pagan and occult notions. Discriminating between the two is everything.

This hardly means that any of these societies have inherently been opposed to pragmatism or scientific inquiry. These cultures have simply accepted the twin pillars of material and nonmaterial reality. Healthy cultures resist the all-encompassing preoccupation with spiritualist ideas; but they don't pathologize all spiritual experiences, nor do they deny the existence of a spirit world—a peculiarly modern temptation.

I wrote this book to clarify these points. I have argued throughout it that there is nothing "unscientific" about the whole subject, that to the unbiased mind the evidence is compelling.

Some years ago, I was contacted by a freelance writer from a popular science magazine who was preparing and researching a piece about demonic possession. Familiar with an essay I had written previously, he asked to interview me. He was respectful and thoughtful. At his request, I voluntarily agreed to send him a description of several contemporary cases who had granted me permission to share their details.

The writer read them and said that he found the accounts utterly fascinating. His editor also wanted to include my case examples in the piece, which was slated to run in the next issue. The editor told me that any serious treatment of demonic possession needed to include the scientifically credible reports and long experience of an academic psychiatrist like myself.

Then I never heard from the magazine again.

I was not really surprised. I believe the piece was rejected for ideological *and* commercial reasons. Its publishing team probably feared they'd receive blowback from their scientifically oriented readership, which I imagine could negatively impact their subscription lists. So much for open-mindedness. Even a "science" magazine, especially one more popular in nature, could not make room to include the argument that possession could even *possibly* be best explained by *real, genuine evil spirits*. There had to be a material cause. The magazine probably found the notion of demons to be either ignorant or just unacceptable to air. Although the publishers may have imagined such a position might "offend" their typical readers, in my experience it would likely have created a lively controversy, as my piece in *The Washington Post* did a few years later.

Some people are taken aback, though, when I say that I understand that mentality. I acknowledge that there *is* a positive element to that resistance. There *are* religious and philosophical periodicals and journals in fields like spirituality, and even the field of "parapsychology," where such a topic can be aired. Maybe one doesn't think much of some of these outlets. Often, I don't.

But we should be respectful of legitimate boundaries here. The concept of the "spiritual" simply goes beyond what our modern and narrower conception of science can legitimately study. And so, understandably, possession and the like are typically ruled out as acceptable subjects in contemporary scientific journals. It is impossible to subject spiritual realities, such as spirits and prayers, to the same kind of scientific scrutiny as metals and clouds.

And in many ways, I concede, the world is better off for sticking to these distinctions. Look at the spectacular advances made in science since the Enlightenment. In my profession as a doctor, these protocols have brought vaccines, antisepsis, the discovery of microbes, immunology, and so much more. We have airplanes, unheard-of feats of engineering, televisions and computers, even space travel. We have a lot to be thankful for in our scientists. My own field of psychiatry has benefited enormously from careful double-blind studies and neuroscientific advances.

We also do not want our scientists pontificating on subjects outside their areas of expertise, however. The late Stephen Hawking was a brilliant astrophysicist, but from interviews he gave, he seemed to know nothing of philosophy, the history of religion, or spirituality. There is a tendency among extreme specialists, as prominent scientists inevitably must be, to have difficulty with interdisciplinary perspectives beyond their field.

A true scholarly perspective of possessions requires a multidisciplinary approach, involving a mix of medical, historical, and spiritual knowledge rare among pure scientists. Specialized geniuses in their field all too frequently feel their brilliance qualifies them to speak out about other fields with equal authority—like some rich and successful businesspeople, skilled in their bailiwick, who think they are experts in life and uncommonly gifted with rare human wisdom to boot. The same can—and should—be said about Sigmund Freud. No one ever accused Freud of being shy in his opinions. His ideas outside his field about spirituality and anthropology, however, were amateurish and outdated. His attacks on organized religion, for example, reflected the prejudices of the nineteenth-century secular positivist. His notion of Christianity reflected mere regurgitations of anti-Christian polemics, thoroughly refuted even in his own day.

As an American, I believe in the separation of church and state. I also believe, in one sense, in the separation of science and religion. The word "science," from the Latin *scientia*, originally meant, simply, "knowledge." Science, as understood in the more modern use of the term, however, does not expect to answer religious questions any more than we should expect the Bible to answer scientific ones.

This does not mean there cannot be a creative, constructive dialogue between the two. Reason and faith can be complementary fields of inquiry and should not contradict each other. Legitimate historical and other religious controversies like religious phenomenological and historical scholarship are subject to nuanced, reasoned discourse. Otherwise, we reduce faith to a world outside of reason, and we allow science in its more constricted sense to dictate every answer, even about spiritual questions or experiences. This narrower definition is labeled "scientism," and its truncated demarcations rule out religious questions from the start as unanswerable in nature.

But religious matters can and should be subject to debate and rigorous scrutiny. If they are not, we might as well stop studying them altogether, even stop talking about them as rational human beings.

The risk in avoiding a sober study of these topics is to leave their discussion to the untrained and the inexperienced, or to the extremists. Absent reasonable scholarship, the interested men and women in these fields are left on their own, without guidance, to make sense of these evident but complex realities. Many of my talks have attempted to make these distinctions to science-minded audiences. Most intelligent people seem open to the argument, when properly explicated.

I have crossed paths with many spiritual seekers. I have found most to be sincere people who ask tough questions about serious matters, though they admittedly sometimes come up with unconventional answers. Though easy to mock, they are among our most sensitive and thoughtful citizens. Some are simply and poignantly desperate. Middle-aged searchers for some proof of continued existence of their dead spouse or other kin sadly turn to mediums who allegedly channel their relatives' spirits. Trite bits of remembrance often emerge. Sometimes darker themes appear, too.

Young people who do not have proper direction in spiritual matters may turn to playing with witchcraft, casting spells, and the like. Some are lost souls looking for excitement or a little spiritual comfort in the wrong places. But at least they are looking.

There are many such people, and to their credit, they are not buying the materialists' message anymore (if they ever did) that "nothing" is going on "out there." They may be looking for something to believe in other than just a dead, senseless universe. The belief systems they come up with may be seriously flawed; but who can blame them, when so few sober and thoughtful guides are available?

• • •

As a physician and a believer in the reality of possession, I came to see I had a responsibility to be willing to speak out and strike a sensible balance between extreme skepticism and naïve credulity, as emphasized throughout this book. In the service of those goals I came to find, a bit surprisingly, that the various media outlets—print, radio, online, podcasts, and television—were eager to inquire about my findings and viewpoint. In their reporting, some are professional and accurate; some distort the realities of this subject. But overall, the media have treated me fairly.

Reactions from media users always vary widely—from hardcore skeptics to firm believers. As I read the reader responses to my article in *The Washington Post*, I recognized once again that no amount of evidence will persuade a radical skeptic that possession exists and exorcisms are needed. Still, I welcomed the mostly respectful debate.

Most people fall into the category of "intrigued but skeptical." And those are the people who I envisaged might find this book the most eye-opening and helpful. It does presume a certain understanding of the limits of a too narrow view of what real science entails as well as a certain openness to the notion of a spiritual realm beyond our awareness. My experience has been that thoughtful people find both assumptions to be valid—a very human impulse—though they often have no one to help them navigate such choppy waters.

THE REALITY BEHIND THESE PHENOMENA

Why Demons Attack

*I write so that knowledge of these important matters may not
fade away like the fleeting memories of a passing dream.*

**—THOMAS HOOKER, PURITAN FOUNDER,
CONNECTICUT COLONY**

Daniel Patrick Moynihan, Harvard professor and longtime US senator, famously remarked that everyone is entitled to his opinion, but not to his own facts. The facts are straightforward and well-documented in this book. I could have discussed many more cases, but multiplying examples, as noted, is unlikely to sway those impervious to an open-minded viewpoint.

The more interesting question to me has always been: How can we understand on a deeper level these phenomena?

I close the book by highlighting the more traditional view, which seems to me by far the most coherent. I have resisted an overly doctrinaire or denominational inclination, because the concept of possession and a spirit realm is accepted and discussed by all the major world religions. But, in the end, one should also fly one's flag by making one's own conclusions known. Here we admittedly enter the realm of human and divine mystery, the ultimate answers being known only to God. In closing, I merely suggest part of an answer.

My own experience and the collective wisdom of centuries suggest that demons are indeed dedicated to destroying human beings—preferably spiritually, but also physically. The whole business seems pretty odd. While acknowledging its inscrutability, can we surmise any rationality to it all? Why, I am often asked, would evil spirits choose to assault and even to take over a person's body?

Sadism and "misery loves company," I'm sure, are parts of the answer. But further, the deeper, time-honored explanation involves the idea of their despising humans because of their ultimate envy and hatred of God. If one is such a proud and envious creature, God (and especially the God-man) stimulates their hatred and bitterness. And, it also seems, their loathsome activity is directed to the image of the divine reflected in all of us human creatures. Yes, they want to corrupt us and win us to their "side," it certainly appears so.

We humans retain a capacity to love, an ability demons seem to have lost or foresworn in their rejection of God. The demonic world seeks to negate our loving personalities, destroy us spiritually, and, if it can, even cause our physical death.

Inevitable speculation about the rationale for these horrific episodes hearkens back to the age-old question, debated in every major civilization, of why evil exists at all. A closely related question involves the notion of free choice. Thinkers of all spiritual traditions have long discussed these conundrums. Why would one expect intelligent spirits—devils *or* angels—to be any different from humans in their ability, and willingness, to freely choose widely divergent moral paths? And, given their superior powers, evil spirits can cause even *more* havoc than we humans seem able to do quite well on our own.

The Romans had a good phrase for that: *corruptio optimi pessima*, "the corruption of the best is the worst of all." As pure, albeit corrupted, spirits, the power and intelligence of demons are greater than the power and intelligence of human beings; hence, they have a higher capacity to create mayhem and misery.

This is so, and indeed normally may occur, I believe, unless they are constrained by forces even superior to them. Many thinkers have taught precisely that, that only divine and holy antagonists—God, angels, saints, holy figures, and effective exorcists especially—have the full power to truly stand up to them and help liberate their victims. And even so, the human victims must normally cooperate in that effort.

One philosopher opined that Satan and evil spirits would kill us all if not prevented. I used to think this view a sort of superstitious, medieval hyperbole. But now I believe it is a statement of fact.

God's *permissive* will—albeit for a *limited* time—should never be mistaken for his *active* wishes. The traditional teaching that God can bring even something good out of evil is hard to accept, of course, especially if one is the unfortunate victim of the kinds of horrific attacks described in this book, or of any tragedy for that matter.

If humans can act in such sadistic ways, why doubt that malign spirits act similarly at times? In the introduction, I called demons "cosmic" terrorists, a term that in the past couple of decades has taken on a more plausible and concrete meaning for much of the public. One could equally choose Nazi guards, Khmer Rouge fanatics, common thugs, or sadists of all kinds as apt figures of comparison.

Given the "risks," philosophers have long pondered whether the creation of such humans or spirits—beings of free will but capable of massive evil—is just, whether it has been "worth it." But for the world of humans and the world of spirits, the notions of love without freedom or good without the possibility of evil seem to many profound thinkers implausible, even logically impossible.

Having rejected goodness and turned to evil, demons have also consciously or implicitly rejected God and chosen "their own place." Philosophers used to talk of the "glamour of evil," however repulsive to the decent-minded. Cruel spirits, which is what they are, obtain their satisfactions where they can, I suppose. And they've made their choices. Hard as it is to fathom, blinkered as they undoubtedly are, there is also no evidence they want to change their stripes.

Along with a wider inclination toward such ideas among many modern believers, there has long been speculation—from early church history, as a minority view, to recent scholarship, in a trend accelerated in the last few decades—about the possibility of an ultimate universal salvation, for evil spirits as well as for (the speculation's main aim) humans. It's a convoluted argument, in my view, and can seem a bit like wishful thinking perhaps. The predominant mainstream tradition has emphasized that the choices individuals—spirits and humans alike— make to reject the divine will, conscious or implicit, may well be fixed and irrevocable in some nearly unfathomable manner, again another "mystery" in traditional religious language.

Also unfathomable is the precise nature of this fate, though most modern religious thinkers who believe in these notions tend to acknowledge that God surely cannot be some sort of sadistic torturer. It's the possibility of an eternal separation from God, the ultimate source of love and happiness, that may represent the most painful and tragic consequence of an unworthy life on earth in the afterlife.

Debates about such heated issues have been perennial, of course. But I simply challenge readers to ponder the further implications of these weighty issues for themselves.

• • •

I am not a clergyman or a guru, nor do I set myself to be any sort of paragon. I am simply a physician who has tried to help people coming to me in immense pain and confusion. I saw myself as eventually getting a glimpse "through a glass less darkly"—a privilege, but also a responsibility. And so, I eventually thought it incumbent upon me to share my findings.

I end with a final story that underscores the stakes here, the *personal* challenge that the honest reader must contemplate in confronting these matters. The Romans had another saying, *tua res agitur*, loosely, "this concerns *you*, too."

Some realm is paying attention to *all* of us, I can see strongly, after all my experiences, including the following one.

On two separate occasions a couple of weeks apart, first a young woman and then a mother and her son came to consult me. Each spoke of a demonic spirit attacking them. The young woman had met with a *brujo*, a sorcerer. Only I could realize a certain significance to her story. On a two-sided token he had given her was written "Scalias," the precise name of the evil spirit harassing Catherine, from chapter 7. Naturally, neither she nor the *brujo* had ever met Catherine, and they lived about eight hundred miles apart. We puzzled over the word on the other side of the token, "Broccoli." She said she had no idea why that word was inscribed there, and she had no special association with or dislike of the vegetable.

I put it out of my mind.

Then about two weeks later, upon referral from a dedicated priest I know, an Ecuadorean woman brought her twelve-year-old son to me to assess whether I could help determine whether an evil spirit may have started to harass him. I told them that I thought, on the basis of certain paranormal elements to his case, that the claim seemed credible. When the boy got up to leave, I asked him whether the evil spirit had ever mentioned its name. He looked at me and said, "Yes, he told me his name is 'Broccoli.'"

No one could have known the significance of those names other than me. It was a message to me, obviously from our demonic foes. To back off, perhaps?

More significantly, the anecdote illustrates that there is a dark world out there that seems to know a lot, hardly only about me, but rather about *each one of us*. It despises us poor mortals and is strangely invested in misleading and harming us. Again, I am not claiming a new or pet theory here.

I hope to have presented in detail strong evidence for this traditional view. Without strong evidence, why would a rational person believe it?

Admittedly, this evidence is intermingled throughout history with exaggerations, confusion, and overreaction, even the uncommon abuses I have described. But this is not unexpected, given the capacity of human beings for ignorance, denial, or a simple loss of perspective.

The mathematical genius Blaise Pascal drew an interesting conclusion about miracles, genuine and imagined alike—a topic equally surrounded with confusion and charlatanism. Pascal was an astute student of religious history and human nature. He wrote, "for it would not be possible that there should be so many false miracles, if there were none true."

His point about historical miracles is analogous to the long record of debates about demonic phenomena, too. Pascal knew that the many false or exaggerated reports about miracles derive a borrowed legitimacy from the real ones; they prove confusing to people and stimulate false hopes and superstitious reactions precisely for the reason that these false claims are based on their mistaken parallels with the rare but genuine ones. Possessions, true and false ones, are nearly an exact analogue in that sense.

It is another traditional belief that either dismissal of or excessive preoccupation with the ugly reality of the demonic world—as opposed to trust in God, his love, and his providence—is unwise. Still, our human obligation should be to take sober account of all aspects of our cosmic situation, even the less savory ones. The wise person doesn't close his or her eyes to realities, however repellant or hard to understand.

I hope to have shown that none of this witness contradicts "science" properly understood, perhaps the key theme of this book. The point of this scientifically credible evidence is to alert us all to these sobering realities.

ACKNOWLEDGMENTS

I thank my past academic chairman for many years, Dr. Joseph English, for his unflagging encouragement regarding a research project that gives new meaning to the term "controversial."

Though I wrote the complete manuscript myself, I thank several individuals whose helpful suggestions were invaluable: my superb editors at HarperCollins, Miles Doyle and Sydney Rogers; my friend and fine writer John Ryan; the talented wordsmith—including of Latin—John Farren; and a colleague in this rarefied field, the European independent scholar of history and anthropology, William Gallagher (no relation).

I extend my posthumous appreciation to three highly experienced and erudite exorcists who remain anonymous but not only gave me the guidance of their wisdom, but also their friendship. They encouraged me, as well, to write this book. I miss them each and this effort would have been impossible without them.

An added set of thanks goes to my book agent Don Fehr and to Stewart Levy, J.D.; *a grazie anche al maestro Sal.*

Finally, a special note of gratitude to several friends and colleagues who read the manuscript for their always supportive comments.

NOTES

p. 2   The first quotation is from Dr. Mark Albanese, assistant professor of psychiatry at Harvard Medical School and a director of mental health and addiction medicine, Cambridge Health Alliance. The second is from Dr. Joseph Masdeu, professor of neurology, Weill Cornell Medical College; a past director of the American Academy of Neurology; and presently the Graham Family Distinguished Chair, Houston Methodist Department of Neurology. The remarks from the exorcist are from Father Gary Thomas of the San Jose diocese; the latter part of the quotation as cited in a CNN online profile of the author (John Blake, "When Exorcists Need Help, They Call Him," CNN Health, August 4, 2017, https://www.cnn.com/2017/08/04/health/exorcism-doctor/index.html).

p. 2   Richard Gallagher, "As a Psychiatrist I Diagnose Mental Illness. Also, I Help Spot Demonic Possession," *Washington Post*, July 1, 2016, https://www.washingtonpost.com/posteverything/wp/2016/07/01/as-a-psychiatrist-i-diagnose-mental-illness-and-sometimes-demonic-possession/.

p. 2   Blake, "When Exorcists Need Help."

p. 6   Jennifer Robison, "The Devil and the Demographic Details," Gallup, February 25, 2003, https://news.gallup.com/poll/7858/devil-demographic-details.aspx. The report found that 70 percent of Americans believe in the devil and hell. A 2007 Pew poll found that "more than one-in-ten Americans [11%] say they have experienced or witnessed an exorcism." Russell Heimlich, "Witnesses to Exorcisms," Pew Research Center, Fact Tank, November 12, 2007, https://www.pewresearch.org/fact-tank/2007/11/12/witnesses-to-exorcisms/.

p. 22   The article referenced here is "A Seventeenth-Century Demonological Neurosis," in *The Standard Edition of the Complete Psychological Works of Sigmund Freud*, Vol. XIX, ed. and trans. James Strachey (London: Hogarth, 1923), 72–103. Subsequent references to and quotations from Freud refer to this edition and appear in the text.

p. 22   Aldous Huxley, *The Devils of Loudun* (London: Chatto & Windus, 1952).

p. 23   Jean Lhermitte, *Diabolical Possession, True and False* (London: Burns & Oates), 1963. Original edition (French): *Vrais et faux possédés* (Paris: Fayard, 1956); first US edition: *True and False Possession* (New York: Hawthorn, 1963).

p. 24   William Blatty, *The Exorcist* (New York: Harper and Row, 1971).

p. 26   Multiple books explain the theories and treatment recommendations of Dr. Otto Kernberg, e.g., Otto F. Kernberg, *Severe Personality Disorders: Psychotherapeutic Strategies* (New Haven: Yale Univ. Press, 1984); and Frank E. Yeomans, John F. Clarkin, and Otto F. Kernberg, *A Primer of Transference-Focused Psychotherapy for the Borderline Patient* (Northvale, NJ: Jason Aronson Press, 2002).

p. 27   Richard Eugene Gallagher, Barbara L. Flye, Stephen Wayne Hurt, Michael H. Stone, and James W. Hull, "Retrospective Assessment of Traumatic Experiences (RATE)," *Journal of Personality Disorders* 6, no. 2 (1992): 99–108.

p. 40   Malachi Martin, *Hostage to the Devil: The Possession and Exorcism of Five Living Americans* (New York: Reader's Digest Press, 1976).

p. 63   The Latin version of the Roman Ritual (*Rituale Romanum*) was first published in 1614. A version of the Latin text (with accompanying English translation) can be found in Philip T. Weller, *Roman Ritual*, 3 vols. (Boonville, NY: Preserving Christian Publications, 2007). The modern rite was approved by the Vatican in 1998 and published in January 1999 as *De exorcismis et supplicationibus quibusdam*. An approved English translation, *Exorcisms and Related Supplications*, appeared in 2017 (Washington, DC: US Conference of Catholic Bishops).

p. 70   The sourcing on the chapter about Julia inevitably relies on historical and observational data, inherent to this subject matter, as argued in the Introduction. I am obviously certain about what I witnessed directly about Julia's "psychic" abilities, her possessed states, and the activity of several of her associates. I am also fully confident in the veracity of the testimony about her exorcisms given by various and multiple impeccable reporters—the pseudonymous Father Jacques and Father A. as well as the many other participants (who are in unanimous agreement as to all details)—whom I interviewed at length. Her story's internal consistency and the striking similarity of her possession and exorcism to well-documented features of other historical cases lend added (and in my view seamless) credibility to this account, despite the details of her case being marked by an acknowledged singular intensity.

The tales about her cult largely depend upon her own reports to me and therefore may possess less epistemic surety. On the other hand, Julia was always coherent and expressed herself soberly and intelligently. Furthermore, she repeatedly claimed she would never lie to me and appeared to have little reason to exaggerate; any cognizance of false claims on her part would have seriously jeopardized the willingness of the two priests to perform the rituals that she was seeking, as noted. I also have documentation given to me by Father Jacques corroborating a number of features of her involvement with the cult. Finally, there was the independent verification of the existence and activity of cult members, including threatening behaviors, alluded to throughout the account in Chapter 3.

p. 76 Isabel Vincent, "I Was an MS-13 Gang Member—and Got Out Alive," *New York Post*, June 10, 2017, https://nypost.com/2017/06/10/i-was-an-ms-13-gang-member-and-got-out-alive/.

p. 79 M. Scott Peck, *Glimpses of the Devil: A Psychiatrist's Personal Accounts of Possession, Exorcism, and Redemption* (New York: Free Press, 2002).

p. 84 I have directly heard about fifteen credible cases of levitation during exorcisms in the contemporary era alone—seen by about thirty-four observers. One was reported to me by a European professor of my acquaintance who witnessed it himself during an exorcism.

p. 85 Colin Wilson, *The Occult: A History* (New York: Random House, 1971), 178.

p. 112 Joseph De Tonquédec, *Les maladies nerveuses ou mentales et les manifestations diaboliques* (Paris: Éditions Beauchesne, 1938).

p. 114 All psychiatric diagnostic terms are from the *Diagnostic and Statistical Manual of Mental Disorders (DSM-5)*, 5th ed. (Washington, DC: American Psychiatric Association Press, 2013).

p. 122 Arthur Kleinman, *The Illness Narratives: Suffering, Healing, and the Human Condition* (New York: Basic Books, 1988), and Kleinman, *Patients and Healers in the Context of Culture: An Exploration of the Borderland Between Anthropology, Medicine, and Psychiatry* (San Francisco: Univ. of California Press, 1980).

p. 123 Frank Hammond and Ida Mae Hammond, *Pigs in the Parlor: A Practical Guide to Deliverance* (Kirkwood, MO: Impact Christian Books, 1973).

p. 129 Thomas Aquinas, *Summa Theologiae*, ed. P. Caramello (Turin: Marietti, 1963).

p. 142 The Earling case was recounted by Carl Vogl, *Begone, Satan: A Soul-Stirring Account of Diabolical Possession* (1935; Charlotte, NC: Tan Books, 1973).

p. 155 René Laurentin, *Le Démon: Mythe ou réalitié* (Paris: Fayard, 1995).

p. 156　Gabriele Amorth, *An Exorcist Tells His Story* (San Francisco: Ignatius Press, 1999).

p. 156　William Friedkin, "The Devil and Father Amorth: Witnessing 'the Vatican Exorcist' at Work," *Vanity Fair*, October 31, 2016, https://www.vanityfair.com/hollywood/2016/10/father-amorth-the-vatican-exorcist.

p. 157　Benigno Pallila, *Rescued from Satan: 14 People Recount Their Journey from Demonic Possession to Liberation* (San Francisco: Ignatius Press, 2018).

p. 157　Matt Baglio, *The Rite: The Making of a Modern Exorcist* (New York: Random House, 2009).

p. 159　Erika Bourguignon, "Introduction: A Framework for the Comparative Study of Altered States of Consciousness," in *Religion, Altered States of Consciousness, and Social Change*, ed. Erika Bourguignon, 3–35 (Columbus: Ohio Univ. Press, 1973).

p. 160　From "In U.S., Decline of Christianity Continues at Rapid Pace," Pew Research Center, October 17, 2019, https://www.pewforum.org/2019/10/17/in-u-s-decline-of-christianity-continues-at-rapid-pace/.

p. 164　T. K. Oesterreich, *Possession Demoniacal and Other Among Primitive Races, in Antiquity, the Middle Ages and Modern Times* (New York: Routledge and Kegan Paul, 1930).

p. 176　"The Mail," *New Yorker*, November 18, 2019, p. 5, in response to Christine Smallwood, "Astrology in the Age of Uncertainty, *New Yorker*, October 28, 2019.

p. 176　"Paranormal America 2018: Chapman University Survey of American Fears," Chapman University, Wilkinson College of Arts, Humanities, and Social Sciences, October 16, 2018, https://blogs.chapman.edu/wilkinson/2018/10/16/paranormal-america-2018/.

p. 177　Anton Troianovski, "A Shaman with a Plan to Cure Russia's Ills: Exorcise Putin," *New York Times*, October 10, 2019, A4, published online as "'An Exorcism Must Be Done': An Anti-Putin Shaman Sets Off Unrest," October 9, 2019, https://www.nytimes.com/2019/10/09/world/europe/shaman-putin-dissent.html.

p. 178　Laura M. Holson, "Witches Are Having Their Hour," *New York Times*, October 11, 2019, last updated October 24, 2019, https://www.nytimes.com/2019/10/11/style/pam-grossman-witch-feminism.html.

p. 183　Herbert Thurston, *Ghosts and Poltergeists* (Chicago: Gateway, 1953).

p. 209　Lawrence Pazder and Michelle Smith, *Michelle Remembers* (New York: Simon & Schuster, 1980).

p. 210   Mike Warnke, *The Satan Seller* (Alachua, FL: Bridge-Logos, 1973).

p. 210   Gail S. Goodman, Jianjian Qin, Bette L. Bottoms, and Phillip R. Shaver, "Characteristics and Sources of Allegations of Ritualistic Child Abuse," Final Report to the National Center on Child Abuse and Neglect, US Department of Justice, 1994, pp. 1–15. Cf. B. L. Bottoms, P. R. Shaver, and G. S. Goodman, "An Analysis of Ritualistic and Religion-Related Child Abuse Allegations," *Law and Human Behavior* 20, no. 1 (1996): 1–34.

p. 211   Lawrence Wright, *Remembering Satan* (New York: Vintage, 1994).

p. 211   Paul R. McHugh, *Try to Remember: Psychiatry's Clash over Meaning, Memory, and Mind* (London: Dana, 2008).

p. 213   Marsha M. Linehan, *Cognitive-Behavioral Treatment of Borderline Personality Disorder* (New York: Guilford Press, 1993).

p. 223   Ernest Jones, *Life and Work of Sigmund Freud*, Vol. 1 (London: Hogarth, 1953).

p. 223   Peter Gay, *Freud: A Life for Our Time* (London: J. M. Dent & Sons, 1988), 94, 96.

ABOUT THE AUTHOR

Richard E. Gallagher, MD, a board-certified psychiatrist, is Professor of Clinical Psychiatry at New York Medical College and a faculty member of the Psychoanalytic Institute of Columbia University. He is a Phi Beta Kappa, magna cum laude graduate of Princeton University and winner of the Stinnecke Class Prize, a scholarship award in classical Latin and Greek. He trained as resident in psychiatry at the Yale University School of Medicine and is in private practice in Valhalla, New York.

Dr. Gallagher is the longest-standing American member of the International Association of Exorcists since its founding in the early 1990s. For a number of years, he served as scientific adviser on its governing council as the only layman and sole psychiatrist. He has also helped train major groups of exorcists in the United States in distinguishing possession cases and other diabolic attacks from medical and psychiatric pathology.

Over the past twenty-five years Dr. Gallagher has consulted for hundreds of ministers, priests, and rabbis (and clergy of other faiths, too) as well as numerous mental health professionals on the subject area of this book. He has published and lectures widely on the topic of diabolic possession from the medical perspective and the critical need to differentiate such very rare cases from the much more common instances of people with mental or medical illness.

None of the above organizations or any other academic or religious institution bears any responsibility for the views expressed or tales recounted in this book. Then again, they haven't witnessed what he has as a doctor who has seen more such cases than any other physician, and perhaps any other person, in the world.